Bluegrass in Baltimore

Bluegrass in Baltimore

The Hard Drivin' Sound and Its Legacy

TIM NEWBY

McFarland & Company, Inc., Publishers

Jefferson, North Carolina

LIBRARY OF CONGRESS CATALOGUING-IN-PUBLICATION DATA

Newby, Tim, 1974–
    Bluegrass in Baltimore : the hard drivin' sound and its
legacy / Tim Newby.
        p.   cm.
    Includes bibliographical references and index.

    ISBN 978-0-7864-9439-2 (softcover : acid free paper) ∞
    ISBN 978-1-4766-1952-1 (ebook)

    1. Bluegrass music—Maryland—Baltimore—History and
criticism.   2. Bluegrass musicians—Maryland—Baltimore—
Biography.   I. Title.

ML3520.N49 2015
781.64209752'6—dc23   2015016208

BRITISH LIBRARY CATALOGUING DATA ARE AVAILABLE

© 2015 Tim Newby. All rights reserved

*No part of this book may be reproduced or transmitted in any form
or by any means, electronic or mechanical, including photocopying
or recording, or by any information storage and retrieval system,
without permission in writing from the publisher.*

Cover image © Tim Newby

Printed in the United States of America

McFarland & Company, Inc., Publishers
  Box 611, Jefferson, North Carolina 28640
    www.mcfarlandpub.com

Table of Contents

Acknowledgments

Every good story needs a voice to tell it and this story had many good voices. I would like to thank everyone who took time to meet with me, chat on the phone, or share some thoughts by email about their time and experiences playing music in Baltimore. My extreme gratitude and thanks go to Jordan August and Phil Chorney and the Charm City Folk and Bluegrass Crew, Anders Beck, Sam Bush, Hugh Campbell, Jerimy Campbell, Heather Coffey, Roy Cole, Steve Cunningham, Arnold "Buddy" Dickens, Tom Ewing, Carl Fleischhauer, Dave Frieman, Alice Gerrard, Chris Hillman, Ed Hough, Cris Jacobs, Travis Kitchens, Patrick McAvinue, Dwight McCall, Del McCoury, Jerry McCoury, Chris Pandolfi, James Reams, Jeff Roberts, Dean Sapp, Ron Cohen, Aaron Smithers and Matt Turi at the Southern Folklife Collection at the Wilson Library at the University of North Carolina at Chapel Hill, Caleb Stine, Carroll Swam, Hank Schwartz, Tony Trischka, Chris Warner, Artie Werner, and Pete Wernick.

Extra special thanks go to Russ Hooper and Sandy Rothman for the time and immense help they provided. Their thoughts, contributions, and contacts were key in helping me with this project.

I would like to thank and recognize the bands, musicians, and people who have made and promoted music in Baltimore over the years and continue to do so today. Without your music and inspiration there would be no story to tell: Bob Baker and the Pike County Boys, Walt Hensley, Earl Taylor and the Stoney Mountain Boys, Del McCoury, Jerry McCoury, Russ Hooper, Jim McCall, Alice Gerrard and Hazel Dickens, Mike Seeger, Frankie Short, Sr., Jon Glik, Kimball Blair, Dee Gunter, Hoppy Ledford, Chris Warner, Bluestone, Mike Munford, Jack Cooke, Warren Blair, Windy Ridge, the Bridge (Cris Jacobs, Kenny Liner, Dave Markowitz, Mike Gambone, Patrick Rainey, and Mark Brown), Caleb Stine and the Brakemen, Dave Hadley, Mookie Siegel, Dave Giegerich, Arty Hill, Ed Hough, Patrick McAvinue, Smooth Kentucky,

Wye Oak, Beach House, Future Islands, All Mighty Senators, Lake Trout, Pigeons Playing Ping-Pong, Brad Selko and the Hot August Music Festival, Believe in Music, Charm City Folk and Bluegrass Festival, Feinwood, Chester River Runoff, Lower Case Blues, Honey Dewdrops, Yellow Dubmarine, Freedom Enterprise, Country Devils, Baltimore Bluegrass Band, Satyr Hill Band, Bald Head Mountain, and Cara Kelly.

Thanks go out to the "email group" for their thoughts, opinions, and critiques of the work in progress. Thanks to Jesse Fendya, Doug Martin, Pat Ryan, John Skozilas, Paul Skozilas, and Matt Sprow.

To my parents and my parents-in-law, thanks for all you do.

And finally to my wife, Melissa, thanks for the unlimited support, help, and encouragement you gave me through this whole process.

Preface

The inspiration for this book was born from an interview I conducted with Del McCoury for an article I was working on for *Honest Tune* magazine. Through the course of our conversation, Del spoke of his early formative years as a musician in Baltimore. I had a vague knowledge of the deep history that bluegrass music had in Baltimore, but through my conversation with Del I learned just how deep that history was. As a long-time Baltimore resident and huge fan of the city, it always excites me to be able to dig into a topic about my hometown that I am also so passionate about. Over the couple of weeks following the interview I began to casually research this rich history. Seemingly every conversation at the time with my wife started with my saying, "You are not going to believe this," or "You know that building on Chapel Street by where you used to live," and ended with a new nugget of Baltimore's bluegrass history that I had recently stumbled across. After a couple of weeks, my wife made a simple yet obvious observation: "This sounds like it would be a great book. You should write it." And she was right.

Baltimore's rich bluegrass history is woefully under-documented. Noted country music historian Bill Malone's pair of books—2008's *Working Girl Blues: The Life and Music of Hazel Dickens* and 2011's *Music from the True Vine: Mike Seeger's Life and Musical Journey*—provided some of the best documentation of the formative years of bluegrass in Baltimore with the chapters that focused on Dickens' and Seeger's time in the city. With a lack of published material on the history of bluegrass in Baltimore I turned to the *Baltimore Sun* newspaper, which over the years had done a good job profiling some of the better-known bluegrass musicians in the area. Another great source of information about the early years of these pioneering musicians in Baltimore proved to be the liner notes of the various albums they released or appeared on. Many of the Seeger-produced albums released at this time included lengthy bios of the performers.

1

I started compiling lists of people to try to speak with. It was difficult at first, as many of the original players in the bluegrass scene in Baltimore from the fifties and sixties were no longer alive or older and tough to track down. I soon made contact with Carroll Swam, who first became immersed in the downtown bluegrass scene while a student at what was then known as Towson College, now Towson University. We met on a chilly President's Day in a house he was rehabbing near my neighborhood of Canton in Southeastern Baltimore, not far from the where the infamous Chapel Café once stood. A cold breeze was blowing through the unfinished house. With a cup of coffee in hand Swam proved to be an invaluable starting point, as he recounted tales from the glory years, those early years of bluegrass in Baltimore. Through his stories he introduced me to an intriguing cast of characters such as Ray Davis, Earl Taylor, Walt Hensley, Marvin Howell and Russ Hooper. Previously these were just names in a story, but after my conversation with Swam they were now more than that. They had personalities and rich colorful histories. Swam got me in contact with one of those characters, Dobro player Russ Hooper.

Russ has been a constant part of the bluegrass scene in Baltimore since his days as a teenager in the early fifties, and he would become a fountain of knowledge and one of my greatest resources as I plowed through this project. He was always available to take my call, answer a question, respond to an email, point me in the right direction, and help connect me with many of the past greats from Baltimore.

The help and guidance of West Coast bluegrass icon Sandy Rothman must also be acknowledged. Sandy is originally from the bay area in California, and still resides there; but he, along with his good friend Jerry Garcia, discovered the sounds emanating out of Baltimore via Mike Seeger's highly influential 1959 album *Mountain Music Bluegrass Style*. The album featured a large number of Baltimore-based musicians, most notably Earl Taylor and the Stoney Mountain Boys, one of the real titans of the close-knit scene of that city. It was the tracks by Taylor and the Stoneys that really captured Sandy and Garcia's attention, Sandy saying those tracks "were the most mind-blowing of all." A few years after discovering Taylor, Sandy would actually go on to play with the Baltimore musician for a short time in the late sixties and early seventies. Sandy was an invaluable resource through the course of my research. His knowledge of not only many of the players in Baltimore, but also bluegrass in general helped to validate the importance of those musicians who first started in Baltimore. Sandy, like Russ, was always there to answer a question and help me make contact with those who could share some thoughts on the subject.

It was the interviews conducted with the musicians who built the scene in Baltimore—those musicians who carried it through the down times, and those current players who helped reinvigorate the scene—that became the backbone of this book. This book is as much about Baltimore as it is the people who made the music first birthed in the rough corner bars where bluegrass seem to flourish so easily and is now an integral part of the city's fabric. *Bluegrass in Baltimore* comprises the stories and memories from the many musicians who took time to meet with me, chat on the phone, answer my many emails, and dig through their old picture collections to find some great photographs to share. It is this personal touch from all of those musicians that serve to bring this hard driving story to life.

Introduction

"It was like meeting God"

Recommended Listening: *Classic Bluegrass from Smithsonian Folkways* is the ideal appetizer, as it is a masterful introduction to the world of bluegrass. It is a compilation album that pulls from influential record label Smithsonian Folkways Recordings (nonprofit record label of the Smithsonian Institution), an extensive bluegrass catalog that spans the last forty years. It features artists from Baltimore and the surrounding area as well as some of the legends of the genre such as Bill Monroe, Doc Watson, the Country Gentlemen and the Stanley Brothers. It is the perfect album to stimulate an appetite for some sweet bluegrass reading.

On a cold night in early February 1963, in a small nondescript neighborhood in Southeastern Baltimore, on the corner of Pratt and Chapel streets in the shadow of Johns Hopkins Hospital, there was a small bar that you would have been hard pressed to find then and does not exist now. Called the Chapel Café, it had a much-too-low ceiling with bad lights that seemed to do nothing but provide a ghostly haze attesting to the heavy cigarette smoke lingering in the dank air. This served to make the ill-mannered, boorish disposition of the locals hunched over the bar even more menacing as they seemed to revel in yelling "play or get out" at the band perched on the small stage every time there was a lull in the music.[1] The fourteen-year-old bassist onstage that night remembers it as "nothing but cigarette smoke and spilled beer, one of them rough places, the kind of place where the bouncer would have to throw out at least one guy a night."[2] Into this atmosphere—across the sticky, beer-splattered floor, beyond the bar area that was just to the right of the door and over towards the stage tucked into the corner on the opposite wall—walked a man.

This bar was much like countless other bars littered across Baltimore: Jazz City just a couple blocks away on Pratt Street in Fells Point, the 79 Club

5

in Federal Hill, the legendary Cozy Inn, and the chicken-wire-covered stage at Oleta's and Marty's Bar KY. All of them were tough beer-and-a-shot joints that were small, worn down, reeking of stale beer, and teetering on the edge of violence each night. But the man who walked into the Chapel Café that night was not like the countless other patrons who inhabited it. He was a tall man who cut an imposing figure and was known to be of few words. He was often referred to as an "ornery old cuss"[3] by those who did not know him, though in reality he was a much more complex man than that simple, limiting description. He also had started a band that lent its name to a still developing sound that had its roots in the mountains of Appalachia, found its way to the city streets, and was now being played in this poorly lit bar, much like it was at similar other bars around Baltimore. This sound was still shaking off its earlier label of hillbilly—so-named for the migrants who brought this music with them when they came down from the mountains or moved from the South to the cities to find work and a better life—and it was beginning to be recognized by another, less derogatory name: bluegrass.

The man who walked into that small corner bar was Bill Monroe, who with his band Bill Monroe and his Blue Grass Boys had first given shape and life to this new and exciting style of music. Bluegrass was born from the old-time string-band music that Monroe learned in his youth back in his rural home in Rosine, Kentucky, and from the fiddle of his favorite uncle, Pendleton Vandiver, whom Monroe went to live with after Monroe's parents died when he was a teenager. Uncle Pen would become a role model for Monroe in all aspects of life, but it was through music that Pen would have his greatest impact on the young budding musician. Years later, after Monroe's musical genius was widely recognized, he would give credit to his Uncle Pen, referring to him as "the fellow I learned how to play from."[4] Monroe would later immortalize his uncle in one of his most famous songs, "Uncle Pen," in which he sang about the late-night hoedowns and dances he played at as a teenager with his uncle.

Monroe mixed his Uncle Pen's fiddle sound with the country, gospel, and blues in the air at the time and ratcheted it up to a breakneck speed with his distinctive trademark mandolin to create what famed folklorist and musicologist Alan Lomax called "folk music with overdrive," in a 1959 article for *Esquire*.[5] Levon Helm, from rock 'n' roll hall of famers The Band, saw Monroe when Helm was a six-year-old and says this new style of music "really tattooed my brain." He recalled how Monroe had taken "that old hillbilly music, sped it up and basically invented what is now known as bluegrass music: the bass in its place, the mandolin above it, the guitar tying the two together, and the violin on top, playing the long notes to make it all sing. The banjo backed

Del McCoury, with son Rob McCoury at left, plays the 2012 Delfest Festival in Cumberland, Maryland (photograph by the author).

the whole thing up, answering everybody."[6] Country music outlaw Waylon Jennings would echo Helms' sentiment about the impact of Monroe and this new style of music he was playing. "In my house, in Littlefield, Texas, it was the Bible on the table, the flag on the wall, and Bill Monroe's picture beside it. That's the way I was raised."[7] And for a brief time, nowhere was this new style of hillbilly music, this folk music with overdrive, played better, faster, or in such a way that it would leave as permanent a footprint on the history and development of bluegrass than in Baltimore.

The teenaged bassist Jerry McCoury, who was on stage that cold February night at the Chapel Café in 1963, recalled with a laugh that when Monroe walked into the tiny Baltimore bar, "I actually didn't recognize him at first. He was wearing his glasses and he had a hat on. Then I realized who it was and I was in total awe." With admiration and high praise in his voice he continues: "It was like meeting God."[8]

Monroe's stop in Baltimore was no accident. He had dropped by to see a former member of his band, Jack Cooke, who was playing the café that evening. Monroe needed a couple of players to fill out his band for an upcoming gig at New York University in New York City for the Friends of Old Time Music on February 8, just a few days later.[9] He was hoping Cooke would join him on guitar, and he wanted to check out the older brother of McCoury, who was a banjo player Cooke had recommended. McCoury's 22-year-old banjo playing older brother remembers that same evening when the man rightly called the "Father of Bluegrass" walked in during their set: "We were playing the Chapel Café in Fells Point one night in 1963 when Bill Monroe walked in front of us. I could have fallen over right then and there. The purpose of him stopping by was to take Jack [Cooke] with him up there to play a show in New York City. He didn't have a guitar player or lead singer at the time. Whoever it was had quit and he thought Jack would do it. He also didn't have a banjo player either so they took me up there to play."[10]

The banjo player, Jerry's older brother Delano, joined Monroe's band, which at the time included Kenny Baker on fiddle and Monroe's longtime partner, Bessie Lee Mauldin, on bass. After the show in New York City Delano joined the band full time, and at the request of Monroe he switched from

The Stoney Mountain Boys onstage at Carnegie Hall in 1959 when they became the first bluegrass band to play at the famed venue. From the left: Curt Cody on fiddle (obscured), Earl Taylor on mandolin, Walt Hensley on banjo, and Sam "Porky" Hutchins on guitar (courtesy Photo-Sound Associates collection, Ronald D. Cohen Collection #20239, Southern Folklife Collection, Wilson Library, University of North Carolina at Chapel Hill).

banjo to guitar and took over lead vocals as well. It proved to be a career-defining break for the young banjo player turned guitarist/singer. Though his time with Monroe was short, it was an influential time, as the bluegrass legend helped introduce the world to the voice of Del McCoury, a voice which might be the most perfect in bluegrass, a voice that is the living embodiment of the "high and lonesome" sound, a voice about which country music superstar Vince Gill declares, "I would rather hear Del McCoury sing 'Are You Teasin' Me?' than just about anything."[11]

Since his brief time with Monroe, McCoury has gone on to establish himself as one of the truly legendary figures in the genre. He was inducted into the International Bluegrass Music Association (IBMA) Hall of Fame in 2011, has released more than thirty albums, won fifteen IBMA awards—including being named Entertainer of the Year nine times (with four straight wins from 1997 to 2000)—and won two Grammy awards in 2006 and 2014 for his albums *The Company We Keep* and *Streets of Baltimore*. He is a man whose roots stretch back to the earliest days but who stands firmly in the now. A man who is not afraid to collaborate with any number of bands who might be assumed to be outside the normal wheelhouse and comfort zone of an aging bluegrass legend, mixing it up with younger bands like Phish, Yonder Mountain String Band, the String Cheese Incident, Old Crow Medicine Show, Leftover Salmon, and Steve Earle—bands that are pushing the sound his one-time mentor Bill Monroe first created so many years ago into new and bold directions.

While some may argue that the music those younger bands are creating is not true bluegrass they are missing the point. These younger bands have been inspired by, and learned from, legends like McCoury and Monroe and are helping to evolve the bluegrass genre, creating something different, but something at its core still old-timey string band music. As Chris Pandolfi, banjo player for the Infamous Stringdusters, argued so passionately in his Bluegrass Manifesto on his blog, and later as the keynote address at the 2011 International Bluegrass Music Association business conference, "Bluegrass is whatever someone says it is. That's all it takes, one person. My only opinion is that all opinions count equally. This is not politics, its music."[12]

For Monroe to stumble upon such an absurdly talented player in Baltimore was no lucky break. During the fifties and sixties Baltimore was teeming with talent and a rare convergence of people. In addition to Del McCoury, a host of other influential pickers and musicians would emerge from Baltimore during this time, including Bill Clifton, Earl Taylor and the Stoney Mountain Boys (the first bluegrass band to grace the stage at Carnegie Hall), the pioneering duets of Hazel Dickens and Alice Gerrard, and the groundbreaking banjo wizardry of Walt Hensley. They would all help to introduce the hard-driving style, best found in its most pure form in those rough, corner bars on the streets of Baltimore, and bring this energetic style to the music world at large.

Mike Seeger, music folklorist, the first person to record and produce a full-length bluegrass album (1957's *American Banjo: Three Finger and Scruggs Style*), cofounder of the New Lost City Ramblers, and half brother to famed folk singer Pete Seeger, was part of this scene when he lived in Baltimore during the 1950s and remembers this vibrant, special time in the city: "There was a folk-song community in Baltimore. It was a meeting of working-class bluegrass people, like Hazel [Dickens] and her brothers, who were reared in old-time music, and urban folk-music people, who were often liberal politically. It was a unique time. This didn't happen much in Washington, and it didn't happen much in other places. It happened with [folk group] The Almanac Singers in New York, but this [Baltimore] was bluegrass."[13]

Baltimore was one of the few places in the United States where musicians from the mountains and the South could meet and play with folks likely outside of their normal social strata. College-educated city folk and hillbilly migrants from Appalachia mingled easily in Baltimore over the common ground of music, and in particular string-band and early bluegrass music. Seeger again provides the best explanation of Baltimore's unique personality as a city: "We were quite conscious in Baltimore of being a place where the city and the country met. You'd have tough bluegrass bars, where the city people were the outsiders. You'd have bohemian parties, where the country people were the outsiders. It was a place where different classes and different cultures were meeting. It was a time of curiosity and discovery and friction and exhilaration."[14]

Hazel Dickens moved to Baltimore as teenager before playing with Seeger in some of the earliest bluegrass bands in Baltimore. She became known for her deeply intense songs about working-class folk and for her groundbreaking work and duets with longtime collaborator Alice Gerrard, which helped pave the way for women in bluegrass and country.[15] Dickens recognized this special bond between hillbillies and educated "northerners," which did not seem to be happening in any other city. She recalled how she often felt inferior around the educated people she encountered when she first moved to Baltimore, but through music she was able to bond with these people from such different backgrounds. Her meeting and eventual long friendship with Seeger was crucial not only to her musical growth, but also to the growth of bluegrass in Baltimore. "Mike [Seeger] was the first person outside of our culture to validate our music," says Dickens, "He looked on it as an art form; while to us it was just what we did. We never thought anyone would be interested."[16]

Much of the focus on bluegrass as it relates to its growth in cities tends to revolve around Nashville, with its well-deserved Music City title, and the bluegrass scene that eventually developed in Washington, D.C., around such genre-defining bands as the Country Gentleman and the Seldom Scene. While there were many other urban settings at the time with a large population of Appalachian migrants and important urban hillbilly scenes, it can be argued that none of them had the lasting impact Baltimore did. During those early years that saw the identity of bluegrass truly formed, it was the vibrant, special scene, a short drive north of D.C. on I-295, in Baltimore that Seeger recalled that truly laid the foundation. With his trademark chuckle, Del McCoury agrees: "There was Nashville, and then there was Baltimore. There were other places. Detroit was pretty big, and Cincinnati—there was a big bluegrass scene in those two cities, and Washington [D.C.] as well—but Baltimore was the hot town for this kind of music back in the fifties and sixties."[17]

Jack Hofer, owner of the Sandpiper Inn, a bar in the Dundalk area of Baltimore, which opened back in the early eighties and used to host regular bluegrass nights, explains: "In the fifties and sixties, Baltimore was the bluegrass capital of the world. People were pouring into Baltimore from West Virginia and Kentucky because we had shipyards, the steel mills, the factories, everything. There were so many mountain people around that you would be talking to somebody, and they'd mention that someone was playing 'hillbilly music' at somebody's house or at a bar. There was more bluegrass in Baltimore than back in Kentucky where I am from."[18]

In the years following World War II, as the factories and industries boomed, there was an exodus from the mountains and the South into the cities, and Baltimore found itself the recipient of an extraordinarily talented crop of musicians who settled into an area ripe with possibilities and opportunities. In a house on Eager Street that held weekly gatherings of like-minded urban folk-music people and hillbillies, in neighborhoods across Baltimore called "Little Appalachia," in "hillbilly ghettos" where migrants clustered in the cramped row houses that hosted nightly pickin' parties, and in the working-class bars that could just as easily erupt in a brawl as they could in live music, the sound of hillbilly or bluegrass music was not only being played but also redefined and pushed in new directions.

These sounds soon started reaching the ears of young, impressionable musicians across the country who were just beginning to find their way musically. Sam Bush, one of the originators of the modern bluegrass sound that began developing in the 1970s, was a teenager in Bowling Green, Kentucky, and one of those young impressionable musicians in the late 1960s when he first came across the "hard-driving Baltimore-style."[19] Bush's band, New Grass Revival, was a revelatory shot in the arm to bluegrass music when they burst onto the scene in 1971. They were a bunch of young hotshot pickers breaking the restrained bluegrass mold at the time, with their long hair, jeans, and T-shirts. Their psychedelic-influenced take on bluegrass fused together everything from jazz, funk and blues to rock. They shook off the shackles that had tethered the genre for too long and changed the face of modern bluegrass. An album Bush came across by Baltimore banjo picker Walt Hensley proved to be the first time Bush felt the spark that would ignite his passion to move bluegrass into new realms and heard a term that would go on to define those early years of his long, storied career. Bush heard Hensley's groundbreaking 1969 album, *Pickin' on New Grass*, and it blew away the young artist—instigating the formation of the band New Grass Revival—and was part of the birth of a new style, "Newgrass." With his own mind fully blown, Bush explained, "He [realized Hensley] was stretching the boundaries there."[20]

For a time in the fifties and sixties, Baltimore was front and center in the development of this new exciting brand of music and was often referred to as the "hotbed" or "hot-spot" of bluegrass and the "epicenter of country music."[21] Dwight McCall grew up around this scene in Baltimore. His dad, guitarist/singer Jim McCall, was an integral part of the scene in Baltimore, playing off and on for years with Earl Taylor and Walt Hensley. As he grew up, Dwight saw firsthand the abundance of talent that resided in Baltimore. His first shows as a professional musician were as a teenager with his dad, Hensley, and many of the other early pioneers of bluegrass from Baltimore. This experience had a great impression on Dwight, as he became a highly respected bluegrass musician in his own right, logging many years as the mandolin player in banjo master J.D. Crowe's band. For Dwight there is no question as to Baltimore's place in the history of bluegrass: "The people that have played and come out of the Baltimore music scene are some of the best that will have ever played this music. It is a special place."[22]

Many of those early Baltimore musicians who inspired young impressionable talent like Sam Bush and Dwight McCall and helped provide such a unique voice to this still developing musical style would seem to have been within arm's reach of making it big, of reaching that musical summit, only to fall short due to a litany of reasons. With a scene built around a large influx of poor migrants with limited education, it is not surprising to hear McCoury say that the bands in Baltimore "were less professional"[23] than those in other cities, and to find so many players who were so talented on the music side fail so easily on the business side. This lack of business acumen or professionalism proved to be the biggest hindrance for many musicians from Baltimore.

Starting in the late 1960s Washington, D.C., slowly began becoming known as the Capital of Bluegrass as band after band there piggybacked on what they first heard in Baltimore at house parties and rough bars. To some people this title of the Capital of Bluegrass is open for debate. Baltimore bluegrass pioneer Russ Hooper makes it clear he completely and utterly disagrees with this. "D.C. claims to be the home of bluegrass or the Capital of Bluegrass," he declares with a defiant laugh, "and that is far from the truth. If it had not been for [D.C. based bands] the Seldom Scene and the Country Gentleman, I don't think they could have laid any claim to that at all."[24] Hooper's strong opinion is born of a lifetime playing in Baltimore, starting as a teenager in the early fifties when he played in some of the first bluegrass bands and jam sessions to take place in the city. He would go on to become one of the most influential Dobro players of all-time, and inspire and play with those same D.C. bands he mentioned. Washington, D.C., rightly gets credit for all it was to become in the bluegrass world. Much of this is due in large part to the musicians and bands from that area, who tended to be more educated and better off economically than their friends to the north in Baltimore, that city's musicians never seeming able to capitalize on their music in the same way. Those Baltimore musicians who helped pioneer this sound and influence many of those D.C. musicians seemed to get left behind. "I don't think Baltimore ever got its due in bluegrass, possibly because before bluegrass began to get really popular its [Baltimore's] heyday had passed," explains long-time Baltimore bluegrass icon Chris Warner.[25]

Baltimore, like other cities during this time, including Akron, Cincinnati, Columbus, and Dayton, had a an extremely active and influential bluegrass community that developed among the working-class Appalachian migrants who flocked to these cities looking for work. Baltimore was bigger than those Ohio cities, with a population of 949,708 in 1950, making it the sixth-largest city in the United States and almost double Cincinnati's population. Baltimore was unique in that, while it relied heavily on the influx of Appalachian migrants in its music scene, it was influenced just as heavily by the modern sounds emerging from Washington, D.C., and the folk-revival scene in New York City. Musician and writer Tom Ewing got his start playing with Baltimore musician Earl Taylor in the seventies before going on to join Bill Monroe's band in 1986. Ewing, one of the leading voices on the history of the genre, explains Baltimore's place among these other midwestern cities that were such vital destinations for hillbilly migrants looking for work: "I think that Baltimore was an extremely vital part of the northeastern scene, where bluegrass really first flourished during that time. There were just a lot of good musicians there [in Baltimore]. In my research, it's also clear that the area was key for the likes of Mike Seeger and Ralph Rinzler, who did so much to further the career of Bill Monroe in the 1960s."[26]

While geographically close, the makeup of Baltimore and Washington's burgeoning bluegrass scenes were worlds apart. Whereas Baltimore was built around the hillbillies who had moved to the cities for work, D.C. was built largely on the college-educated individuals, commonly referred to as "folkies," who took a fancy to folk and string-band music and co-opted this sound being created in Baltimore. Alice Gerrard was one of these folkies who first became enamored with, then became an integral part of, the Baltimore scene, and saw these differences between the two cities up close: "The difference was the people who came to Baltimore came for work, and a lot of them were very poor. They were working class who came up from the South because the coal mines were played out and they couldn't get work. So that is why they migrated to these pockets of Appalachia in Baltimore and got jobs in the factories. That wasn't the case in D.C. There younger people were finding this music [bluegrass in Baltimore] and really becoming drawn to it for whatever reason. They were seeking it out."[27] For these folkies, this music was not about culture, heritage, or a way of life, it was simply about the music and their affection for this homespun sound.

For every Del McCoury or Hazel Dickens who clawed their way out of Baltimore and achieved that lofty legendary status there are countless stories of those who could not quite obtain what their seemingly unlimited talent placed within their grasp. Whether due to lack of education, poor business sense, too much drink, a lack of faith in one's abilities, or quite simply bad luck, many of these Baltimore pickers found that, instead of etching their name in big letters on the roll call of greats, they were more often than not consigned to the overlooked role of early innovator or forgotten influence. The scope of these musicians' influence was wide and far-reaching, but unfortunately, as bluegrass musician Artie Werner (who years later played with many of the early pioneers from Baltimore in Cincinnati) says, "people don't realize how much bluegrass was influenced by Baltimore-area musicians."[28] It seems with the passage of time this has come close to being forgotten, as Baltimore is often overshadowed by its big brother to the south, Washington, D.C., and the impact of these pioneering musicians is relegated to a passing memory or a simple mention in a lyric. But Baltimore's story is the story of early bluegrass. Without it and the musicians who lived and played there, what we know and hear today would not be the same.

1

"Hillbilly haven"

Recommended Listening: The Bill Monroe compilation album *The Early Years* is the perfect complement for Chapter 1. The album is a collection of early singles and some of the first songs ever recorded in the bluegrass style. It provides great insight into what was inspiring the musicians in Baltimore.

No Dogs or Hillbillies. Those four words were printed in large bold letters at the bottom of a "For Rent" sign, and they hit a young Hazel Dickens like a ton of bricks. Dickens, who was just barely out of her teens at the time, was looking for an apartment upon her move back to Baltimore in 1954. This followed a brief return to her native West Virginia after her original foray into Baltimore as a sixteen-year-old in 1951.

Dickens was born in 1935 in Montcalm, West Virginia, in the heart of coal-mining country. The Dickens family claimed to be distant relatives of British author Charles Dickens, but the West Virginia Dickenses were world's away from their distant relative. They were hard-working folk, albeit very poor, with their major livelihood coming from the local mines and the industries associated with it.

Upon her return to Baltimore, Dickens was living with her sister Velvie in a typical Baltimore row house in a neighborhood near Eutaw Place originally built for workers in the sail-making industry. The neighborhood now was made up of migrant hillbilly-folk much like Dickens and her family. Dickens had ventured out of her neighborhood looking for an apartment when she encountered the sign. The sign recalled past immigrants from around the world, as they ran into warnings like "No Irish Need Apply" or similar derogatory statements. Dickens quickly realized she "knew [she] fit one of those descriptions"[1] on the sign she saw. Those four simple words helped breed a growing feeling of resentment in her. It was a feeling she would not lose until she began to find new friends among these city folk who were as passionate as she was about the music she had learned as a child in the

15

hills of West Virginia. She recognized that music was a "wonderful common ground on which to build and nurture new friendships." These friendships she would make with these city folk would go on to be some of the most important personally and musically for Dickens in her life, and they were at first built on that common ground of music. "We were a lot more willing to keep the cultural differences in the background and deal with one another more on a musical level until we learned to begin trusting the fact that we could be good friends despite the differences in our upbringings," she explained. "Many of those same friends are still some of my best friends all these years later."[2]

Situated off the Patapsco River, an arm of the Chesapeake Bay, Baltimore has long been an important shipping port. The Port of Baltimore was founded in 1706 at Locust Point for the tobacco trade and grew quickly. The town of Baltimore, named after Lord Baltimore—who was the first proprietary governor of Maryland—was founded shortly thereafter, on July 30, 1729. It was a key city during the Revolutionary War, serving as the capital of the United States from December 20, 1776, to February 27, 1777, when Congress met at the Henry Fite House located at the corner of Baltimore and Liberty streets. It also played a vital role in the War of 1812 (and perhaps landed itself for

View of Baltimore's Inner Harbor from atop Federal Hill. At one time the Inner Harbor was the second largest port of entry for immigrants to the United States. Today it is the centerpiece of Baltimore's downtown area (photograph by the author).

the first time on the national music scene), as Fort McHenry, located on Baltimore's Inner Harbor, served as the backdrop for Frances Scott Key as he watched the fort successfully defend Baltimore Harbor from attack by the British navy and was inspired to compose the words to "The Star-Spangled Banner." His poem was set to the tune of "To Anacreon in Heaven" and would later become the national anthem. While this may have been the first important musical event to originate in Baltimore it was not the last, as many prominent musical acts have emerged from the city over the years. Innovative rock guitarist Frank Zappa, famed songwriter Jerry Leiber, legendary soul singer Billie Holiday, popular composer and ragtime pianist Eubie Blake, jazz singer Ethel Ennis, controversial rapper Tupac Shakur, singer/songwriter Tori Amos, and Talking Heads front man David Byrne all have called Baltimore home during early parts of their lives. Baltimore was also home to the earliest known commercial manufacturer of banjos, William Boucher. Until Boucher began manufacturing banjos in 1845, all banjos were homemade and varied greatly. Boucher standardized the wooden frame and design of the instrument, thus helping create the modern design of the banjo.

Present-day Baltimore is still the largest seaport in the mid–Atlantic region and closer to midwestern markets than any other seaport on the East Coast. At one time its Inner Harbor was the second largest port of entry for immigrants coming into the country, trailing only New York City's Ellis Island.[3] Baltimore is less than 200 miles from New York City, located between Washington, D.C., and Philadelphia, and because of its larger and more prosperous neighbors it is often overlooked today. In the 1950s Baltimore was at the peak of its population growth and the sixth-largest city in the United States, trailing New York City, Chicago, Philadelphia, Los Angeles and Detroit. It was then, much as it is now, a working-class city that still bears the rugged imprint of the longshoremen, laborers, and factory workers who came before, many of them from the Appalachian hills and mountains. These early migrant workers represent what Baltimore is at its core: hardworking, genuine, and unafraid to tell it like it is.

The Great Depression had a crushing impact on the Appalachia region's economy, one already in dire straits. For many people of this economically depressed region, moving to the cities to find work was their only option. Historian John Alexander Williams writes in his book *Appalachia: A History*, "It has been said that all mountain regions must import capital or export people."[4] For much of the 20th century Appalachia did just that. With the region's labor force far exceeding the limited opportunities available in its core industries of agriculture, forestry, and mining, many Appalachian residents had little choice but to flee the mountains in search of steady work and a paycheck. And flee they did, an estimated two million people making the exodus from mountain to city.[5] Much like other cities at the time—Dayton, Cincinnati, Detroit, Columbus, and Pittsburgh—Baltimore saw a huge influx of migrants from the eastern mountain region starting during the Great Depression and continuing through the manufacturing boom that came with the development of New Deal-era jobs and World War II.

Baltimore in the forties and fifties had a thriving manufacturing, shipping, and textile industry, being home to 75 percent of all jobs to workers in the region. Bethlehem Steel, located in Sparrows Point near the Dundalk neighborhood just east of the city, was the economic giant of the region in the 1950s. It was one of the largest steel plants in the world at the time, employing more than 31,000 people. Many of those workers first came to the city from the Appalachian Mountains. In addition to Bethlehem Steel, Baltimore was home to a number of other huge plants and factories that were a big draw for people from Appalachia looking for work. General Motors, Western Electric, and the Martin Bomber Plant were thriving at the time and located on the same spit of land at Sparrows Point as Bethlehem Steel. Eastern Avenue, which runs from downtown Baltimore to Sparrows Point, was a primitive two-lane road at the time and the only option to and from the factories. This small road would become choked each morning and afternoon as these Appalachian migrants left the city to head to the factories for work, then retreated to the safety of their neighborhoods at the end of the day.[6]

The discrimination that Hazel Dickens encountered on her search for an apartment would have been fairly common for these hillbilly migrants. Down South the term hillbilly was often used as a familiar, affectionate self-description, but up North in the cities where these migrants had moved, it took on an offensive, derogatory meaning as a slur for rural, working-class people. Much as these hillbilly people faced prejudice and discrimination, so did the music they brought with them. James Hobart Stanton, one of the earliest owners of an independent record company that released albums of hillbilly-bluegrass type music, recognized the preconceived negative bias people held towards this music. He said, "People tied a banjo and a fiddle with Kentucky, with coal mining, with rural hillbillies, and socially people that were more educated, maybe more socially prominent, they turned their nose down at it."[7] Into the 1950s some record labels still advertised this type of music with offensive caricatures of hillbilly folk as barefooted, corn-cob pipe smoking, long-bearded mountain men in overalls.[8]

In a 1953 article in the *Baltimore Sun* titled "Hillbilly Music and Epilepsy," Dr. Samuel C. Little took this negative attitude toward this style of music a step further, trying to use science as a way to prove what he saw as the limited redeeming qualities of hillbilly music, saying he believed "an [epileptic] attack in one of his patients was induced by listening to a 'hillbilly' jam session." He added, "Music-induced epilepsy—called 'Musicogenic'—has been reported by two other researchers. And while scientific proof remains to be established, it seems possible that music can 'trigger' an epileptic seizure in certain cases, because it's already known that 'hallucinations' of music can do so." Of course, Dr. Little's "hypothesis" may have been based more on unfair stereotypes of this type of music and people, as he also goes on to blame such random events as poorly working televisions, driving past trees at sunset, and the reflection of the sun on ocean waves as other potential "triggers."[9]

The discrimination and prejudice these migrant folks faced in their new homes cultivated a sense of isolation among them and forced them to congregate and live in neighborhoods built upon the cultural similarities they shared. These areas were called "little Appalachia" or "hillbilly ghettos." In Baltimore, which had an extremely large influx of such migrants, these areas were clustered across the city in the neighborhoods of Hampden, Dundalk, Highlandtown, Lower Charles Village, and just outside the city in Middle River. A 1974 article in the *Baltimore Sun* called the city a "hillbilly haven" and explored these neighborhoods, the large hillbilly migrant population that found a permanent home in Baltimore, and the lasting impact they had on the culture of the city. The article posed the simple question of "Why Baltimore?" to one of these migrants, an elderly woman who first came to the city with her husband in 1951. Her simple answer, "for work," revealed the most pressing need of these people who were forced to flee the poverty of the mountains.[10]

The children who were either born in the cities to migrant parents or had moved with their families at a young age seemed to suffer an even greater disconnect than did their parents. They never truly had a connection to their parents' home in the mountains and they never truly felt part of the cities they grew up in. To try to maintain the connection to their "old home place" people brought with them parts of the culture they had known in the South and mountains. One of the easiest and most common ways to maintain this connection was through music.

The people of the Appalachian region were a mix of English, Irish, Scottish, and Welsh immigrants who settled there in the eighteenth century. The music that developed there over the years reflected this with its reliance on primarily stringed instruments, especially the fiddle, all of which were a regular part of the musical repertoire of these settlers from the British Isles. Melodically, this early hillbilly sound was very similar to the ballads and jigs commonly found among these settlers and would go on to form the backbone of bluegrass music.

Like Hazel Dickens and her family, who moved to Baltimore in the early fifties, these migrants who came into Baltimore and similar cities maintained their connection to their roots and rural homesteads through music they might have learned as children at the knees of their parents on their front porches or in the pews of their churches. While this might be an overly romanticized image of where the music came from (Bill Monroe was in fact from rural farmland in Kentucky—not the mountains) the sentiment was the same. It was a shared rural music. This shared music helped foster a sense of belonging and power for the migrants. The music they brought down from the mountains was still referred to as hillbilly and included strains of country, gospel, and old-time string-band tunes, mountain ballads, and the earliest seeds of what Monroe and his band had started to create in the 1940s. These various strains of music, when combined with the desperation of folks taking a chance by moving away from their homes to the harsh life in the city, would eventually blossom into the sound we recognize today as bluegrass.

Despite outward appearances and most preconceived notions, bluegrass is a relatively modern musical development. While its roots lie deep in the hills and mountains, it can be argued that bluegrass as we know it today did not exist until the hillbilly migrants left their homes in those hills and ventured into the cities looking for work and a better life. The music they brought down from the mountains at the time was more the bastard cousin of country music than bluegrass. Like country, early bluegrass tunes shone a light on the everyday lives of those singing them, but when the music moved into the cities it changed to reflect its new environment. Tom Mindte, owner of Patuxent Records, a music label based out of Rockville that specializes in bluegrass music, grew up in the Baltimore-Washington area in the sixties and seventies and saw this transformation of the music: "Down South the musicians played in church halls and school auditoriums, but up here they played in bars and the songs changed accordingly. Instead of just playing those nostalgic songs about the cabin on the hill and mother's grave, they started adapting drinking and cheating songs from mainstream country and arranging them for bluegrass bands."[11] This new style was similar musically to the rural music found at the time, with a large portion of the early bluegrass songbook dependent on traditional ballads and hymns passed down from generation to generation. Many of these early traditional songs were first organized into a songbook called *150 Old Time Folk and Gospel Songs*, written by country/bluegrass singer Bill Clifton in 1955. This widely influential book has been dubbed the "Bluegrass Bible" for its huge impact on this developing brand of music.[12]

Bill Clifton was born William August Marburg in 1931. Unlike most other early bluegrass pioneers he came from a wealthy family. He was raised on a farm just outside the Baltimore city limits in what is now considered part of Towson. He showed an early interest in music and would form his first band, the Dixie Mountain Boys, while attending the University of Virginia. He used the stage name Bill Clifton when performing, as his well-off parents were opposed to his musical endeavors. After college he joined the Marines, during which time he compiled *150 Old Time Folk and Gospel Songs* when he found he had little opportunity to play

Russ Hooper with his first Dobro, purchased from Ted's Used Instruments on Charles Street (courtesy Russ Hooper).

music in any kind of meaningful way with other similarly inclined musicians. Upon his discharge from the Marines Clifton immersed himself in the burgeoning bluegrass scene, which he helped spur on with the publication of his songbook. He began playing with many of the early pioneers in Baltimore and Washington, D.C., and organized one of the first ever bluegrass festivals, in 1961 in Luray, Virginia. Clifton was one of the first non-rural stars of country and hillbilly music, and because of this he was often referred to as a "citybilly."[13] He would go on to become one of the leading voices of this new sound, eventually gaining induction into the International Bluegrass Music Association's Hall of Fame in 2008.

The music found in the traditional hymns in Clifton's book began to evolve after the migrants started arriving in cities like Baltimore, Dayton, and Columbus. Much of the lyrical content started to address the hard life found in the city, the daily grind of working in the factories, and a longing for the old home place and a simpler time. Journalist and songwriter Jon Weisberger, in an article for *No Depression* magazine, argues, "Old habits die hard, and one of the hardest to shake is the tendency to assign bluegrass to the Appalachian Hills and hollers. Though understandable, it's inaccurate, almost as quickly as Bill Monroe's brand of country music turned into a genre; it found a home in the smoky nightclubs that served thousands of hillbilly transplants in the industrial centers east of the Mississippi."[14]

With its thriving manufacturing industry and the giant presence of Bethlehem Steel Baltimore was one of those important industrial centers in the 1950s. Russ Hooper moved there in 1952 from Washington, D.C., as a fifteen-year-old to help take care of his grandparents who were in poor health. He lived with them first on Bank Street near Patterson Park before moving to nearby Lakewood Avenue. Hooper compares his move to Baltimore to riding a turnip truck: "It stops, you get off, and you're here for the rest of your life."[15] In his case this was very true, as he has called Baltimore home ever since. As a twelve-year-old he discovered a passion for music when his father bought him a six-string Rickenbacker lap steel guitar for Christmas. He got his first taste of playing live in front of a crowd a few years later while still living in Washington as a fourteen-year-old when he and a friend persuaded the administration at McKinley Tech High School to allow them to play in the gym after a basketball game. It was an experience that had a lasting impact on young Hooper, as playing and performing became an integral part of his life.[16] Shortly after moving to Baltimore he bought his first Dobro—which would become his primary instrument—from an old, now closed music store on Charles Street called Ted's Used Instruments.

Hooper is often affectionately referred to in a down-home kind of way as a "very likeable fellow"[17] and seems to be universally adored by everyone he comes in contact with for his friendly, easygoing manner, and unmatched knowledge of the history of bluegrass in his hometown. It is a deep, firsthand knowledge, born from a lifetime of playing music in Baltimore. It is a knowledge that he will gladly recount with a humorous story or an interesting tale to anyone who wishes to chat. He is a musician's musician, valued not only for his immense musical talent, but also for his extreme professionalism onstage.[18] Baltimore-based guitarist Frank Joyner, who played with Hooper throughout the sixties in the Franklin County Boys, says, "I can tell you that you won't meet a more humble, genuine guy than he is. In all the years we played music together, not once did he ever do anything that wasn't good for the group."[19]

Through his long career, Hooper went on to play with seemingly everyone in Baltimore at one time or another, including Bob Baker, Charlie Waller,

Danny Curtis, Del McCoury, Walt Hensley, and Marvin Howell. He also has become a highly requested bluegrass session player. On Rebel Records' 1965 compilation album *70 Song Bluegrass Spectacular,* Hooper played on almost half the tracks, which represents only a small fraction of his studio work.[20] By Hooper's count, as of June 2013 he has played on 427 tracks, spanning fifty years and countless albums.[21] Through his tireless session work and his unparalleled skills onstage, Hooper has emerged as one of the truly preeminent Dobro players of all time, being named in the International Bluegrass Hall of Fame as a pioneer of the sound and instrument. *Bluegrass Unlimited* magazine says he has achieved "legendary status among those people familiar with the adolescent years of bluegrass."[22] However, like so many of his music playing peers, he would come consistently close to the big time but for one reason or another seemed to avoid making that final step. In Hooper's case, over the years he would turn down multiple invitations to join legendary bands Flatt and Scruggs and the Country Gentlemen. In the early fifties, though, upon his arrival in the city he was just another young kid looking to play music with like-minded folk and did what many migrants who moved into Baltimore did; he searched out similar musicians who were playing the earliest strains of what would become bluegrass.

When Hooper turned sixteen he discovered a music store on Howard Street called Fred Walker's. Fred Walker's was a large store that stretched out over two floors. The first floor was devoted to albums and sheet music and the second to instruments. It was the second floor where the instruments were sold that really excited the young musician. "Anybody could go there and take any instrument out of the case and play all day long if they wanted," remembered Hooper.[23] He spent countless hours there picking away in the afternoon. He soon met two "fellas" doing the same thing. Fellow teenagers Dickie Rittler and Bob Arney were both also whiling away their afternoons at Fred Walker's, Rittler usually picking away on a banjo while Arney was strumming a guitar. Arney's family lived just outside the city in Woodlawn and had an unused tenant farmhouse on their property. The three young musicians started getting together on weekends to rehearse there, Hooper and Rittler taking the long bus trip out of the city, and a close musical bond was formed among them. Tiring of picking at Fred Walker's and practicing at the Arneys' farmhouse they soon began playing in front of an audience as part of "Rhodie's Revues."

"Rhodie's Revues" were mini traveling variety shows that were a mix of singers, dancers, and musicians who would play at local schools and nursing homes. The three young musicians developed a short set of country songs and some traditional tunes and were soon a regular part of these revues. During a revue at Fort Meade, a military base just outside of Baltimore, they spotted another young musician carrying both mandolin and guitar cases. Intrigued, they approached him and asked him if he happened to know how to play bluegrass. The young musician, Danny Curtis, answered, "Yeah." Hooper, not wanting to miss out on an opportunity, dragged Curtis, Arney, and Rittler into a supply closet and the three practiced together for thirty minutes, working up a short set they would play later during Hooper's regular spot at the revue. Curtis was as capable on the guitar as he was on the mandolin, but it was with the mandolin that he would go on to make a name for himself. The relationship that started from that chance encounter would evolve into one of the most important of Hooper's life, as he and Curtis would go on to have an extremely long, productive musical partnership and deep friendship that lasted for more than fifty years, until Curtis's death in 2006. Their relationship extended well beyond music, as Curtis served as best man at Hooper's wedding, and Hooper would fondly say the two of them were "like brothers."[24]

In the tightly packed row houses that lined the streets in the "hillbilly ghettos," late-night jams and pickin' parties would erupt on the weekends and fill the hot, humid Baltimore air with the sounds of the mountains as mandolins, banjos, fiddles, and guitars played the songs of their old home place all night long. "You had all these people in the mid-forties moving up north from Appalachia trying to find work and they brought music with them," explains Hooper. "They would work all week in these factories, and then on the weekends they would manage to contact these people and have jam sessions at their houses."[25] Hooper and his new music friends soon became part of these late-night parties.

In the mid-fifties, in a brownstone house on Calvert Street, a guitarist from Blacksburg, Virginia, named Bob Baker, who had recently moved to the city, began hosting regular jam sessions on the weekends. Baker had moved to Baltimore in search of work and had found steady employment at the Crown service station on the corner of 21st and Charles streets. He was born in 1931—and hailed originally from Pike County, Kentucky—into a musical family and was well versed in the old-time string songs that made up much of the foundation of bluegrass. He had a brother, Billy Ray, who played bass and had moved to Baltimore shortly after Bob in search of work.[26]

Baker's time in Baltimore was short, as he moved back to Virginia in 1961. Despite the brief time in Baltimore his stay in the city was influential; his house jam sessions and the musicians who congregated and played there would go on to form much of the nucleus of the earliest bluegrass bands in Baltimore and the surrounding area. Hooper and his new friends met Baker,

Mike Seeger shows off his skills on the resonator guitar in the early 1960s (Photo-Sound Associates collection, courtesy Ronald D. Cohen Collection #20239, Southern Folklife Collection, Wilson Library, University of North Carolina at Chapel Hill).

and they soon became regulars at his all-night gatherings. The Dobro player fondly recalled, "We used to go over there on weekends on a Saturday night and come out Sunday morning when the sun was coming up. We would just play all night long."[27]

At first the music played at these all night pickin' parties simply helped bond the migrant folk who populated the neighborhoods and kept them connected to their rural homes. The players at these early parties soon realized the music they were creating might do more than just simply help them stay connected to the places they came from. Jerry McCoury, who was still in high school at the time, traveled to Baltimore with his older brother Del from their home in Lancaster County, Pennsylvania, to hear the new exciting music firsthand and eventually joined in as the two became regular fixtures of the scene. He remembers its gradual evolution: "All these musicians coming from the South for work at the seaport or something like that started playing together. They soon realized they could make a small amount of money getting together with friends and playing in these clubs. It mushroomed, and people loved it. People would come out to hear this music and have a good time."[28]

Hooper admits that not all of those who began playing out in the bars were in it solely for the money. With a laugh he elaborates, "For some, it [playing music] was just an excuse to drink. A lot of the guys I knew playing who had their own groups—who shall remain nameless—that was the reason [drinking] for them, to just get out from home and to play and have that access."[29]

At the same time that Hooper was playing with his friends at Baker's house, Hazel Dickens and her brothers Arnold and Robert had begun to spend time and play with a conscientious objector to the Korean War who was doing his alternative service at the Mount Wilson Tuberculosis Hospital in Pikesville, Maryland, about ten miles outside of Baltimore.

Mike Seeger was born in 1933 in New York City but grew up near Washington, D.C. He was the half brother of iconic folk singer Peter Seeger and had developed a love of old-timey traditional folk music at a young age from his parents, who were both heavily involved in the preservation of traditional American folk music. This love blossomed into a lifelong passion that would see him go on to become one of the most influential voices in not only preserving but also keeping alive the traditional folk songs and old-timey music from the mountains. The next generation of American folk singers, who were coming of age in the fifties and sixties, looked to Seeger as a guiding spirit who reaffirmed their own passions with his unquenchable thirst for this most American of music.

In the early 1960s Bob Dylan was a struggling young songwriter who looked up to Seeger's work with his band the New Lost City Ramblers, a band whose music was a straightforward interpretation of this old-time sound. The New Lost City Ramblers were at the forefront of the folk revival and they and Seeger were a major influence on the budding songwriter in Dylan. You can catch glimpses of the New Lost City Ramblers and subtle strains of the bluegrass Seeger loved so much in Dylan's early work. In his autobiography, *Chronicles* (volume 1), Dylan acknowledged how massive an impact it had on him when he first encountered Seeger at a house party in the early 1960s at Alan Lomax's loft on 3rd Street in Manhattan:

> When I saw him my brain became wide awake and I was instantly in a good mood…. He was extraordinary, gave me an eerie feeling. Mike was unprecedented. He was a duke, the knight errant. As for being a folk musician, he was the supreme archetype…. He played all the instruments, whatever the song called for—the banjo, the fiddle, the mandolin, autoharp, even harmonica in the rack. Mike was skin-stinging…. He played on all the various planes, the full-index of the old-time styles, played in all the genres and had the idioms mastered—Delta blues, ragtime, minstrel songs, buck and wing, dance reels, play party, hymns and gospel—being there and seeing him up close, something hit me. It's not as if he just played everything well; he played those songs as good as it was possible to play them. I was so absorbed in listening to him that I wasn't even aware of myself. What I had to work at, Mike already had in his genes, in his genetic make-up. Before he was even born, this music had to be in his blood.[30]

But before house parties with Bob Dylan and Alan Lomax, Seeger was just a kitchen orderly working at Mount Wilson Hospital in Pikesville, Maryland, where he had started in February 1954. Upon his arrival he made it clear he was a musician looking to play, and he soon met Robert Dickens, Hazel's brother, who was a patient at the hospital. By this time the entire Dickens family, mom, Sarah, dad, Hillary (who went by H.N.), and their eleven children (five girls and six boys), which included Hazel, Arnold, and Robert, had relocated to Baltimore after the decline of the coal industry in their hometown in Mercer County, West Virginia. Shortly after meeting Seeger, Robert invited his new friend over to his parents' house one evening to pick some tunes. The Dickens house was located in the Little Appalachia area of Baltimore, bordered on the east and west by Charles and Calvert streets and on the north and south by 20th and 25th streets, near what are today the neighborhoods of Remington and Charles Village.

Hazel reckons that the Dickenses "were the first hillbilly family he [Seeger] met in Baltimore, maybe the first ever,"[31] and she was wary of this interloper into her world. Hazel—who had begun to get deeply into music, even spending her first ever paycheck since her arrival in Baltimore to buy a guitar—was unaware of how serious or knowledgeable Seeger was about the music he was playing with her brothers in their living room. Acting unimpressed and trying to gauge the true motives of Seeger, Hazel, who had inherited her father's sometimes short temper, turned up the radio while they were playing in an attempt to drown them out, insisting this was how what they were playing should sound. Seeger continued to play, unperturbed by her childish attempt to interrupt. Hazel eventually wore down and joined in with them, and an extremely long and meaningful friendship was born.[32] Hazel would become drawn to Seeger when she discovered his genuine love and knowledge of the music she grew up with, saying, "Mike validated my culture."[33] Seeger also truly appreciated her immense talents and treated her with respect as an equal. This sort of respect would have been different from how she was treated by many of the men she played music with or encountered in the bars where she played at the time.

Seeger, Dickens, and her brother Arnold were soon regularly taking part at the jam sessions that took place at Bob Baker's house. On any given night you could find the Dickenses, Seeger, the Baker brothers, Hooper, Rittler, Arney, and a fresh-faced seventeen-year-old, Frankie Short, who had recently moved to Baltimore from West Virginia, among many others playing all night until the sun came up. Out of those late-night jam sessions was birthed one of the first working bluegrass bands in the city, Bob Baker and the Pike County Boys. Taking their name from Baker's birthplace in Kentucky, the Pike County Boys featured Seeger on fiddle, Dickens on bass, Rittler on banjo and Bob Shanklin (Dickens' one-time boyfriend) on mandolin.

The music at this time that Hooper and his friends and Seeger, Baker, and the Dickenses were playing was more likely still referred to as hillbilly or country. It was still in the earliest stages of the music Bill Monroe began to popularize with his Blue Grass Boys in the 1940s and had not yet taken on a fully established identity. That identity had first started to blossom upon the resignation of banjo player David "Stringbean" Akeman from Monroe's band in 1945. At this time Monroe was experimenting with a wide variety of sounds and instruments in his band, including a short-lived stint that saw an accordion join. The accordion dropped soon enough, but Monroe continued to try out new sounds in search of what he heard in his mind's ear. Stringbean struggled to find a role in this new sound and shortly afterward handed in his resignation to Monroe. Stringbean was a better comedian and showman than musician, and he would eventually go on to gain fame as one of the early comedy/music acts of the Grand Ole Opry. He would parlay his time on the Opry into even greater fame as he became one of the original stars of the long running country music/comedy TV show *Hee-Haw*.[34] According to Russ Hooper, upon Stringbean's resignation guitarist Lester Flatt, who was in Monroe's band at the time and had become completely disillusioned with the banjo as part of the group, told his bandleader with a frustrated sigh, "If you never hire another banjo picker I'll be tickled to death."[35] Monroe, as was his norm, did not heed the advice of anyone but himself and soon hired a banjo prodigy from North Carolina.

Born in Shelby, North Carolina, in 1924, Earl Scruggs is known for his revolutionary work in developing and popularizing the three-finger style of playing that, because of his innovative approach to the banjo, would become known as "Scruggs style." Country singer Porter Wagoner, recognizing Scruggs' monumental impact on a new generation of banjo pickers once declared, "Earl was to the 5-string banjo what Babe Ruth was to baseball."[36] While Monroe gave bluegrass its identity, it was Scruggs' one-of-a-kind banjo roll that gave bluegrass its easily identifiable sound, a sound that every banjo-picker since has tried to emulate. Scruggs' massive impact still reverberates loudly among musicians today. Chris Pandolfi, the Dartmouth College and Berklee College of Music-educated banjoist for the jam-grass stars Infamous Stringdusters, says, "I can't think of another musician who did so much for an instrument.... It was that banjo roll that sorta catapulted the music forward conceptually and in its popularity." Pandolfi says that as a young, developing band they look to those playing styles pioneered by the unbelievable genius in Earl Scruggs and "try to apply them to things that are meaningful to us today."[37]

Scruggs' addition to Monroe's band in 1946 would cement the classic Blue Grass Boys lineup of Monroe, Flatt, Scruggs, Cedric Rainwater on bass, and Chubby Wise on fiddle, which would help create and define the sound that gave bluegrass its now distinctive style and would go on to influence every bluegrass musician who has grabbed an acoustic instrument and picked a tune since. This classic lineup was only together for a short time, but it was a highly influential time, highlighted by the group's performances at the Ryman Auditorium as part of the *Grand Ole Opry* radio show. Russ Hooper recalled the impact that this new, exciting lineup had: "You think this country went bananas over the Beatles when they hit in '64? It was the same way at the Ryman whenever Earl came out to do a number with Bill. The crowd would just go crazy."[38]

Monroe's growing influence with the new sound was far-reaching, and began to find the ears of those who were first starting to play what would soon be dubbed rock 'n' roll. At the time, there was a lot of crossover and overplay between what was becoming bluegrass and the first strains of rock 'n' roll. Called rockabilly, it borrowed the rhythm and guitar work from rock 'n' roll and combined it with the hillbilly style of country music prevalent at the time. An upbeat, bluesy version of Monroe's "Blue Moon of Kentucky," set to a rocking 4/4 beat by Elvis Presley in 1954, was a minor hit for Presley and inspired rockabilly pioneer and legendary guitarist Carl

Perkins to head to Memphis to kick-start his music career. Perkins was greatly influenced by Monroe's work and recognized the bluegrass pioneer's impact on the developing sound of rock 'n' roll, explaining, "Some of those old Bill Monroe songs are so close to rockabilly it's scary."[39] Monroe may have not consciously realized it, but as he was creating this electrifying, cutting-edge sound with his Blue Grass Boys, he was breaking an old tradition to make a new one.

Grateful Dead guitarist and longtime bluegrass aficionado Jerry Garcia was another young musician greatly influenced by Monroe's sound. Garcia spent the spring of 1964 on a cross-country road trip with friend and fellow picker Sandy Rothman to see and record bluegrass at some of the legendary hot spots of the music. The trip included a stop in Alabama to see Jim and Jesse McReynolds, a stop in Ohio to witness the Osborne Brothers up close, and a stop at fabled Sunset Park in Pennsylvania, just a short drive north from Baltimore.

Sunset Park was home to many of Baltimore's best pickers on the weekends, hosting shows for more than fifty years until it closed in 1995. Due to its reputation as a bluegrass hot spot at the time, Rothman would later admit he wished they had possessed the presence of mind to actually stop in Baltimore itself and ask around about what was going on there while they were in the area. He said it was a "big mistake" not to stop by and poke around and get a chance to try to meet some of the city's famed pickers.[40] The pair's stop at Sunset Park, though, allowed them to see some of those pickers up close, and that fact would eventually provide much musical fodder for Garcia and the Grateful Dead throughout the course of their long career, as they dipped heavily into the treasure trove of traditional songs he would have heard played on Sunset Park's hallowed stage and on the tapes he and Rothman recorded of all the bands and performers they saw throughout their trip. The argument can be made that the Grateful Dead in their always changing set lists helped introduce a whole new generation to bluegrass with the inclusion of many songs that had their roots in the traditional and bluegrass world.

The stop at Sunset Park would also prove to be the first time Garcia crossed paths with one of his lifelong musical partners, David Grisman, courtesy of an introduction from Rothman. Rothman had encountered the future mandolin guru on an East Coast trip the previous summer. But the real focus of the trip was the time Garcia and Rothman spent at Bill Monroe's Brown County Jamboree, better known as Bean Blossom, outside Bloomington, Indiana, watching the master play up close. The duo harbored dreams of auditioning for Monroe's band during their time at Bean Blossom. Despite the quality time spent there listening to the ornery legend, Garcia was never able to actually muster the courage to break out his instrument and try out for him.[41] As Garcia and Rothman's trip came to an end Garcia returned to California, where he soon started the Grateful Dead. Rothman stayed East and ended up actually landing the spot he and Garcia coveted so much, and he played banjo and guitar for a short time with Monroe and the Blue Grass Boys in the summer of 1964.[42] Rothman would go on to establish himself as an important player in the bluegrass world, playing with everyone from Monroe, Clarence White, and Earl Taylor, to a number of Garcia-inspired acoustic bands.[43] Garcia's inability to introduce himself and audition for Monroe did not deter his admiration for him, as he stated, "He [Monroe] is the creator of this music. The guy who after which all other bluegrass bands are patterned, who set the formula so to speak."[44]

Despite the massive influence of Monroe and his band, the use of the term bluegrass was still far from common or accepted at this time. It appears the use of the term bluegrass to describe this growing style of music increased after Flatt and Scruggs left Bill Monroe's band and started their own. It was an acrimonious split that found the men on opposite sides of a growing rift. Monroe did not speak to his former bandmates for years, while Flatt and Scruggs did not even like to hear their former band leaders name mentioned in their presence. Because of this, the term bluegrass was sometimes thought of as a feud word. People who wanted to hear Flatt and Scruggs play some of the songs they had done with Monroe, yet feared saying his name in front of them, would ask the duo if they could play "one of the old Blue Grass tunes,"[45] using the name of the band, instead of Monroe's name as a way to request the music. People seemed to latch onto this idea of calling the music Monroe made by the name of his band instead, as it became more and more common for people to refer to this style of music as bluegrass.

Louise Scruggs, whose husband was Earl Scruggs, worked as manager and booking agent for her husband and Lester Flatt after they left Monroe's band in 1948. She remembers the slow evolution of the term bluegrass, saying the first time she heard it called bluegrass was around 1958. She said she "absolutely" avoided using the word bluegrass; instead she still called their music "country." Scruggs sensed the all-too-common prejudices against bluegrass music and the people who played it: "No bluegrass was played, really, all over the country. So I kept them, in their publicity [materials] in the country music field and they got airplay. Whenever they had a single released, it always got played. You couldn't get a bluegrass album or record played."[46] Historian and folklorist Neil Rosenberg argues that another reason for the limited use of the word bluegrass is that for many of these musicians—who later were identified as first-generation bluegrass musicians—the music they were creating then did not differ that greatly from much of what was called country music at the time.

An article from the *New York Times* in August of 1959 tried to explain this growing musical trend and examined bluegrass as a "form" of "hillbilly music" because of its growing popularity and "vogue in city folk music circles." It derided hillbilly music as being the "poorest example of poor man's music," while praising the new bluegrass sound as a "virtuosic ensemble instrumental and vocal style of white American folk music." The description it gave of the music was spot-on and still holds true for what is thought of as the traditional bluegrass lineup:

> Played in groups of up to six performers, it involves a complex set of string-instrument patterns and an almost acrobatic high-range vocal line, usually taken at staggeringly fast tempos. Its instrumentation, all non-electrified is generally the five-string banjo, mandolin, fiddle, guitar, and string bass. Splashes of technical display and semi-improvisational format are used in solos and ensembles. It is an energetic vehicle for a great variety of traditional mountain blues, ballads, songs and breakdowns.[47]

The article named some of the leaders and cutting-edge musicians of the new sound, and the list, unsurprisingly for the time, was dominated by Baltimore musicians. Earl Taylor and the Stoney Mountain Boys, Mike Seeger, and Russ Hooper's old pal Bob Baker and his band, the Pike County Boys, were all prominently mentioned. It would seem likely that given the lack of national exposure most bluegrass acts had at the time, the musicians from Baltimore had gained national attention through their inclusion on the *Mountain Music Bluegrass Style* album released in 1959. The groundbreaking album was one of the first full-length bluegrass albums ever released and the first introduction to the genre for many people.

For some, there was a very clear distinction between bluegrass and the hillbilly/country music played down South and in the mountains. Journalist and writer Hunter S. Thompson was a Kentucky native and had grown up listening to this type of music. While living in New York City in 1961, he went to Greenwich Village to write an article about the bluegrass music being played there. After seeing a Greenbriar Boys show (which included a young Ralph Rinzler on mandolin), Thompson came to the conclusion that bluegrass was a city-created version of the country music he heard back in Kentucky: "Here in New York City they call it 'bluegrass music' but the link—if any—to the bluegrass region of Kentucky is vague indeed. Anybody from the south will recognize the same old hoot-n-holler, country jamboree product that put Roy Acuff in the 90 percent bracket. A little slicker, perhaps; a more sophisticated choice of songs; but in essence, nothing more or less than 'good old fashioned' hillbilly music."[48]

It is quite possible the term bluegrass started to find traction and become more commonly used in Baltimore in the mid-fifties, a bit earlier than other parts of the country, as one of the earliest known instances of the word being used onstage was during a show at New River Ranch in Rising Sun, Maryland. New River Ranch hosted weekly events that many of the locals in Baltimore frequented on a regular basis. In May 1956, Monroe thanked the promoters of New River Ranch during his performance for supporting "bluegrass type music."[49] Some folks in the Baltimore area claim an even earlier use of the word, as they remember local radio DJ Don Owens using the term in 1948 on his show *Radio-Ro-Day-O* on local station WGAY.[50] The term seemed to start working its way into the vernacular of the musicians, appearing in various interviews and comments made from stage, but it was not until the mid-sixties, during an interview with long-time Grand Ole Opry Show announcer Grant Turner, that Monroe seemed to crystallize his desire to call this brand of music he helped create bluegrass, so as to distinguish it from country music. He told Turner he was dissatisfied with the direction country music was taking and wanted his music to be separate from it.[51]

The actual first use of the word in print is generally accepted as appearing in 1957 in the liner notes to *American Banjo: Three Finger and Scruggs Style*.[52] The album was recorded and produced by Mike Seeger while he was living in Baltimore. The accompanying liner notes by folklorist Ralph Rinzler attempt to clarify when this developing music moved from what was thought of as country to bluegrass: "This style of music became somewhat of a rallying point for musicians and fans of the older forms of acoustic southern country music, and in the mid-fifties it acquired the name 'bluegrass' since it was initially played by Bill Monroe and the Bluegrass Boys. Monroe was from Kentucky, The Blue Grass State. The term 'bluegrass' basically refers to an acoustic southern string band."[53]

American Banjo: Three Finger and Scruggs Style was an important album, the first stop on the long journey to introduce and legitimize the new sound. It is an album that took its shape from the unyielding interest of Mike Seeger in this most American of music and an extremely tight production budget that forced Seeger to rely on the close relationships he had developed with many of the local pickers in his adopted town. It is an album that, unsurprisingly, had its roots deep in Baltimore, roots that first sprouted in a row house on Eager Street.

2

"Laughing with our banjos"

Recommended Listening: The Mike Seeger-produced *American Banjo Three Finger and Scruggs Style* was released in 1957 and is the first full-length bluegrass album ever recorded. It is a compilation of music by various banjo pickers. It has an earthy flavor to it, as the album was recorded with a portable recorder in non-studio settings. The homespun warmth and the ragged, loose edge the album possesses are reminiscent of the music being made in the row-houses and bars in Baltimore in the 1950s. Many of the tunes played on the album would have been regular parts of the jam sessions and house parties that were flourishing across the city.

"It was kind of a brownstone, Baltimore-type row house. It became kind of a hub of musical activity," remembers Alice Gerrard. Today the California-bred Gerrard is the matriarch of women songwriters. Her work with Hazel Dickens can be heard in every female song of empowerment, in every heartfelt note sung by Emmylou Harris, in the old-time revival sound of Gillian Welch, the prodigious talents of Alison Krauss, or whenever Naomi harmonizes with Wynonna; but in the mid-fifties Gerrard was still simply a college student at Antioch College in Ohio. She had learned how to play piano as a child in California, but she did not discover old-timey and folk music until she was in college and began to listen to the tapes her boyfriend Jeremy Foster had collected of like artists. The pair had recently relocated to Washington, D.C., as part of their co-op job through Antioch College. They worked during the week and headed north to Baltimore on the weekends to meet up with Foster's good friend from high school, Mike Seeger. Their destination was usually a "brownstone, Baltimore type row house" at 1325 Eager Street in the south-eastern corner of the city, near Johns Hopkins Hospital.[1]

"Mike [Seeger] lived there, and there were always a lot of people there. There was folk music and there were parties. It seemed to be almost every weekend there was some kind of party; though it probably wasn't that often, that is how I remember it," says Gerrard with a wistful laugh. "It would be a

Carl Chatzky in 1978 at the Baltimore Blue Grass Inc. store. Chatzky was an important link between the more folk music-centric scene and the developing bluegrass scene in Baltimore (courtesy Russ Hooper).

real mix of people. It was an amazing collection of people. There would be country people and city people. Younger, sometimes radical, left-wing political young people or just plain young people from the upper middle class, and then the hillbillies would come. We would all just sit around and play music, eat, and there would be these parties that would go all night. Sometimes the police would come and close them down. It was wild, and we were all really young."[2]

At the time, Gerrard was still a few years away from her groundbreaking work with Hazel Dickens, and she admits that she was "more of a hanger-on at that point," just "kind of soaking it all in." But despite Gerrard's lack of participation, the house on Eager Street was an exciting, thriving, pulsating hub of musical activity that saw a widely disparate collection of people coming together and bonding over a shared love of music. This house was at the center of the vibrant scene Seeger recalled so fondly, and it was made up of those same people Hazel Dickens had said bonded over the "wonderful common ground" of music, and became some of her closest friends.

The house at 1325 Eager Street was the home of Willie Foshag and his wife, Alyse Taubman. They lived in a modest apartment on the third floor which was conservatively furnished with mostly used furniture and hand-me-downs. Foshag had been in the army but had since left and was working as an aeronautical engineer. He was well-known for his deep, un-matched knowledge of bluegrass. Jefferson Airplane and Hot Tuna guitarist Jorma Kaukonen grew up in the Washington, D.C., area and had discovered bluegrass after he graduated high school in 1959. Kaukonen recalled hearing tales of Foshag, who he remembered as "the older guy that everybody looked up to, who was the go to guy that knew all kinds of stuff about bluegrass." Foshag's wife Taubman graduated from local Goucher College and was working on her master's degree in social work. She was drawn to people in need, particularly those migrants who had moved to Baltimore from the surrounding Appalachian region. She was the daughter of a wealthy Baltimore businessman whose family had founded Advance Auto Parts, in 1932, which today is one of the largest auto supply retail chains in the United States. But in the 1950s Taubman lived a life completely at odds with her privileged upbringing. The couple were part of the local bohemian community of writers and artists and hosted parties, musical gatherings, and other events at their apartment. Both of them were deeply into music, Taubman learning to play the fiddle and Foshag the autoharp. Foshag had recently befriended Seeger, over their shared interest in the autoharp, at the home of another prominent couple in the Baltimore bohemian folk-music scene, Myron Edelman and Lisa Chiera.

Edelman and Chiera lived in a small carriage house behind a large apartment building on St. Paul Street near North Avenue in what is now the Station North Arts District. To access the house, you had to walk down a small path past the apartment building into a large open area where the house sat. Edelman and Chiera hosted various get-togethers and folk music events at their house in the late fifties and the early sixties. Most of the music-making took place in the main front room, with the assembled folks playing everything from old time tunes to protest songs to bluegrass. It was a wide-ranging bunch who assembled in the small carriage house. On any given night "Mike Seeger, Hazel Dickens, Alice Gerrard, Pete Street, Carl Chatzky, and a girl named Fay with hair down to her toes" might all be present.[3]

Chatzky, a regular at Edelman and Chiera's house parties, hosted many of his own musical gatherings on the weekends. Chatzky was an interesting character who provided an important link between the college-educated folkies and the true-blue pickers from Appalachia. He was an extremely bright individual who was attending Johns Hopkins University when he first discovered bluegrass in 1958. Chatzky never quite achieved the success of some of his more famous friends from Baltimore, but he would prove to be an important and long-standing part of the Baltimore scene. He regularly played with Mike Seeger, Hazel Dickens, Russ Hooper, Betsy Rutherford, and Alice Gerrard throughout the sixties and seventies. Chatzky was also very close with Dickens family. Hazel's brother Arnold named one of his sons Carl after his good friend. Later Chatzky developed a relationship with the famed Stanley Brothers and played with them when they needed someone to fill in. Equally adept at the banjo, mandolin, bass, and guitar, Chatzky was a valuable utility player to bands in need. His greatest fame came when he toured in the seventies with Peter Rowan. Chatzky stayed in the Baltimore area until the late nineties, when he moved to the West Coast.

Mike Seeger had first become acquainted with Edelman and Chiera through another mutual musician friend, Andy Ramsay, who also lived on Eager Street. Seeger had met Ramsay through the folk singer and Bob Dylan idol, Rambling Jack Elliot.[4] Edelman worked as an attorney, while his partner, Chiera, was very active in taping and recording traditional, old-time string band and bluegrass music throughout the region. She would travel with Mike Seeger on many of his recording trips through the sixties gathering and collecting music from some of the original musicians in the Appalachian Mountains and other areas of the South. Through her work taping she would go on to produce an album, *Galax, VA: Old Fiddlers' Convention*, in 1964 for Smithsonian Folkways.[5]

It was at Edelman and Chiera's house in 1957 that Seeger would first meet eventual New Lost City Ramblers bandmate and cofounder Tom Paley. The two would play together informally at Edelman's house for a few years before deciding to start the highly influential folk-revivalist band New Lost City Ramblers.[6] Despite the inclusion of such talent and so many future leaders in the folk and bluegrass world at Edelman and Chiera's gatherings and similar house parties

Bob Baker and the Pike County Boys, one of the first working bluegrass bands in Baltimore. Standing (from left): Mike Seeger, Hazel Dickens, and Bob Shanklin; kneeling (from left): Dickie Rittler and Bob Baker (courtesy Russ Hooper).

around Baltimore, there were no stars at the time; they were simply young friends learning and enjoying music together. Seeger, with his famous last name, might have been the closest thing there was to a celebrity.

As with many folk music communities at the time, this one was made up mostly of a younger college-educated crowd who had an interest in this type of music. The music played at these bohemian gatherings tended to be an idealized view of the working-class people who made the music and a sanitized version of the folk songs and traditional ballads they sang. Musician and writer Pete Kuykendall, who was from the Washington, D.C., area and through his friendship with Seeger was familiar with the scene at Edleman and Chiera's, snidely referred to those who gathered there as "bohacks"— bohemians who made hackneyed music.[7] The inclusion of Seeger, Hazel Dickens and her brothers, Robert and Arnold, into Edelman and Chiera's gatherings provided a taste of authenticity and helped elevate the quality of music being made there. The playing moved from simple folk songs and old timey music to something closer to the bluegrass and hillbilly music being played by Bill Monroe, Flatt and Scruggs, and Ralph Stanley. For many at these gatherings this would be the first time they heard the music they adored so much being played by a "real" person from that region.

Through the introduction provided by Andy Ramsay, Seeger began regularly attending the musical happenings at Edelman and Chiera's house and it was there he was first introduced to Taubman and Foshag. Dickens, who was playing with Seeger at the time, would have also first met Taubman and Foshag around the same time. Dickens and Taubman would grow to become extremely close, and their relationship became what Dickens declared was "one of the closest I've ever had."[8] Taubman became a mentor to Dickens, helping to bring her out of her shell, overcome her natural shyness and adjust to life in the city.

Foshag and Taubman also held regular parties at their house and Seeger and Dickens soon became a regular part of these gatherings as well. The gatherings were not only musical in nature, but also included long, in-depth discussions about political and social issues. Dickens was still too shy and unsure of herself to participate in these discussions but she listened intently and absorbed all she heard. The talk had a profound impact on the young, naïve Dickens. "I just exploded during that period," she later recalled, "It was the beginning of me being politicized."[9] This politicization of the burgeoning songwriter would eventually show itself in some of her most famous protest songs, such as "Black Lung," "The Mannington Mine Disaster," and "They'll Never Keep Us Down," and she would go on to become known as the voice of the working class. Dickens represented the working class so well because there was no doubt, given her background and upbringing, that her music was real and spoke the truth. Her music was not made for the mainstream; it was made to express emotion. Her time spent listening to the late-night political discussions at Taubman's house only helped intensity the soulful honesty with which she sang.

Since their initial meeting at the Dickens house a few years earlier, Seeger and Dickens had grown close and they began playing regularly together. They first played in a variety of informal settings, often at Hazel's house, but soon branched out to play at other parties around the city with Hazel's brothers. This led to the occasional gig at the bars around town, though Dickens preferred to tell her mother they were clubs "because that sounded a little better."[10] They usually worked the gigs for nothing more than tips.

These gigs around Baltimore at locations like the Cozy Inn or the 79 Club—where the aroma of stale beer mingled with the smell of the men who had returned from a long day working in the factories and plants and who were looking to drown their overworked souls with too much drink—would have been an eye-opening time for Dickens. She did not drink and the rough, drunk and ready-to-fight crowd that inhabited these bars would have been an affront to her, especially in the brutish, dismissive way they treated the women who frequented these places. "I didn't have to work in a factory to see how badly women were treated," said Dickens. "Playing in bluegrass, a male-dominated form of music was enough."[11] She took it all in, observing and remembering. These memories would eventually manifest themselves in some of her most powerful songs, including the feminist classic "Don't Put Her Down, You've Helped Put Her There."

Dickens and Seeger had also become part of the jam-sessions held at Bob Baker's house on Calvert Street, where Russ Hooper, who was also a regular member of the sessions, encountered Seeger for the first time. With a laugh, Hooper remembered the first time he laid eyes on Seeger: "He came in with a T-shirt with holes all over it and he just looked like a typical hippie."[12] Baker, Dickens, and Seeger started one of the earliest working bluegrass bands in Baltimore during this time, Bob Baker and the Pike County Boys. Baker played guitar and sang, Seeger played the fiddle, and Dickens was on the bass. Hooper's pal Dicker Rittler on banjo, and Bob Shanklin on mandolin completed the lineup. For Dickens the Pike County Boys were a "smoother" sound than the music she made with her brothers at home. Keeping in line with the more professional approach, Dickens purchased a "couple of used cow-girl shirts with the bow-ties and some pants to match, to try and look the part."[13] Regular gigs were tough to come by, but they did find the occasional paying job at the seedy Blue Jay Bar on South Broadway in the Fells Point area of the city. Seeger remembers these early gigs with Baker and Dickens as being at "some of the worst downtown dives" in Baltimore.[14] In addition to her regular gig with Baker and the Pike County Boys, Dickens began to freelance with other musicians in the city, including regular jobs with Jack Cooke and Danny Curtis.

With the addition of Seeger and Dickens to the music scene evolving in Taubman and Foshag's house, and the extraordinarily close friendship that developed between Dickens and Taubman, the house on Eager Street soon morphed into that hub of activity Gerrard recalled becoming the center of all their musical happenings. Many times they would hold parties at the Eager Street house and use all three floors for different types of music: "old-time on one floor, bluegrass on another, and folk-music on another."[15] Dickens would help prepare for the evening by calling up all the musicians she knew and then set the mood in the house by lighting candles and placing cushions on the floor for people to sit on while they played or listened to the music being created.

Lamar Grier was another local musician who was a regular part of the house party music scene in Baltimore. "I remember those days," says Grier. "We'd play all night long. At Eager Street we would play on the second floor … [but] we had to break when the Osborne Brothers came on WWVA [famed country-music radio station out of Wheeling, West Virginia]. The parties were treasures. We did that just about every weekend, and I looked forward

Party at Tom Gray's house for his birthday in 1966. Bill Monroe and his band had a gig in the area that night and they stopped by afterward. Russ Hooper says they jammed until 5:30 in the morning. Bill Monroe, with mandolin plays with Russ Hooper (center) and Hazel Dickens (courtesy Russ Hooper).

to that weekend."[16] Grier soon left the friendly environs of Eager Street to play banjo in Bill Monroe's band in 1965. After leaving Monroe in 1967 he reunited with old friends Hazel Dickens, Alice Gerrard and Mike Seeger and played and recorded with them for a few years. After leaving Dickens and Gerrard's band he would join Washington's Buzz Busby for a stretch before playing in Peter Rowan's band. Grier retired from music in 1984.

Seeger "believed that bluegrass music was the logical and inevitable outgrowth of the music made by old-time string bands,"[17] so it was only natural that when he began to play with Dickens and her family he would gravitate towards a more bluegrassy sound. Whereas many of their friends' parties around the city tended to focus more on folk music and labor-protest songs, the musicians who gathered on Eager Street found that through the strong-willed influence of Seeger and the authentic, Appalachian touch of Dickens they began to play with more of a bluegrass feel. This difference was highlighted by the inclusion of some of the local hillbilly musicians. Through

Tom Gray's birthday party in 1966. The night was packed with some of the region's best players. In the crowd (from left): Tracy Schwartz (fiddler in plaid shirt), Richard Greene (fiddler), Tom Morgan (between Schwartz and Greene, leaning on wall), Peter Rowan (guitar player with back to camera), Alice Gerrard (with drink in hand), Bill Monroe, James Monroe (bassist obscured by Bill Monroe), Russ Hooper (bottom right with back to camera) (courtesy Russ Hooper).

Seeger and Dickens and their association with Bob Baker and all the hillbilly musicians who gathered at his house for those late-night jam sessions, many of those migrant hillbilly musicians found themselves part of the parties on Eager Street. "It was all these different kinds of people who might not have found one another," Gerrard says. "There was a lot of tolerance on both sides. It was the music that cemented it all together."[18] Consequently, the music played at the house on Eager Street reflected this, the focus being on a more bluegrass sound and less folk-type songs. The bluegrass parties at Eager Street tended to be rowdier than those of their friends singing folk songs at Edelman and Chiera's house, and the Eager Street crew enjoyed breaking up their friends' parties. Gerrard remembers how they would gather up their instruments and "intrude on their little circular group of being cool where they were singing labor songs," blasting into Chiera's house "laughing with our banjos."[19]

Inadvertently, through the house parties on Eager Street a more authentic bluegrass sound started finding its way to Washington, D.C., and the college-educated folkies from there who were so deeply into learning about this kind of music. Seeger was originally from the Washington area before he moved to Baltimore for his alternative service at Mount Wilson Hospital. When he joined in with the Eager Street crowd, many of his friends from Washington, including high school friend Jeremy Foster, his girlfriend, Alice Gerrard, Pete Kuykendall, and Dick Spottswood, began to travel north to Baltimore to take part in the exciting new music scene. Kuykendall referred to this group from Washington as the "suburban hillbillies."[20] They would take the music they heard and learned on Eager Street back to Washington and it would become incorporated into their own bands, many of which became highly influential in their own right. In addition to the bands these suburban hillbillies would form, their influence would reach much farther than just the music they would make. Kuykendall and Spottswood would both go on to help found and publish the long-running *Bluegrass Unlimited* magazine. "It was an incredibly real time of learning and openness," remembers Gerrard. "It was a real education; it was a really amazing time. It was a very unusual phenomenon. It stays in my memory as a kind of wonderful, unusual experience with a lot of mixtures of people and wild parties."[21]

Another important connection made at the time was the friendship and eventual musical partnership that developed between Hazel Dickens and Alice Gerrard. Just as meeting Taubman and receiving her guidance had done for Dickens, the meeting between Dickens and Gerrard had an important impact on Dickens' life, as the two would develop a musical voice together that would make them the first women of bluegrass. They both differ on their memories of when they first met, though they agree it was around 1955 or 1956. Gerrard recalled the meeting coming about through an introduction from her then boyfriend, Jeremy Foster, at Bob Baker's house. Gerrard had just started learning how to play the banjo and guitar and Foster felt the two would "hit it off musically." Dickens thought the pair met at a party at Foshag and Taubman's house. Regardless of how they met, what Foster first told Gerrard about Dickens always stayed with her: "There is this little girl with an incredibly big voice that you've got to meet."[22]

Upon meeting, Dickens and Gerrard discovered their voices meshed together in a wholly unique way that must have been jarring to those unaccustomed to hearing women harmonize in a bluegrass style. The way their voices came together was perfect, with Gerrard's deep, haunting, husky singing providing a low harmony and rock-solid foundation over which Dickens' high, wavering, "incredibly big" voice colored with dust from the coal mines could dance freely. "We found our voices matched," Dickens said, "matched better than my singing with a lot of men."[23] The pair created something new and unheard of: two powerful female singers harmonizing together in a genre long dominated by men. Their partnership provided the blueprint for countless women singers and songwriters who followed in their large footprints. Bill Friskics-Warren, in No Depression, declared, "Since the folk revival of the 1950s, no two women have exerted as much influence within bluegrass and old-timey circles as Hazel Dickens and Alice Gerrard."[24] Their influence would not only be seen in women songwriters and musicians, but men as well. Jerry Garcia was fond of old war songs and songs about brothers and especially liked an old tune called "Two Soldiers," which had been around since the Civil War. Garcia first discovered it through Dickens and Gerrard's self-titled 1973 album and included it as part of the Jerry Garcia Acoustic Band repertoire in the 1980s.[25] Bob Dylan was another fan of the song and has been performing "Two Soldiers" as part of his live set since 1988. He included it on his 1993 album World Gone Wrong, admitting in the liner notes he first learned it from Garcia, acknowledging Dickens and Gerrard's contributions to the development of the song.[26]

Dickens and Gerrard did not immediately begin to perform together after their initial meeting, and when they did it was generally only for a few friends at the house parties they frequented around Baltimore. Their first big public appearance was at the annual Old Fiddlers' Convention in Galax, Virginia, in 1962, a few years after their initial meeting. The Old Fiddlers' Convention is acknowledged as the world's largest and oldest fiddlers' conventions and has regularly been a gathering of bluegrass fans for years. Dickens and Gerrard's set was made of up mostly Carter Family songs, with the duo performing on autoharp and guitar.[27] Around this same time, Gerrard and Dickens met Peter Siegel and David Grisman at one of the house parties in Baltimore. At the urging of Siegel and Grisman the pair eventually set out to record their first album, *Who's That Knocking?*, released in 1965. The album was hailed for its unique and successful pairing of two female singers, something quite rare in bluegrass and country music at the time.

During their first ever public performance at the Old Fiddlers' Convention, Dickens and Gerrard would have seen some familiar faces in the crowd, as their good friend Lisa Chiera was in attendance recording tracks for the album *Galax, VA: Old Fiddlers' Convention* she would produce and release in 1964. It would also been very likely that Seeger and some others from their scene in Baltimore would have made the trip down, as they were a constant presence at the convention in Galax over the years. Chiera was very active in recording at this time, making the annual trip to the Old Fiddlers' Convention in Galax as well as continuing to record at the house parties that filled the weekends back in Baltimore. But she was not the only person in their group who was capturing the music being made. Seeger had long been lugging around his Magnecorder M-33 tape recorder documenting whatever music he came across.

The Magnecorder M-33 was a large reel-to-reel machine built to be a consumer version of the larger professional model. Seeger became omnipresent at New River Ranch and Sunset Park, the two dominant music parks in the region, with his forty-pound beast of a tape recorder perched on the edge of the stage with its lone microphone stationed at the center of the stage aimed at the PA mike. He had first obtained the tape recorder in 1955 and shortly afterward was regularly bringing it with him on his trips to New River Ranch and Sunset Park. Seeger would ask permission of the owners, if they minded if he recorded there, and then would ask the individual musicians before they performed for permission to record as well. Famed country singer Grandpa Jones became the first person to allow Seeger to record him at a show at New River Ranch May 1, 1955. Bill Monroe became the second person to grant permission a week later at another show at New River Ranch.[28]

The attention that many of the early bluegrass pioneers received in Baltimore was in no small part due to the diligence of Seeger and his ever-present tape recorder. San Francisco musician Sandy Rothman appreciates Seeger's recordings and all the music it introduced Rothman to: "If it wasn't for Mike's recordings we might have never known about Earl Taylor in a far place like the Bay Area."[29] Songwriter and Hot Rize mandolinist Tim O'Brien was another musician who greatly appreciated Seeger's tireless efforts to record this old-time sound at its source. "I'm always looking for repertoire," says O'Brien, "and I'd like to say that I've always gone directly to the source, but I needed—and most people need—a complier. Mike's one of those. Whether it's his recordings of other people singing and playing or whether it's his own recordings, I've definitely learned a thing or two from him."[30]

Recording contracts and full-length albums were extremely rare for bands of this ilk, so to have someone like Seeger capturing the music being made was extremely important. The bands would have been able to make decent money on a consistent basis from playing live shows and getting a regular residency spot at a local club or bar. Recordings and albums at the time were created for marketing and promotional purposes so that bands could get exposure on radio to help build audiences for their live shows. Seeger had gained an interest in the preservation of music from his parents. His father, Charles, was an ethnomusicologist with a focus on American folk music, while his mother, Ruth, worked closely with John and Alan Lomax at the Archives of American Folk Songs at the Library of Congress. Mike's recordings were at first informal and sporadic, capturing the sound of bluegrass in its infancy, with bands still finding their way on stage creating new styles and sounds every time out. He would catch bits of conversation and chatter onstage that helped give insight to the bands and performers and showcase how this new musical style was developing. His recordings were not limited to the stage either, he was known to corner musicians after shows in the parking lot or backstage or even sometimes at their homes to get the performance or song he wanted. Seeger's interest in recording would take on a greater importance in the summer of 1956 with the arrival of a letter from Moses "Moe" Asch.

Moe Asch was the founder and owner of Folkways Records in New York City. Folkways was an influential label, releasing over 2000 albums of old-time, world, folk and similar types of music since Asch first started the label in 1948. Folkways introduced a generation of folk singers and old-time music enthusiasts to the songs of such legendary figures as Woody Guthrie, Lead-Belly, and Pete Seeger, as well as the traditional songs that had been passed down for countless years in the South and Appalachian regions.

Asch was friends with Seeger's older half-brother Pete and became aware of the younger Seeger's interest in recording and documenting this growing style of music. He especially took note of the younger Seeger's interest in Scruggs-style banjo, which Mike had been teaching Pete. This bluegrass style of music was starting to catch on with some of the enlightened city-folkies and Asch wanted to make sure he properly documented it. In the summer of 1956 he sent Seeger a letter asking, "How would you like to do an album for us on Scruggs-style banjo?" An excited Seeger leaped at the opportunity. "It changed my life putting together an album of musicians that I knew were all around me, who couldn't be heard in any other way," he said.[31] Asch offered Seeger $100 to help cover expenses, and with that in his pocket and his forty-pound tape recorder in tow, Seeger set out in his Chevrolet Carryall (a large truck-type station wagon) to record some of the earliest pioneers of the banjo. Because of his tight budget and limited resources he was able to make only one trip through the South and would have to rely on many of his musician friends in the Baltimore and Washington, D.C., area to help fill out the album. Fortunately he hung out with some of the most talented musicians in the area.

American Banjo: Three Finger and Scruggs Style (**author's collection**).

Before setting out on his southern recording trip Seeger talked with his friend Pete Kuykendall, who was an avid music collector and musician and had discovered country and bluegrass music as a young child through the radio stations that regularly played it in Washington. With his deep knowledge on the history of the genre, Kuykendall was able to point Seeger in the right direction regarding whom he should try to see and record on his trip. Despite being able to put together only one five-day trip through the South, it was an extremely fruitful trip. Dates with some of the oldest pioneers of the banjo were arranged and Seeger was able to record performances from Smiley Hobbs, Junie Scruggs (Earl's older brother), Snuffy Jenkins, Oren Jenkins, and Larry Richardson among others. Most of the recording sessions took place at the player's home, with any backing accompaniment coming from Seeger and some of his friends who had accompanied him on the trip, usually Tom Morgan and Pete Kuykendall. Upon his return to Baltimore Seeger called on his friends to provide the final tracks to the album.

He enlisted his Pike County Boys bandmates Bob Baker, Hazel Dickens, and Bob Shanklin to help showcase the traditional tune "Cindy," played by Baltimore banjo picker Dickie Rittler. Seeger also recorded a performance from a teenaged Veronica Stoneman. Better known as Roni, she was the youngest child of the musical Stoneman family. The Stonemans are one of the truly legendary families of country and bluegrass music. The father, Ernest "Pop" Stoneman, wrote country music's first million seller, "The Sinking of the Titanic," in 1924. As with many families at the time, the Great Depression forced the Stonemans to move from their rural Virginia home to the Washington, D.C., area in search of work, and they eventually settled in Carmody Hills, Maryland. The entire Stoneman family was extremely musical, many of the 23 children going on to prominent recording careers. The family was led by daughter Roni and son Scotty. Roni would gain fame and go on to a long career as one of the stars of the long-running country music comedy TV show *Hee-Haw*. Roni's appearance on Seeger's album was the first recorded performance of a woman playing three-finger Scruggs style on an album, and a life-changing event for Roni. Despite having played in the some of the rough-and-tumble Baltimore bars as a precocious twelve-year-old with her older brother Scotty, she was aware how much more important her appearance on the album was. "It was sure a big deal for me. After that record came out in 1957 with me playing, 'Lonesome Road Blues,'" recalls Stoneman, "I became known as the First Lady of the Banjo, and that's what people call me today."[32]

The finished album, *American Banjo: Three Finger and Scruggs Style,* was released in 1957 and was the perfect recorded history of Scruggs-style banjo playing. The first half of the album was devoted to early pickers such as Hobbs, Jenkins, and Junie Scruggs, who would have influenced a young Earl Scruggs' developing three-finger picking style. The second half of the album was filled with younger players who had been first influenced by Scruggs and emulated his revolutionary style of picking. Many of these younger pickers were virtually unknown at the time, but would go on to make a name for themselves as well. Seeger would appear on many of the tracks as a backing musician. "Many of the pickers wanted backup bad enough to ask [Seeger] to play," and his tight budget often left him as the only one available.[33] To those tracks he contributed his workmanlike playing. His playing, while never flashy, was the perfect complement to the rustic feel of the album with his simple, melodic flourishes. *American Banjo* was the first full-length album devoted to bluegrass and "brought the music into a revolutionary new recorded sound medium. Instead of six minutes worth of two songs, the record had close to an hour's worth of music, with thirty-one separate selections."[34] A reissue of the album in 1990 added an additional sixteen to tracks to the overall length of the album.

American Banjo was released with an extensive set of liner notes. It included detailed bios on each of the performers by Seeger that helped to introduce the listener to each performer. The liner notes also included a comprehensive description of bluegrass by Seeger's friend and fellow folklorist Ralph Rinzler. Rinzler's notes are generally the accepted first use of the word bluegrass in print, and as such he tried to define the word: "The term 'bluegrass' basically refers to an acoustic southern-string band consisting of a guitar and string bass, used primarily for rhythm, and a mandolin, banjo and one or two fiddles for backup 'breaks' or instrumentals. The musicians are also singers, solo or in a combination as large as a quartet. Instrumentals and vocals are performed in specific new styles evolved in Monroe's band that are built on the foundation of old-time southern string and vocal music."[35]

As the record was released on the Folkways label it was geared more to the urban, educated folkies who were so enthralled with the burgeoning folk-revival movement. Rinzler's notes would have been the first time many of them heard the word bluegrass and its connection to Bill Monroe. At the time, they would have most likely still referred to the music Monroe made as country or hillbilly. In an article for *Bluegrass Unlimited* magazine in 1985, Dick Spottswood reflected on the importance of the album, calling it "a significant influence in spreading the bluegrass sound to an emerging generation of young city pickers."[36] Clearly recognizing who the album was geared towards, Seeger included a subtle reference to those young city pickers with the inclusion of Eric Weissberg on the final two tracks on the album. Weissberg was a trained musician who had attended the Juilliard School of Music before becoming an integral part of the New York City folk scene. He would become one of the most influential players in that scene, though to many he would be best known for playing the iconic "Dueling Banjos" in the 1972 movie *Deliverance*. "Dueling Banjos" would be the first exposure to banjo and bluegrass music for many people.

Around the same time he was working on *American Banjo*, the twenty-four-year-old Seeger moved into a second-floor apartment in the same building as Foshag and Taubman. The friendship between Seeger and Taubman began to intensify upon his moving in, eventually blossoming into a romantic relationship that hastened the end of Foshag's and Taubman's marriage. Fos-

Mountain Music Bluegrass Style (**author's collection**).

hag soon moved out of their shared apartment on Eager Street. Seeger and Taubman's relationship lasted about a year and was the first serious one of his life. Their relationship would come to an end when Taubman began to pressure Seeger about marriage. Seeger, who did not feel he was ready for marriage, ended the relationship

After the success of the *American Banjo* album, Seeger continued to find new projects and unheralded musicians to record for Folkways Records. He began taking regular trips through the South, often accompanied by Taubman when they were still together. His two projects immediately following *American Banjo*, 1957's *Negro Folk Songs and Tunes* and 1958's *The Stoneman Family: Old Time Tunes of the South*, were important documentation of this very regional music, but both failed to have the same broad impact as *American Banjo*. That would change with his next project, 1959's *Mountain Music Bluegrass Style*, which would grow out of his time in Baltimore and the friendships he made with many of the local bluegrass musicians.

Recognizing the enormous amount of talent around him in Baltimore playing bluegrass and sensing a real and growing interest in this style of music in the burgeoning folk-revival scene happening at the time, Seeger wanted to introduce the folk-revival scene to his friends in Baltimore. "I had this feeling of a mission," said Seeger.[37] For many in the folk-revival scene they loved hillbilly and bluegrass type music, but tended to drift towards safer, more staid versions of these old-timey songs, versions that were made by musicians who came from their scene and were more likely college-educated like themselves. These college-educated folkies found many of the stars of hillbilly and bluegrass music at the time a bit too "ethnic."[38] Seeger, having the always valuable cache of his famous last name in folk circles, aimed to bring the mountains to the masses. Or at the very least help introduce some of the true performers of bluegrass to the gatherings of folk-revivalists who huddled cross-legged on the floor of their tiny apartments in gatherings as they tried to learn how to pick the old-timey tunes. Seeger would succeed in doing that, as the album ended up influencing a generation of folk-revival pickers across the country. West Coast folkie, burgeoning bluegrass head and future Jerry Garcia road-trip partner Sandy Rothman recalls the impact *Mountain Music Bluegrass Style* had on the folk-scene in the Bay area: "The whole album was a revelation, feeding us folkies a major slice of bluegrass culture, well known in the Mid-Atlantic [region], but unknown here in the Bay Area."[39]

Upon its release, *Billboard* magazine gave *Mountain Music Bluegrass Style* a favorable review, awarding it three-stars and saying, "A top collection of hill numbers are performed here in sparkling and authentic style by a group of artists including Smiley Hobbs, Tex Logan, Don Stover, B. Lilly,

Chubby Anthony, Earl Taylor and the Stoney Mountain Boys, Bob Baker and the Pike County Boys and others. The set is annotated in knowledgeable and interesting fashion by Mike Seeger who goes into the history and background of the music and artists. For fans of the genre it's a mighty rewarding set."[40] Seeger would also inadvertently cause a major shift in bluegrass—though one that would take years to notice—with the release of *Mountain Music Bluegrass Style*. He had asked the bands that appeared on the album to play their more traditional songs, as he hoped to expose these songs to a wider audience; but, as he noted in the album's extensive liner notes, "Not all of the selections on this album are strictly bluegrass since they may omit several instruments or treat a song differently than Bill Monroe might have. But they are all in the stylistic area presently agreed to be called 'bluegrass,' which to some means 'not old-time, not commercial country, but somewhere in between.'"[41]

For many in the folk-revival scene this was the first bluegrass album they had heard. This very traditional style of music on its first chance at influencing a whole new scope of pickers was doing it in a way that deviated from the standard Bill Monroe lineup and playing style. These folkies would go on to form countless bands themselves and morph and mutate bluegrass into what suited them, what some people may argue is not "true" bluegrass. "When people from the South were moving into the cities they were still remembering what they heard on the opry and they were trying to copy it," explains Russ Hooper. "They were copying what some of the very early bluegrass bands like the Lonesome Pine Fiddlers, Sonny and Bobby Osborne, and Jimmy Martin were doing. They were still playing that traditional sound. But it has changed because the new groups, the younger generations coming up now who are playing this stuff, have managed to put their own signature on it. Very seldom do you find a group now that does traditional bluegrass."[42]

As with *American Banjo*, Seeger called upon his friends to play and perform on the album. He got fiddler Tex Logan to provide a pair of tracks, "Katy Hill" and "Natchez Under the Hill," which both highlighted Logan's influential tuning techniques. These two songs featured Seeger on banjo and his New Lost City Ramblers bandmate John Cohen on guitar. Seeger also recruited banjoist Don Stover and guitarist Bea Lilly, who were on hiatus from the Lily Brothers while Everett Lilly was touring with Flatt and Scruggs, to play a handful of songs for the album. Two local Baltimore bands who were friends of Seeger's would account for half of the tracks on the album, and it was these tracks that really caused *Mountain Music Bluegrass Style* to spring to life and catch fire.

Seeger first looked to friend and bandmate Bob Baker, who he and Dickens played with in the Pike County Boys, for help with the album. The band at this time consisted of Bob Baker on guitar, Bob Shanklin on mandolin and Seeger on banjo when he was available. Dickens had since left the band and was replaced by Baker's brother Billy Ray on bass. Russ Hooper, who was long part of the jam sessions at Baker's house, had also started playing with the band, but he had not yet joined them full time and was therefore not part of the recording sessions for *Mountain Music Bluegrass Style.* Since Dickens' departure from the group they had also recruited fiddler Jimmie Grier to round out the lineup.

Grier was originally from Washington County, Tennessee, and had joined the army in 1946. Upon his discharge, he, like so many of his southern brethren, settled in Baltimore to look for work. He lived on William Street not too far from the legendary 79 Club on Cross Street in Federal Hill. In Hooper's estimation Grier was one of only two fiddler players (the other being Curtis Cody) who were "making the rounds" and capable of playing with the skilled pickers in Baltimore at the time.[43]

Baker and the Pike County Boys contributed five songs to the album. As it was Seeger's goal to have the album help introduce many of the old-time songs that were a regular part of these bands' repertoires, he asked them to play some of those traditional numbers for the album. The five songs Baker recorded for the album were all older traditional songs, some dating back to the 1920s, and had been given new life by Bill Monroe when he began playing them in his new bluegrass style. The five tracks allowed Baker and his band to show off their talents as they showed their range, moving from the slower hymn-like tempo of "Drifting Too Far from the Shore" to the driving cadence of "Little Willie" to the frantic picking of the classic "Rabbit in a Log" (titled "Feast Here Tonight" on the album), which showcased the skillful fiddle work of Greer. All of the songs were recorded in Taubman's living room at 1325 Eager Street. Despite this intimate setting Seeger encouraged Baker to introduce the songs as if he were on stage. Baker did just that and the spoken word introductions he provided for each track helped give a little history of the songs, as well as giving the listener a better sense of what it would be like to see the band onstage at one of its regular gigs around Baltimore. Baker and the Pike County Boys were not the only band that used the comfy environment of Taubman's living room in which to record their tracks for Seeger.

Another local band that had been around since the earliest days of the growing bluegrass scene had captured Seeger's attention, as they had that of many folks around town. Seeger had recently made their acquaintance after catching one of their shows at the 79 Club and being blown away by what he heard. The band featured a hot-shot banjo player who would go on to influence countless pickers who followed in his large but extremely modest footsteps. It was led by a mandolin player with a "razor-edged high tenor"[44] who was sometimes referred to as the "the poor man's Bill Monroe."[45]

Like Bob Baker and the Pike County Boys they would record the majority of their tracks for the *Mountain Music Bluegrass Style* album in Taubman's living room. The rest of their tracks were recorded at a 10:00 a.m. recording session in a room above the 79 Club. Their six-song contribution was the most by any single band on the album. But it was two of the tracks in particular, "White House Blues" and "Short Life of Trouble," that were played with an energetic style, delivered with an incredible, intricate picking that grew out of unmatched interplay within the band, and blasted forth with paint-peeling vocals that would leave a lasting impact on so many other musicians who first heard those tracks when they were developing their musical chops as young, impressionable musicians.

3

"A high octane explosion"

Recommended Listening: 1959's *Mountain Music Bluegrass Style* recorded and produced by Mike Seeger. The album was one of the first full-length bluegrass LPs ever produced. It was a compilation album that highlighted much of the local flavor Seeger had become immersed in while living in Baltimore. Over half of the tracks feature Baltimore bands Earl Taylor and the Stoney Mountain Boys or Bob Baker and the Pike Country Boys. This, combined with the lo-fi recording style that Seeger used, which found him recording in kitchens, living rooms, or whatever open space he could find, make it easy to close one's eyes while listening to the album and instantly find oneself in the midst of a tasty pickin' party in some crowded living room on a hot, humid Baltimore evening.

"I was just floored," recalled David Grisman on the discovery of the song that led him to ditch his rock 'n' roll leanings as a sixteen-year-old and inform his classic piano teacher that he was picking up a new instrument: the mandolin. Grisman would go on to become one of the most influential mandolinists of all time, creating a sound that combined the classic bluegrass he discovered as a teenager and the complex Django Reinhardt-styled jazz he loved into a hybrid affectionately called "Dawg Music." It was named after Grisman's nickname, "Dawg," which had been bestowed on him by Jerry Garcia, his longtime friend and bandmate in the bluegrass super group Old and in the Way. But in 1960 he was just a rock 'n' roll-loving teenager in New Jersey when a friend returned from a trip into New York City with the highly influential bluegrass compilation album *Mountain Music Bluegrass Style*, which featured an electrifying new style of music he had been trying to introduce to Grisman. "I remember the first cut that he played. It was 'White House Blues,' by Earl Taylor with a guy named Walt Hensley playing the banjo," Grisman says. "It was the fastest thing I'd ever heard."[1]

"White House Blues" was a high-octane explosion of the traditional song about the assassination of President William McKinley, first made famous through the version by old-time string-band Charlie Poole and the North

Carolina Ramblers in 1926. Poole played with a three-finger banjo picking style which would later be adopted as a familiar component of the bluegrass sound. Noted historian Bill Malone describes the Ramblers' sound as "a bluesy fiddle lead, backed up by long, flowing melodic guitar runs and the finger-style banjo playing of Poole. Predictable though it might be it was nonetheless outstanding. No other string band in early country music equaled the Ramblers' controlled, clean, and well-patterned ensemble sound."[2] Poole and the Ramblers had a string of minor hits in the twenties, including "Don't Let the Deal Go Down," "Milwaukee Blues," "Sweet Sunny South," "Hesitation Blues," and "White House Blues." "White House Blues" featured Poole's trademark plainspoken tenor style singing and the Ramblers classic banjo-fiddle-guitar lineup, both of which proved to be early influences on a young Bill Monroe and later Mike Seeger and his folk-revival string band, the New Lost City Ramblers. Taylor's version of "White House Blues" was a completely different beast than Poole's restrained reading of the traditional tune. He had most likely been influenced by Bill Monroe's speed-up version of the song, but Taylor's unhinged take seemed to move at an even faster pace than Monroe's. In less than two minutes, Taylor and his band, the Stoney Mountain Boys, laid waste to all that had come before and in the process helped reshape the direction of bluegrass by introducing the world to the hard-driving Baltimore sound.

Grisman says that *Mountain Music Bluegrass Style* "was the first bluegrass [he] ever heard." In addition to the life-changing music he discovered on the album, he used to read the extensive liner notes "over and over."[3] At the same time he was discovering the Mike Seeger-produced album, another group of young musicians across the country in the San Francisco Bay area were having their own mind-blowing experience with the same album. Before their cross-country road-trip to see bluegrass up close, Sandy Rothman and Jerry Garcia were just a couple of folkies picking tunes in coffeehouses and working on their bluegrass chops. Along with Robert Hunter (who would go on to become the Grateful Dead's lyricist) and David Nelson (who would later form the New Riders of the Purple Sage), Rothman and Garcia played in some of the earliest bluegrass bands on the West Coast, the Wildwood Boys and the Black Mountain Boys. During this time, Rothman and Garcia were introduced to the *Mountain Music Bluegrass Style* album by another musician friend, Ray Scott, who was particularly enthusiastic about the Stoney Mountain Boys' sound and made sure Rothman "got it." The Stoney Mountain Boys were featured on the album's cover, providing a rare glimpse of the band, and just as with Grisman it was the tracks by the Stoneys that really set Rothman and Garcia's hair on fire. To Rothman these tracks "were the most mind-blowing of all." He said he and Garcia wanted to emulate the musical "group mind" that Taylor and the Stoney Mountain Boys seemed to play with, but despite their best efforts they never felt they could truly replicate it.

Whereas Grisman was "floored" by "White House Blues," Rothman and Garcia were captivated by the slower tempo of "Short Life of Trouble," another Stoney Mountain Boys track from the album. The song featured Walt Hensley using the tuning pegs on his banjo in a unique style that had a major impact on the budding banjo-picker Rothman. "'Short Life of Trouble' burned itself so deeply into our collective consciousness that when Jerry [Garcia], David [Nelson], and I sang the song in the Jerry Garcia Acoustic Band [tour] of 1987 that was the version [Earl Taylor's] we were still flashing on twenty-eight years later," Rothman says, "and still would be if we could do it again."[4] The song was so important to the trio they included it on both live albums released from that brief Jerry Garcia Acoustic Band tour in 1987—1988's *Almost Acoustic* and 2010s *Ragged But Right*. Rothman says they "were all crazy about Earl Taylor from the records, [because] he was a legendary figure."[5] Rothman would later realize his dream and go on to play in the Stoney Mountain Boys with Taylor in the late sixties and early seventies.

Both tracks were recorded by the classic early lineup of the Stoney Mountain Boys that included Taylor on mandolin, Hensley on banjo, Sam "Porky" Hutchins on guitar, and Vernon "Boatwhistle" McIntyre on bass. The band was led by Taylor's wavering tenor and propelled along by Hensley's hyperactive, maniacal picking that sounded like it could derail at any moment. Hensley would later say that when they recorded "White House Blues" they played it too fast, admitting he felt they "gaffed it."[6] But it was exactly this tenuous balancing act between Taylor's tenor and Hensley's picking, combined with the gas-pedal-mashed-to-the-floor speed that gave this new fiery sound its power.

You did not have to be a bluegrass enthusiast to recognize the awesome, explosive way in which the Stoney Mountain Boys delivered their take on "White House Blues." It was readily apparent on first listen to anyone. Their version of the song featured all the classic parts that one would expect to find in bluegrass, but it harnessed an entirely different energy than before. It was laced with the desperation of men who might have no other option but music and tapped into the dangerous atmosphere that was so pervasive in the smoke-filled corner bars where it was birthed. This recording was a defining moment for the Baltimore sound, as it was one of the first times the new, exhilarating sound could be heard outside of those dangerous corner bars in Baltimore. The mid–1950s were an important transition period in the development of bluegrass, and Taylor and his Stoney Mountain Boys were at the forefront of this transition, as they applied a hard-driving spirit onto the countrified hillbilly music with which they had grown up.

Earl Moses Taylor was born in the southwest corner of Virginia, in Rose Hill, Lee County, near the Kentucky/Tennessee border on June 17, 1929. His parents died when he was young and he was raised by his four older brothers and two sisters. He discovered music at an early age through the pioneering sound of the Monroe Brothers and the banjo playing of his brothers, all of whom used the clawhammer style. But young Earl was moved by a different sound and persuaded his sister Bernice's boyfriend to show him how to play guitar. After mastering the guitar he then learned how to play both the harmonica and mandolin. The mandolin would become his primary instrument over the years. Taylor was part of the flight from the mountains to the North in the mid-forties, looking for work and an opportunity in the big city. He left home at seventeen in 1946 and first tried his luck in Monroe, Michigan. While the work was not plentiful, Taylor did find opportunities to play music. He had developed a singing voice described with the highest of compliments in the bluegrass vernacular as being able to "peel paint."[7] A friend from Rose Hill who was living in Monroe at the time took notice of his powerful voice and incredible stage presence and persuaded Taylor to enter a local talent contest. His good showing at the talent contest got him an offer from "Bud" Bailey to join the Rhythm Mountaineers and shortly thereafter he played his first ever gig at the Bubble Bar in Toledo, Ohio.[8]

Realizing that he might have more to offer musically than just as a complementary role player, Taylor decided to form his own band. He headed south to Cincinnati in 1947, which, like many other working-class cities that stretched from Baltimore to Detroit, had a large influx of southern hillbillies and plenty of places that offered the opportunity to play this type of music. He planned to meet up with "Lucky" Saylor, a guitar player from back home in Rose Hill whom he knew lived in the area. The pair decided to start a band and recruited fiddler Elmer Kinsler to complete the lineup. They named their new band after a landmark near Taylor and Saylor's Rose Hill home in the Virginia coalfields, and the first incarnation of the Stoney Mountain Boys was launched. The trio gained a small amount of notoriety in the area, landing a regular spot on a local radio show in Flint, Michigan. By 1948 the band had run its course, and Taylor, disillusioned with his chances up North, returned home to Virginia for a short spell. The opportunities back home were even bleaker than they were in Michigan and Ohio, and Taylor moved again the following year to Rockville, Maryland. His ex-bandmate Saylor would eventually leave the Cincinnati area as well. He would go onto play with Bill Monroe in 1956 for a short time and, like Taylor, also end up in the Baltimore area, becoming a mainstay in the close-knit music community that blossomed there.

Taylor found the occasional odd job upon his move to Maryland, working for a stretch hanging drywall, but he never seemed to have the drive to hold a steady job. He had an infectious smile that was usually augmented by a Kool cigarette dangling from his mouth, and he possessed an easygoing nature that endeared him to his bandmates. His lack of education would at times limit his employment opportunities, but that did not matter, as the pull of music always was always too strong for him to be tied down to one job for too long. Jeff Roberts, who played banjo in Taylor's band in 1975 after Taylor had moved to back Cincinnati, saw this firsthand: "He was extremely laid back, not a care in the world. Music was all he knew. He was also illiterate which of course would have limited him from pursuing much of anything else."[9] But in the 1950s, despite his inability to hold down a real job for any extended period of time, Taylor gave his laid-back all to music.

A couple of years after moving to Rockville in 1952, Taylor fell in with a couple of younger musicians, Sam Hutchins and Charlie Waller, both of whom were seventeen. While eating lunch in his car one day Taylor heard the duo playing on a small radio station broadcasting out of Wheaton, Maryland, and was instantly smitten by their sound. The next day he tracked the pair down at the radio station and convinced them they should join him. They agreed and a new version of the Stoney Mountain Boys was started.[10] Taylor's music worked best when he had a strong vocal presence to help balance his pure, clean tenor, and in Waller he found just such a partner.

Charlie Otis Waller was born in a small east Texas town in 1935. He moved north at the age of ten to join his mother, who had taken a job with the Potomac Electric Power Company in Washington, D.C. Much like Taylor, Waller decided at an early age that music was his passion and his way to possibly earn a living. Upon his arrival in D.C. he was tutored for a short while by Scotty Stoneman of the famous musical Stoneman family to help with both his musical and performance skills.

Scotty had long been trekking from his home in Carmody Hills, Maryland, to Baltimore and was a regular playing in the bar scene there, oftentimes with younger sister Roni joining him on banjo. He established himself as one of the pioneers of bluegrass fiddle and was referred to as the "bluegrass Charlie Parker"[11] by Jerry Garcia. In an interview with Elvis Costello for *Musician* Garcia credited Stoneman with influencing his adventurous style of guitar playing: "I get my improvisational approach from Scotty Stoneman, the fiddle player. [He's] the guy who first set me on fire—where I just stood there and don't remember breathing."[12] With the experience and tutelage of Stoneman,

Waller landed his first paying professional music gig in 1948 at the young age of thirteen. Shortly thereafter he hooked up with Hutchins, and the duo soon landed a regular spot at that small radio station in Wheaton.

James Samuel Hutchins, known to everyone as "Porky" was a tall, easy-going banjo picker born in Forest Hills, North Carolina, in 1935, into a large, musical family. He picked up the guitar and banjo around age ten, becoming highly proficient on both. Like so many others from the South, Hutchins found his way to Baltimore in search of work, where he landed a job at the Davidson Chemical Company. Early in his career he was known mostly for his impressive banjo work, even winning the highly competitive Sunset Park Banjo contest in 1958, but he later would switch to playing primarily guitar.[13]

Waller's voice and guitar were the perfect complement to Taylor's expressive singing and straightforward approach to the mandolin, and along with Hutchins' steady playing the trio soon developed a strong musical bond. In 1953 Taylor convinced Hutchins and Waller that they should make the short drive north to Baltimore to look for gigs. Upon their arrival in Baltimore they came across a man on the street carrying a violin case. Intrigued at the possibility of expanding their band, they approached him. After a brief audition, in which he wowed them, fiddler Louie Profitt joined the Stoney Mountain Boys, Taylor declaring it was "just like he'd been playing with us for ten years."[14] The new lineup scored their first paying professional gig shortly thereafter when, after cruising up and down Baltimore Street in Waller's car one evening, they were able to convince a local bar owner to let them play a short set. They were an immediate hit with the small crowd, whose rapt attention and high praise, both figuratively and monetarily, had an immediate impact on Taylor. He recalled the show years later in an interview with *Bluegrass Unlimited*: "Just in a few tunes, we had dollar bills throwed around the stage, looked like where leaves had fell off an oak tree."[15] It proved to be a defining moment for Taylor, who then pursued gigs with a vengeance in his new town of Baltimore.

After that first gig, Taylor looked to round out the Stoney Mountain Boys lineup and added bassist Vernon "Boatwhistle" McIntyre. Taylor and Boatwhistle had met at a party when Taylor first moved to Maryland, and they had remained friendly since that time. When Taylor approached Boatwhistle, who was running a used car lot at the time, about the bass vacancy in his band the bassist was more than excited to join.[16] From that day forward Taylor and Boatwhistle formed a rock-solid musical partnership that would be the longest of their lives, as they would play together off and on for over thirty-five years.

Originally from Asheville, North Carolina (born in 1919), Boatwhistle

A true entertainer, bassist Vernon "Boatwhistle" McIntyre performs at the Folksong '59 concert (courtesy Photo-Sound Associates Collection, Ronald D. Cohen Collection #20239, Southern Folklife Collection, Wilson Library, University of North Carolina at Chapel Hill).

was a bit older than his new bandmates. He had been in and out of various bands for years, gaining a measure of notoriety from his time playing with the Morris Brothers in the late 1930s. Boatwhistle was the inheritor of the old comedy tradition from the Blue Ridge Mountains in North Carolina and was one of the truly great bluegrass comedians. A true entertainer, he performed in baggy pants, a sailor hat, and a big bow tie. He always stressed that entertainment was a big part of the business and that fans could listen to music anywhere, so they also had to see the musicians were enjoying themselves on stage as well. He said he developed his comedy act so there was more to him that just standing there and playing.[17] Beloved by all who met him, he was one of those people it seems everyone has nothing to say about him but great things. Boatwhistle was described by Sandy Rothman, who played with Boatwhistle in the late sixties, as "a big bear of a guy who would take you in as though you were family. He was just like an immediate uncle or grandfather. He was warm, friendly, and totally supportive, and musically just tremendous fun to play with. A totally joyous individual."[18] Boatwhistle's loose, relaxed personality always served to keep the band in good spirits, even during those long nights when on the road traveling between gigs. Artie Werner played with Boatwhistle in the late seventies in Cincinnati, and appreciated this trait in the bassist:

> Vernon always kept the band in stitches while traveling, telling his jokes and keeping us awake. He insisted on riding shotgun, and no matter what the temperature his window was wide open. For the long road trips we had a Dodge Travco motor home, like Jimmy Martin had in the old days. I remember him sitting in the front seat while I was driving, his head bobbing up and down, fighting sleep. But if you were to hit a bump or swerve the least little bit, his head would pop up and he would ask what in the heck you were doing.[19]

This new lineup of the Stoney Mountain Boys began to make some noise in the Baltimore area, getting noticed for their high-energy shows. They were soon working full time, what they called "nine shifts" (seven nights and two matinees) a week. A brief setback ensued when Profitt took his leave from the band to pursue other opportunities. (Profitt hooked up with Melvin Goins, best known at the time for his stint with the Lonesome Pine Fiddlers, to form a new band.) Undeterred, Taylor searched out new musicians to fill the ranks of the Stoney Mountain Boys. For a brief stretch they added fiddler Art Wooten, who had crossed paths with Taylor in 1953 in Baltimore. (Wooten, called the "First Fiddler of Bluegrass," was the first ever fiddler in Bill Monroe's band. He had developed the now distinct sound associated with the bluegrass fiddle when Monroe, using his mandolin (tuned the same as fiddle), showed him how he wanted it to be played. Wooten was with Monroe's band when he made his first appearance at the Grand Ole Opry in 1939. He left Monroe in 1942 and enjoyed short stints with both the Stanley Brothers and Flatt and Scruggs. He appeared on early recordings for both bands, helping cement his place as a truly legendary bluegrass pioneer.[20] Wooten left the Stanley Brothers in 1952 and ended up in Baltimore. His time with Taylor was short, with no known recordings existing of their time together. He left Taylor in 1954 to return to his native North Carolina.)

Taylor, Hutchins, Boatwhistle, and Waller worked their nine shifts for two years, until 1955 when Waller started playing with Louisiana native Buzz Busby and his band, the Bayou Boys, in Washington, D.C. Once Waller picked up with Busby he quit the Stoney Mountain Boys and was replaced for short time by guitarist Fred Keith. While Waller was playing in Busby's band he met and befriended banjo player Bill Emerson. After a car accident in 1957 that hospitalized Busby, Emerson recruited Waller, John Duffey, and Larry Leahy for a July 4 show at the Admiral Grill in Bailey Crossroads, Virginia, to play as a temporary band to fill in while Busby was recovering from his injuries. Waller and Duffey, who had never met before, were so impressed by their immediate chemistry that their temporary band soon became something more permanent. Duffey, Emerson, Leahy, and Waller took the name the Country Gentlemen, and one of the most important and most influential bluegrass bands of the last fifty years was born. At this same time Waller was leaving the Stoney Mountain boys and starting the Country Gentlemen, Taylor and Hutchins were being recruited by a young, hot-shot singer in Detroit to join his new band.

Jimmy Martin, known as the "King of Bluegrass," had gotten his start, as so many others had, as a Blue Grass Boy with Bill Monroe. He served as lead vocalist and guitarist for Monroe starting in 1949, but the two frequently clashed, as Martin's over-the-top personality seemed to be the antithesis of Monroe's buttoned-down approach and challenged Monroe's rigid, stubborn authority. Martin left Monroe in 1953 and began working with the Osborne Brothers, Sonny and Bobby, in Detroit. In their only recording session together they cut six songs. Despite the unmistakable talent and chemistry the band possessed, their time together was short-lived, as Martin's larger-than-life personality always struggled to share the spotlight with others. The Osbornes left Detroit in August of 1955, Martin staying behind, intent on starting his own band.

Rufus Shoffner, who played briefly with Taylor in 1948 in Flint, Michigan, had gained a small sense of celebrity himself and had become friendly with Martin in Detroit. Hearing that Martin was looking for some new players he recommended his old bandmate Taylor to him. Taylor and Hutchins had recently relocated to Detroit at the beginning of August 1955 to play with Hutchins' brother, Carace. Much like Baltimore, Detroit was a real destination for the early hillbilly players because of the thriving Appalachian community there. Taylor and Hutchins' plans soon changed after the two arrived in Detroit when Martin started recruiting them. Seven days after arriving,

Walt Hensley, the tall, lean, banjo player with the deadpan stage presence whose addition helped solidify the lineup of the Stoney Mountain Boys. Hensley is onstage at the Folksong '59 concert with Earl Taylor to his left, and fiddler Curt Cody (obscured by Taylor) (courtesy Photo-Sound Associates Collection, Ronald D. Cohen Collection #20239, Southern Folklife Collection, Wilson Library, University of North Carolina at Chapel Hill).

Hutchins and Taylor played an all-night audition for Martin at Casey Clark's club. Martin was thoroughly impressed and asked the pair to join his band. Taylor and Hutchins agreed and became part of the earliest version of Jimmy Martin and the Sunny Mountain Boys.[21]

Their time with Martin was short but fruitful. They traveled to Bradley

Studios in Nashville, Tennessee, with Martin in May of 1956 and recorded four sides for Decca Records, "Before the Sun Goes Down," "Skip, Hop, and Wobble," "You'll Be a Lost Ball," and the classic "Hit Parade of Love."[22] These sessions also included Bill Monroe's old bassist Cedric Rainwater, who was part of the classic Blue Grass Boys lineup in the mid-forties. Rainwater had left Monroe's band in 1948 to work with Flatt and Scruggs after they split from Monroe. Hutchins would leave the Sunny Mountain Boys within the year to return to Baltimore and was replaced on banjo by a teenaged J.D. Crowe. Crowe would play with Martin for four years before leaving to start a solo career. During his fifty plus years as a solo artist, bandleader, Grammy winner, and banjo innovator, Crowe has become an icon in the bluegrass world. His band, J.D. Crowe and the New South, is one of the most influential bluegrass groups of all time, with a roster that reads like an all-star bluegrass team: Jerry Douglas, Doyle Lawson, Tony Rice, and Ricky Skaggs among many others who have played with the banjo master.

Taylor stayed behind after Hutchins left and played for a while with Martin and Crowe. His easy going nature was evident as the legendary banjo picker Crowe called him "one of those you guys couldn't help but liking."[23] In December of 1956, Martin, Crowe, and Taylor headed to Nashville for a recording session that produced another handful of songs; but as would become a pattern for him that he would often repeat, Taylor left shortly after the sessions—right as Martin seemed to gain a wave of popularity—and headed back to Baltimore. Taylor may have been a musical genius, but he was no businessman and always seemed to be one step behind opportunity. He would pick up with some big-name star but last only a short time—often because he had grown weary of the hard times on the road that bands at the time had to endure—and soon find himself back in the same working-class bars he had been in before as a long procession of musicians passed through his band on their way to often bigger things.

Returning to Baltimore, Taylor reunited with Hutchins, Boatwhistle, and for a short time Waller, and set about reestablishing the Stoney Mountain Boys. Waller left permanently soon after Taylor's return to devote his energy full time to his new band, the Country Gentlemen. Taylor found the final, crucial piece of the classic Stoney Boys lineup after Waller's departure, when on a night off from his semi-regular gigs at the Jazz City Club in the Fells Point neighborhood in Baltimore he wandered into the Cozy Inn.

The Cozy Inn on West Baltimore Street was one of the truly infamous Baltimore bars of the time. It had a notoriously rough reputation and was known for its shady atmosphere and even lost its liquor license for a short time in 1957 for serving alcohol to minors.[24] It was a place Russ Hooper referred to as a "dump."[25] Mike Seeger said it was the place that everyone always remembers from that time: "You had a stage about six feet deep and eight feet wide that three or four people could crowd onto, and a sound system that barely got the sound out there. There were maybe a dozen tables and all those low-down barroom smells of smoke and drink. Occasionally there were fights, but people were usually too old or too drunk to fight."[26] Taylor walked into those low-down smells that evening. Crowded onto the small stage was a pick-up bluegrass band whose tall, lean, banjo player with the deadpan stage presence blew him away that night. "Lord have mercy," Taylor later roared, "[he] just knowed so know much on that neck … it was impossible to make him miss a note!"[27] It was immediately evident to Taylor why the tall banjo player would soon garner the nickname "Banjo Baron of Baltimore." Bowled over and impressed, Taylor asked the tall banjo player, Walter Hensley, on the spot if he wanted to join the Stoney Mountain Boys. Hensley, who also played guitar and banjo in rock-a-billy band, the Black Mountain Boys, admitted to Taylor that he could make more money playing rock 'n' roll, but "bluegrass was the music of my [Hensley's] roots, the music I loved."[28] So with a quiet "yeah," the banjo player joined Taylor, completing the classic Stoney Mountain Boys lineup. With the addition of Hensley, Hutchins switched from banjo to guitar, allowing the world to be introduced to the otherworldly pickin' of the shy banjo player.

Like Taylor, Hensley was originally from the southwest corner of Virginia, raised in the small town of Grundy. It was thought by some people at the time that Taylor helped instigate Hensley's move to Baltimore so he could join the Stoney Mountain Boys, but Hensley claims he "didn't really know who Earl was" until he moved to Baltimore.[29] Hensley was born in 1936 and was a few years younger than his mandolin playing bandmate. While Hensley was still young, his family moved to Pike County, Kentucky, where his dad, Finn, had taken a job in the coal mines. Shortly after moving, Finn ordered musical instruments from the Montgomery Ward catalog for Hensley and his brother. Walt got a banjo, "a $24 job,"[30] older brother Jim a guitar. At this same time, Hensley heard the music that would come to shape his life forever: "I first heard Bill Monroe when I was ten, eleven, twelve years old and it was a sound that hit me like a bolt of lightning. It was so different. I knew right then it was a sound I liked. I used to listen to Flatt and Scruggs on the radio. I guess if it wasn't for Earl Scruggs I would never have played banjo. I would probably not have played music if it wasn't for Earl Scruggs. It really influenced me."[31]

With no access to records or songbooks, Hensley had to learn from listening to the radio and copying the licks and rolls he heard Scruggs playing, which he practiced constantly. "Drove my dad crazy," Hensley said, "because he worked in the mines, and he'd have to get up at four in the morning. He said, 'If you are going to play that thing, I want you to learn it, but go out to the barn.'"[32] Hensley was a quick student, a musical sponge, soaking up whatever he heard and quickly making it his own on the banjo. He was not only great at adapting musically, but also became great at adapting whatever he could find into strings or picks. When times were tough for the Hensley family or the thirty-five mile trip into town to replace broken strings or picks became an insurmountable obstacle, Hensley would fashion finger picks from PET Milk cans or strings from blasting wire. His modest, hard scrabble upbringing had a lasting impact, giving him an extremely humble demeanor and very little tolerance for those who did not share this approach to life. It was a trait James Reams (who played with Hensley on 2002's *James Reams, Walter Hensley and the Barons of Bluegrass*),[33] recognized and admired in his one-time bandmate, remarking, "He didn't cotton to those musicians that seemed to be full of themselves."[34] By 1952 Hensley and his brother Jim had landed a regular gig playing on a popular radio show on WLSI in Pikesville, Kentucky. Around this same time, Walter also started playing with pioneering bluegrass band Lonesome Pine Fiddlers. His time with the Lonesome Pine Fiddlers was sporadic, and the search for work not in the local coal mines— a job whose long hours, low pay, and extremely dangerous conditions was not an appealing option for Hensley—forced him to move north like so many of his Appalachian brethren. He ended up in Baltimore in 1956, where he soon fell in with the Black Mountain Boys and shortly thereafter accepted Taylor's offer to join the Stoney Mountain Boys.

Hensley's bold, audacious work on the five-string banjo proved to be the perfect complement to Taylor's simple and classy traditional style of mandolin playing. "Earl was not a fancy mandolin player, but he played real good and clean. Good timing. I loved his singing," remembered Hensley with fondness. "He was kind of like Bill Monroe with his high shrill voice."[35]

Hensley's ability to constantly change and evolve, to coax new adventurous and inventive licks out of his five-string, easily set him apart from every other banjo picker at the time who slapped a couple of finger picks on and tried to emulate the pioneering work of Earl Scruggs. Hensley used the Scruggs style like so many other hillbilly bluegrass pickers of the time, but the unbelievable speed with which Hensley was able to play served only to enhance his reputation as a stylistic pioneer. It was not just the pure speed he was able to play with, but also the clarity and spaces he left in his music. Sandy Rothman, a long-time Hensley fan, always admired this trait in his playing: "There was Walt Hensley's incredible banjo picking with its perfect note separation that to this day has never been equaled. Nobody else besides Walt—and I don't know if he tried to get it or made a conscious effort to get it—but he had that thing. It's just a mind-blowing space between notes. It's like the beat at which someone talks."[36]

Russ Hooper, who played with Hensley on his groundbreaking 1969 album, *Pickin' on New Grass*, says simply, "I would put him up against anybody. I don't think anybody could touch him back in those days, he was so creative."[37] The superlatives thrown Hensley's way from bluegrass elite over the years are numerous. Masters of Bluegrass bassist Jerry McCoury calls him "top-notch."[38] "One of bluegrass music's geniuses," proclaims James Reams.[39] Folklorist Alan Lomax declared, "There is true folk magic in every note he plays."[40] Dean Sapp, bandleader of the Harford Express, who first met Hensley when Sapp was a fourteen-year-old and has been involved in the Baltimore scene since he was just a teenager in the early sixties, insists, "In the mid-sixties Walter was considered to be the equal to Earl Scruggs. He was, and still is known as one of the greatest to ever come out of the Baltimore area."[41] Rothman agrees with Sapp's assessment: "There is nobody more important to come out of the Baltimore bluegrass scene than Walt Hensley. J.D. Crowe will tell you, Del McCoury will tell you, everybody will tell you how incredibly influential he was to everyone, not just to banjo pickers."[42]

Hensley's influence would stretch far beyond traditional bluegrass borders, Russ Hooper recalled a conversation he had with Hensley about some famous fans. "Walt once asked me 'Do you know who one of our biggest fans is?' I said, 'No.' He said, 'Jerry Garcia.' He [Hensley] said Garcia absolutely loved his banjo picking."[43] Garcia's close friend Sandy Rothman confirmed this: "Jerry was a huge fan of Walt Hensley."[44]

Despite the universal praise and genuine admiration that Hensley's peers and famous fans had for his unmatched abilities, he was painfully shy, almost to a fault. An introvert, he found it hard to open up to even to his bandmates, instead confiding mostly in just his immediate friends, though longtime friend Russ Hooper remembers that despite his shyness when Hensley was younger he still seemed to have a different girlfriend every time Hooper saw him.[45] Hensley seemed to possess a lack of confidence and belief in his abilities, never grasping how talented he truly was, shying away from opportunity and the big stage, and instead feeling more comfortable in the small corner bars where he got his start.

Even with the abundance of corner bars and clubs that dotted the city, finding a regular paying gig was extremely tough; many places did not offer pay or would allow bands to work only for tips or drinks. The atmosphere in these clubs was usually less than ideal, and the constant fistfights at these violent, rowdy bars were just part of the added attraction the bands had to deal with. In addition to the local bands scrapping for a chance to play, there was the influx of national acts that came through Baltimore on a regular basis playing at the same clubs and bars as the local bands, thus allowing even fewer gigs for local bands. Competition for these few remaining low-paying jobs was cutthroat. Roy Cole started playing in Baltimore in the mid-fifties and over the ensuing decades would play with everyone from Del McCoury, Russ Hooper, and Earl Taylor to Jack Cooke, and would experience firsthand the cutthroat way of doing business in Baltimore: "We were playing for $5 or $6 a night, and if you were getting $6 you didn't tell anybody because they would come in and play for $5."[46]

While playing with Bob Baker and the Pike County Boys in the late fifties Russ Hooper witnessed the violent tensions that could flare up between bands as they competed for gigs. Earl Taylor and the Stoney Mountain Boys had been working regularly at a place in West Baltimore on Edmondson Avenue called the Franklin Town Inn. Taylor had an offer to play an out of town show and asked Baker if he and his band could cover their gig at the Franklin Town Inn over the weekend. Baker agreed and covered Taylor's gig at the Franklin Town Inn. The owner of the Franklin Inn ended up liking what he heard from Baker and the Pike County Boys so much he hired them to take over Taylor's regular spot without bothering to inform Taylor of this. Taylor and the band showed up to play the following weekend only to find the Pike County Boys onstage in their place. The Stoney Mountain Boys hung around all night glaring at the band onstage. After Baker's set ended, Taylor and the rest of the Stoney Mountain Boys followed Baker and his band out to the parking lot. As Hooper was putting his instrument away in the trunk of his car he saw "Earl, Boatwhistle, Porky, and Walt," approach Bob Baker and his brother Billy Ray, who "was a pretty big boy," and start arguing. "Well, before you know it they are beating the hell out of each other," remembers Hooper, "and I'm thinking, you know, this just isn't worth it.... But, you know, that's the way it was back in those days, cut each other's throats for another dollar."[47]

Despite the success they had found earlier in the decade with their two-year run of nine shifts weekly, Taylor and Hutchins discovered on their return to Baltimore they had to reignite the passion and excitement the Stoney Mountain Boys had created previously. They began to search for regular gigs and slogged through the treacherous bar environment, again creating quite a positive buzz. Part of the draw and attraction of the Stoney Mountain Boys was their realness; they had all grown up in the south in poor, desperate conditions with an instrument in their hands from an early age. This mountain-bred authenticity bled through in their music. "The Stoneys are sure-enough country boys, from way up the crick, and for them every chord and every verse tells a story of mountain life," said folklorist Alan Lomax.[48] This would have been very appealing to the folks who frequented the bars in Baltimore where the boys played and who longed to hear some music that reminded them of their old home place.

The Stoneys' sets at the time were crowd-pleasing affairs featuring everything from traditional songs that made up most bluegrass bands sets to original tunes penned by Taylor and Hensley to the lyrically suggestive content of the Boatwhistle song "Nuts, Nuts, Red Hot Nuts" to contemporary songs like "Purple People Eater," a number-one hit in 1958 for Sheb Wooley. Hooper also recalls that "Earl would do a lot of Jimmy Martin tunes and he would do a lot of old mountain ballads. He would do the up-tempo thing, the Flatt and Scruggs thing."[49] With this wide-ranging and entertaining repertoire at their disposable they ultimately secured a seven nights a week spot at Lindy's Club 79 for $6 a night.

Lindy's Club 79, more commonly known as the 79 Club, was located in the Federal Hill area of the city and had a setup pretty typical for the time. It was in an old row house, at 7–9 East Cross Street on the corner of Cross and Charles streets near the historic Cross Street Market (near where the 8x10 Club—one of Baltimore's current premier live music venues—now stands). The 79 Club had a small stage built into the wall opposite the bar. In between the bar and the stage was a small dance floor with a few tables and stools littered around it. The club was owned by Ollie Mae Boggs, who took over ownership in 1954.[50] It was one of the few places that featured true bluegrass seven nights a week. While the term bluegrass was still a few years away from common usage, Boggs recognized the similarities between what Taylor and the Stoney Mountain Boys and other like-minded bands who played the 79 Club were doing and what Bill Monroe was playing with his Blue Grass Boys, and she advertised with a sign out front that said, "Lester Flatt & Earl Scruggs and Bill Monroe Type Music Played Here."[51] Hensley remembers that it was a unique place in that it seemed to attract a more diverse crowd: "Even though it was in a rough neighborhood, it was a safe place to go. And we'd attract not just mountain people and beatniks, but also doctors and lawyers."[52] Of course, "safe" may be in the eye of the banjo player, as Russ Hooper remembered the place being a bit rougher than Hensley did. Hooper recalled one evening, while playing a show there with Bob Baker, when a man walked into the bar while Hooper was onstage and shot and killed another man right in front of him.[53]

Despite the hazards and dangers that were present at these corner bars and clubs, Taylor and Hensley began to carve out a niche as one of the hottest and hardest-working bands in town. Del McCoury was a young struggling musician at the time trekking down to Baltimore from his home in York County, Pennsylvania, to check out many of the band's regular sets at the 79 Club and Jazz City. With a laugh, McCoury jokes, "I think they played the clubs in Baltimore like eight nights a week."[54] It only seemed like they were playing that much, but they had greatly increased their workload since their return to the Baltimore streets. In addition to their regular seven nights a week gig at the 79 Club, they had again picked up at least two afternoon sets a week and seemed to be an omnipresent presence on the bar circuit. Looking to capitalize on their newfound popularity, the band wanted to get into the studio to record a couple of sides.

They discovered their old bandmate, Charlie Waller, had a friend from high school who cofounded and owned a small record label that was putting out country records and looking to release a bluegrass single. Waller's friend Dick Freeland had, along with Bill Carroll and Sonny "Zap" Compton, founded Rebel Records in Mount Rainer, Maryland, in 1959. Rebel Records would go on to become "the first label of enduring consequence to concentrate on bluegrass"[55] and one of the preeminent bluegrass labels of the last fifty years. When they started Rebel Records they first released a couple of country singles, but the three owners were all serious bluegrass aficionados and looking for a new band to record for the label. Through Waller, proper introductions were made with Taylor and the Stoney Mountain Boys, and the band entered the studio and recorded two sides, "Stoney Mountain Twist" and the sad love song "The Children Are Cryin'."

There is some confusion as to whether this Stoney Mountain Boys recording session in 1959 was for Rebel Records or part of a session recorded by Alan Lomax upstairs at the 79 Club (as a version of "The Children Are Cryin'" would be released by Lomax on the 1959 album *Folk Songs from the Blue Grass*). The band definitely met Freeland at this time though, courtesy of an introduction from Waller. According to current Rebel Records owner Dave Frieman, "there was little kept in the way of files and recording ledgers by Rebel in its earliest years,"[56] and many of the early recordings for the label have been lost forever over time. In 1962 the two songs from the 1959 session were definitely rereleased by Rebel with a reworked version of "The Children Are Cryin'" titled "Calling Your Name," and the original "Stoney Mountain Twist." It was the first bluegrass single ever released by Rebel. Copies of the 1959 version are very hard to find, but the 1962 version can be found on the Rebel Record box set *35 Years of the Best in Bluegrass*.

The Stoney Mountain Boys, who Del McCoury in his typically understated manner calls "a really good bluegrass band,"[57] were a huge influence on the young McCoury. His younger brother Jerry recalls how influential those sojourns to Baltimore were for his big brother's music development, remembering he would study how the band played, how they sang, and what they did onstage. Jerry says that Del, who at the time was still a banjo player, was especially enamored of Hensley and paid particular attention to him and his unmatched talents. In 1957 Del even purchased a used Gibson banjo previously owned by Hensley. It was to become Del's banjo of choice until he switched to guitar when he joined Bill Monroe's band.[58]

Earl Taylor and the Stoney Mountain Boys were making a lot of noise in Baltimore, rightly gaining the title of the hardest-working band in town at the time, and it turned out the McCoury brothers were not the only ones paying close attention to what Taylor and crew were doing. Mike Seeger had begun seeing the Stoneys playing at their nightly gigs at the 79 Club and had become captivated by the hard-driving spirit of Taylor and the Stoney Mountain Boys. He recorded an album's worth of material with the band upstairs at the 79 Club in 1958, some of which appeared on the 1959 album *Mountain Music Bluegrass Style*. But before their release, Seeger shared the tapes with a famous friend of his who was looking for a bluegrass band to fill a slot at a festival he was organizing in New York City.[59]

4

"Like ... standing in a sea breeze"

Recommended Listening: *Alan Lomax Presents: Folk Song Festival at Carnegie Hall* would provide the perfect complement for Chapter 4. Unfortunately the album is long out of print and extremely hard to find. Instead check out the online resource *Culturalequity.org*, a free collection of thousands of songs and interviews that Alan Lomax collected over the years. This collection allows the discovery of the "war-whoops" that inspired Lomax to assemble the Folksong '59 concert.

"I believe we should go back and get a little drink of that whiskey," Walt Hensley said to fiddler Curtis Cody. The normally nondrinking pair was preparing to play a show—like they had countless times before—or so they thought. The rest of the Stoney Mountain Boys—Earl Taylor, Sam "Porky" Hutchins, and Vernon "Boatwhistle" McIntyre—were off elsewhere backstage sharing some whiskey with blues masters Muddy Waters and Memphis Slim, who were also on the same bill. When they agreed to play this gig in New York City, the Stoney Mountain Boys assumed the hall they were booked to play was like any other place they had played. Hensley even casually remarked, "I thought well, what the heck, I have played all the bars and halls in Baltimore, so it's no big deal to me." But as they stood backstage they realized that this hall might be a little different from what they were used to in Baltimore. A "big noise, like a bee swarm," started emanating from the other side of the curtain.

Curiosity got the best of Cody and he slowly pushed back the curtain and peeked out from behind the stage to find out what was making this "big noise." As he pushed back the curtain he saw "five balconies, lights on the ceiling, a big plush bar on the side, carpet that was six inches thick, and all these seats and a big stage."[1] Hensley remembers it as a place "where you look up at the lights and it looks like the sky it's so high."[2] It was at that moment Hensley realized that Carnegie Hall in New York City was not like the halls and firehouses he played back in Baltimore. Opened in 1891, Carnegie Hall is recognized as one of the most important and esteemed music venues of all time; and as Hensley peered out from behind the curtain and got his first glimpse of the world-famous theatre he was discovering just that. As Cody and Hensley stared in amazement at the gorgeous architecture of the world-famous Carnegie Hall, they discovered the buzzing was the sound of what became a packed house slowly filling up for the evening's show. With breath-less awe in his voice Cody finally answered Hensley: "Walt, I believe I want to go back there and have two drinks."[3]

The Stoney Mountain Boys had ended up at Carnegie through an invi-tation from Alan Lomax to play as part of his Folksong '59 concert he had organized. The Folksong '59 concert proved to be an important turning point in the history of folk music and music in general, as Lomax attempted to bring attention to all these various genres of music he loved: blues, folk, blue-grass, gospel, and rock 'n' roll. Rock 'n' roll was still in its infancy at the time and the Folksong '59 concert unintentionally served to show how rock 'n' roll was the sum of all those other styles. The bands onstage that night demon-strated how rock 'n' roll borrowed subtly from each of those styles and genres to create the sound that would come to dominate the musical landscape over the ensuing decades.

Alan Lomax was one of the most important folklorists of all time and had recently returned to the United States in 1959 after almost a decade living in exile in Europe. He was born in 1915 in Austin, Texas. His father was John Lomax, one of the pioneers of recording early folk music for preservation. The elder Lomax had long been interested in American folklore and ballads. But because of the limited technology at the time there was very little in the way of recordings of these songs, and much of the history surrounding them was being lost over time. At the urging of one of his Harvard professors, George Kittredge, himself a leading figure in ballads and old cowboy songs, John began to get out into the field to document these ballads and cowboys songs firsthand from the musicians themselves. This field work lead to the publication of a book, *Cowboy Songs and Other Frontier Ballads*, in 1910. The book was an anthology of early American folksongs and included a foreword by former president Theodore Roosevelt.

John's study and book were groundbreaking because of the inclusion of African American musicians, whose contributions had long been overlooked. This inclusion was important, as John discovered and was able to introduce many important African American blues and folk singers to the world. The most prominent of these African American singers was Huddie Ledbetter, better known as Lead Belly. The inclusion of African American singers in

John's work was a trait his son Alan would embrace as well. The acclaim from his book and his continued pursuit of early American folk music led John to a partnership with the Archive of American Folk Song at the Library of Congress. The library's collection of recorded material was woefully inadequate and John wished to rectify that. With the aid of a 315-pound behemoth of a phonograph that was state-of-the-art for the time, and often with his eighteen-year-old son Alan by his side, John set out through the Deep South to record music at its roots. The younger Lomax caught his dad's recording bug immediately and became a ubiquitous figure on many of John's recording trips.

While working with his father, Alan Lomax began to establish himself as a musicologist of merit and a serious folklorist in his own right. He helped author two books, 1934's *American Ballads and Folk-Songs* and 1936's *Negro Folk Songs as Sung by Leadbelly*. Much like his father, Lomax continued gathering field recordings at a torrid pace through the thirties and forties. In addition to his archival work for the Library of Congress he also began to get involved in commercial recording. He helped put together two groundbreaking sessions for RCA Records during this time, Woody Guthrie's *Dust Bowl Ballads* and Lead Belly's *Midnight Special and Other Southern Prison*

Alan Lomax (far right on guitar) performs at the Folksong '59 Concert at Carnegie Hall with (from left) Mike Seeger, Pete Seeger, and the Selah Jubilee Singers (courtesy Photo-Sound Associates Collection, Ronald D. Cohen Collection #20239, Southern Folklife Collection, Wilson Library, University of North Carolina at Chapel Hill).

Songs. While the sales for both were sluggish upon their initial release, they have been hailed as important milestones in the history of recorded music, as they have gone on to influence a generation of songwriters who followed, with everyone from Bob Dylan to Bruce Springsteen to the Grateful Dead to Van Morrison to Nirvana covering the songs they first learned from those albums, in concert and on their own albums.

As the 1940s drew to a close the younger Lomax, because of his liberal political views, was accused of being a communist sympathizer, along with many others in the entertainment industry. Realizing the potential impact this would have on his career, Lomax quickly settled his affairs and headed off to London, England, where he already had a deal in place to do some work with Columbia Records in Europe. He would spend the bulk of the 1950s living in Europe, not returning to the U.S. until the end of the decade. Upon his return to the U.S. Lomax claimed he was impressed with the change in popular music and the folk-revival scene's embrace of the music he held so close. He said he now heard "war whoops coming out of juke boxes that I used to have to go down to Mississippi to record." Lomax wished to celebrate and highlight this new music so Americans would "not to be ashamed of what we go for musically, from primitive ballads to rock 'n' roll songs."[4] So he set about organizing a lineup for a concert that he felt would encompass those ideals.

Despite having the moniker Folksong '59 attached to it, the lineup Lomax assembled for the April 3, 1959, event at Carnegie Hall was wide-ranging and strayed far from the limiting label of folk music. The program handed out to patrons the night of the show said there would be "a whole panorama of contemporary folk and folk popular music presented by the finest artists in each field." The lineup included country singer Jimmie Drift-wood, who was riding a wave of popularity at the time with his chart-topping "Battle of New Orleans." The song's popularity would continue to grow after his appearance at Folksong '59 and go on to win the Grammy Award for song of the year the following year with Johnny Horton performing it. Also on the bill were blues masters Muddy Waters and Memphis Slim, gospel singers Selah Jubilee Singers and Drexel Singers, and early rock 'n' rollers the Cadillacs, who were best known for their 1955 hit "Speedoo." Lomax also included his friends and folk-revival leaders Pete and Mike Seeger on the bill. Lomax served as emcee for the evening and performed "some of the prison work-songs that he and his father had collected."[5]

Lomax had wished to include a bluegrass group on the bill as well. Bluegrass was a still a relatively unknown style of music in the north at the time and Lomax hoped to help introduce his audience to the music he praised by saying, "Out of a torrent of folk-music that is the backbone of the record business today, the freshest sound comes from the so-called Bluegrass band— sort of mountain Dixieland combo in which five-string banjo, America's only indigenous folk instrument, carries the lead like a hot clarinet."[6] Despite misunderstanding the history of the banjo, which actually had its origins in Africa, Lomax believed that bluegrass was "an updated form of the music he'd heard in the southern mountains back in the thirties and forties."[7] His belief further reinforces the idea and notion that bluegrass did not fully form until it left the mountains and entered the cities. His first choice for a bluegrass band was rightly Bill Monroe.

Monroe's popularity had cooled off a bit since Lester Flatt and Earl Scruggs had left his band in 1948, but despite this wane in popularity Lomax still recognized the importance of Monroe as the catalyst and founding father of the bluegrass genre. But to Monroe, Lomax was just a "northern intellectual and folk song collector and outside the commercial country music circuit"[8] Monroe was familiar with. Worse than that, the straightlaced Monroe thought, because of Lomax's left-wing politics and what he was involved with earlier in the decade, he was a communist. With that in mind Monroe turned down Lomax's offer. Lomax next called on Monroe's former bandmates Flatt and Scruggs but made the costly error of calling Lester Flatt. Anyone who dealt with the pair knew that Earl Scruggs' wife, Louise, handled their booking and was the manager in charge. While waiting to hear back from Flatt, Lomax talked with his friend Mike Seeger, whom he knew was into bluegrass and had just recorded and produced two albums highlighting the music. He asked Seeger for suggestions and without hesitation Seeger recommended a Baltimore band that had completely captured his attention, Earl Taylor and the Stoney Mountain Boys. Seeger passed on the tapes of the band he had made during the recording session for the *Mountain Music Bluegrass Style* album to Lomax to introduce him to the Stoney Mountain Boys.

Impressed with what he heard, Lomax accepted Seeger's invitation to come to Baltimore to check out the band in person at their stomping grounds, the 79 Club. Taylor seemed to recall that night years later as he said he remembered seeing an unfamiliar man who sat off by himself at a small table and had only a few drinks throughout the night, which made him stick out from the rest of the regular crowd.[9] The man who sat by himself was indeed Lomax and he was instantly smitten with the sound of the Stoneys. They were the perfect, pure representation of how he heard bluegrass in his mind's ear and they appealed to him because of their "straight from the cabins in Appalachia"[10] background. Lomax later described the band's sound in the liner notes to *Folk Songs from the Blue Grass*:

Mike Seeger and his half brother Pete perform at the Folksong '59 Concert at Carnegie Hall (courtesy Photo-Sound Associates Collection, Ronald D. Cohen Collection #20239, Southern Folklife Collection, Wilson Library, University of North Carolina at Chapel Hill).

There may be somewhat more accomplished players in other groups, there may be smoother orchestrations, but to my ear nothing quite matches the wild, free, rambunctious rant of the Stoneys. They attack every song and every note as if they were a wing of jet fighters on their last mission. When they finish with a tune, there is a sort of roar that reverberates for a few seconds in the studio, as if the molecules in the air had been dancing a hoe-down and had to scurry back to their proper places before quiet could fall.[11]

Hensley thought it was simpler than all that. He believed it was the band's ability to play so rapidly—in a "hyper-grass" style as they had done with their recording of "White House Blues" on the *Mountain Music Bluegrass* album—that attracted Lomax to the band.[12] Russ Hooper, who was playing with Bob Baker at the time, felt what truly hooked Lomax on the Stoney Mountains Boys and separated them from Baker's band was the special talent of Hensley. Regardless of what inspired him, Lomax was awed by the band and asked them to come to New York City and play at his Folksong '59 concert. The band, who, Hensley said, was "green as grass"[13] and unaware of whom Lomax was, agreed to play. In doing so, Earl Taylor and the Stoney Mountain Boys would become the first bluegrass band to grace the hallowed stage at Carnegie.

The fact that any bluegrass band was playing there was a huge milestone, as it further cemented the genre's growth and acceptance as a separate style of music. Izzy Young, a prominent New York folk figure who owned and operated the Folklore Center in Greenwich Village in New York City, called the Folksong '59 concert "the turning point for folk music"[14] as a genre and a marketplace, helping to cement all the different sounds represented onstage that night—folk, blues, gospel, bluegrass, and rock 'n' roll—as viable forms

Musicians wait onstage for their time to perform at the Folksong '59 Concert (from left): members of the Drexl Singers, members of the Selah Jubilee Singers, Jimmy Driftwood (in hat), Pete Seeger, James Driftwood, Jr., Mike Seeger, unknown (courtesy Photo-Sound Associates Collection, Ronald D. Cohen Collection #20239, Southern Folklife Collection, Wilson Library, University of North Carolina at Chapel Hill).

of popular music. From the stage that night, Lomax tried to sum up his feelings about why he was so positive about the direction he saw music taking after his return from Europe:

> A stampeding herd of youngsters—hillbillies, citybillies, rockabillies—had broken through the gates and set America singing, dancing, rocking to its own rhythms. The juke boxes were pouring out the wild expressive singing that I once had to hunt for in the Mississippi Delta. I saw geetar and banjo-pickers on every subway train. Ballad singers packed the concert halls.... I saw rock and roll audiences clapping time on the off-beat and watched the kids dance more expressively than ever in my memory.[15]

The evening's proceedings were generally well received by both fan and critic. The *New York Times* said the evening was a "panorama of the contemporary American folk song revival" and compared the evening's concert favorably to the influential "From Spirituals to Swing" concert held at Carnegie Hall twenty years earlier.[16] Writer Aaron Rennert, in *Gardyloo* magazine, said he "admired the performers, but criticized the sound system, the obvious lack of rehearsals, and jumbled program."[17] Rennert also claimed that Lomax seemed "discourteous to both the performers and his audience."[18] Despite what some perceived as Lomax's rude behavior, the evening was considered a resounding success, with Baltimore being well represented on stage that evening. Mike Seeger wound up playing with both his half-brother Pete and Jimmy Driftwood, in addition to a short set he played by himself. Mike Seeger's sets were very well received, with Ralph Rinzler, who was in attendance, declaring that Seeger was "very cool, very musical and very old-timey" and that he thought Seeger "was spectacular."[19]

Interaction and sit-ins between bands were easy throughout the night, as all the bands were gathered onstage, sitting in chairs that circled the back of the stage, just behind where the bands performed. All the bands present took advantage of being seated on the stage and so close to the performers and they would take the opportunity to get up at various times throughout the show to sing and play with each other throughout the night. They also spent the time in between songs socializing with each other in their seats on the stage. But despite Seeger's "spectacular" performance and the collaborations and sit-ins by the other bands on the bill, the unquestioned highlight of the evening was the appearance of the bluegrass band from Baltimore, the Stoney Mountain Boys. The Stoneys had added fiddler Curtis Cody to their lineup recently, and he played with them that night at Carnegie Hall, adding a brand-new dynamic to their overall sound.

Cody was born in 1930 in Sneedville, Tennessee, and grew up with— and remained close his whole life to—famed bluegrass singer and one-time

Earl Taylor bandmate Jimmy Martin. He was a quiet, easygoing, laid-back guy who, while never known as the most technically proficient fiddler, was always valued for his rock-solid reliability. His addition brought a lively dynamic to the Stoneys' sound, and he was instrumental in their set at Folksong '59.

The Stoneys followed Pete Seeger, Muddy Waters, and Jimmy Driftwood, hitting the stage after some remarks from Lomax, who commented that "bluegrass is as exciting as the village bands of Romania and Yugoslavia,"[20] which he meant as a high compliment. Then he introduced the band as the "Stoney Mountain Boys from Baltimore," dropping the usual "Earl Taylor and the" from their name. Unsure what to expect from the Baltimore quintet, the crowd was more than a bit standoffish and cool in their initial reception of the band. Taylor said that when they took the stage "you could have counted the hand-plause we got."[21] This did nothing to help with Hensley and Cody's already frayed nerves, which had not eased despite the aid of some liquid courage. "When we started playing it was like a windstorm in that place our pants was shaking so badly," said Hensley. "It looked like we were standing in a sea breeze. We was all scared to death."[22]

Lomax had asked the band to start their set with the fastest tune they knew, so when they got onstage Taylor flashed the infectious smile he was known for to the band, giving them the shot of confidence they needed before counting it down and kicking off with "Fire on the Mountain."[23] The traditional fiddle tune exploded from the stage and saw Cody light the crowd on fire with his blistering bow work. On recordings from the show you can almost hear the crowd levitate as Cody plays with unrestrained speed and energy. The band "hit the mics running"[24] and Cody recalls that, despite the frayed nerves, Hensley then played something on banjo and "tore the place up."[25] Hensley's mind-blowing banjo roll to start "Roll in My Sweet Baby's Arms" would have been the first time the majority of folks in the audience would have heard, let alone seen, picking like that. Taylor, ever the showman, was not going to be left out and held one high note near the end of "Mule Skinner's Blues" for a throat-numbing fifteen seconds. The crowd's reaction was immediate and intense. Their wild reaction and unabashed amazement bleeds through the stage microphones and can be heard and felt on the recordings from that night. The crowd may have been standoffish at first, "but whenever that bluegrass hit them microphones in that Carnegie Hall, that beat anything I ever have seen in my life," recalled Taylor. "When we would end a number, I know that it would take five minutes before we could go into another one—that was how much rarin' and screamin and hair pullin' there was."[26]

The Stoney Mountain Boys perform at the Folksong '59 Concert. Standing (from left): Curt Cody, Earl Taylor, Walt Hensley, Porky Hutchins, Boatwhistle, seated (from left): Jimmy Driftwood (in hat), his son James Jr. (with guitar), Mike Seeger (in plaid shirt) (courtesy Photo-Sound Associates Collection, Ronald D. Cohen Collection #20239, Southern Folklife Collection, Wilson Library, University of North Carolina at Chapel Hill).

The Stoney Mountain Boys brief but electrifying performance was released on an album, the long-out-of-print *Alan Lomax Presents: Folk Song Festival at Carnegie Hall*, a few months after the show, in October 1959. The album featured three tracks each from Jimmy Driftwood, Memphis Slim, and the Stoney Mountain Boys, and an additional two tracks from Muddy Waters. The inclusion of three tracks from the Stoneys shows how truly astonishing and eye-opening their set was. Lomax's third-choice bluegrass band, which did not even get mentioned on the evening's program, billed as simply "Bluegrass Band," had such an impact that they would have three cuts on the A-side of the concert album. Hensley's nerves before the show clouded his memory of the night and it was not until he heard the live recording of their set that he realized how special it was. "I wondered after I heard the live record how we got through it and had it come out as well as it did." Of course Hensley had to qualify that with a typical self-effacing comment that downplayed how great they were that night: "We wasn't good, but we were a lot better than I thought. We was a scared bunch."[27]

The Stoney Mountain Boys during their electrifying appearance at the Folksong '59 Concert (from left): Curt Cody, Earl Taylor, Walt Hensley, Porky Hutchins, and Pete Seeger (seated) (courtesy Photo-Sound Associates Collection, Ronald D. Cohen Collection #20239, Southern Folklife Collection, Wilson Library, University of North Carolina at Chapel Hill).

Lomax's interest in the Stoneys extended beyond including them on the concert album. He felt the reaction from the crowd was so intense and there seemed to be so much interest in the band and bluegrass music from the growing folk-revival scene that he wanted to capitalize on it immediately. Using his contacts in the recording industry, Lomax got Taylor and the Stoney Mountain Boys a recording deal with United Artists. The band stayed in New York after the Folksong '59 concert and promptly set to work on recording

Folk Songs from the Blue Grass (**author's collection**).

songs for a full-length album. Over a nonstop, seven-hour marathon session the band recorded sixty-four songs, seventeen of which were chosen for 1960's *Folk Songs from the Blue Grass: Earl Taylor and His Stoney Mountain Boys.* Calling the album *Folk Songs from the Blue Grass* was simply a way of trying to appeal to a wider audience. The songs the Stoney Mountain Boys played on the album were the same songs they had always played, country and bluegrass at its core, but calling them folk songs allowed the album to be marketed towards a younger, larger audience.

With the release of the album, the Stoney Mountain Boys became one of the first bluegrass acts from outside of Nashville to record an album for a major label. The album was given the Lomax stamp of approval: "Alan Lomax

Presents." Lomax also penned the liner notes, and much like the liner notes for Seeger's groundbreaking bluegrass albums these notes were not aimed at the hardcore bluegrass fan that would catch the Stoneys at their home base at the 79 Club. The notes were instead geared towards introducing those in the folk-revival movement to them. The album was a solid collection and representation of who Taylor and the Stoney Mountain Boys were at the time as a band. The seventeen tracks on the album consisted of mostly traditional songs that would have been familiar to anyone who had listened to bluegrass before. It also included two Taylor originals, "Lee Highway Blues," named after a stretch of road in Southwest Virginia, and the sad lament "The Children Are Cryin'." The latter would be rerecorded for Rebel Records, renamed "Calling Your Name," and released as the label's first ever bluegrass single in 1962.

In addition to helping the Stoneys secure a recording contract, Lomax wanted to get them out on the road and began setting up tour dates for them. Lomax believed they could cross over into the folk revival scene and wanted to take advantage of the positive press and reviews they were getting from their appearance at Folksong '59. This led to a humorous exchange between Taylor and the band. Taylor was illiterate and because of that would sometimes mishear words. Boatwhistle recalled the day when Taylor approached the band and said with excitement that "Alan Lomax said he wanted to put us on the bluegrass circus." It took the rest of the band a moment to figure out that Lomax had told Taylor he wanted to put them on the bluegrass circuit and that they would not be performing with clowns and lions as Taylor's initial comment led them to believe.[28] Lomax arranged for a tour of Europe for the band, but unfortunately they would not get a chance to undertake that trip.

The Stoney Mountain Boys returned to Baltimore following their recording session in New York with visions of Europe, endless horizons, and limitless opportunities dancing in their heads. They went right back to work, playing their normal weekly spot at the 79 Club. Upon their return, Hensley remarked to the crowd, after they had barreled through a few numbers, "Well, last week we were playing Carnegie Hall, and this week we are back in this dump again."[29] The excitement from New York would quickly wear off. Shortly after their return, Porky Hutchins informed the band he wanted to quit. His reasons were not entirely clear. Some people believed he had just tired of the regular grind playing the clubs. He and his wife had befriended an older local man and were acting as his caregivers, so his free time was not as abundant as it once was. Del McCoury provided a different explanation. He said that shortly after the Stoneys returned from New York and the

Carnegie Hall show he bumped into Porky and asked him why he was no longer in the band. Porky told McCoury that while they were in New York recording the *Folk Songs from the Blue Grass* album he and Taylor had gotten into an argument over writing credits for some of the songs. Porky claimed he had written or helped write "The Children Are Cryin'" as well a couple of other songs, but Taylor refused to give him credit for them and did not list his name on the album as a cowriter. Porky declared to McCoury, "I'll never play with him again."[30] With both Taylor and Porky long dead, the answer to which of them wrote what music for the songs will probably never be known. But what is the real shame is that Taylor's wife, Ellen, is generally accepted as having written the lyrics to the majority of his songs, yet she never received credit for her work. Given Taylor's illiteracy, his wife's help would not be surprising. Porky held true to his word and never worked with Taylor again. He began playing around Baltimore with another band, but eventually the man he and his wife cared for died and left everything he had to them and they moved back to North Carolina. With a potential tour Lomax had set up looming, the band had to find a new guitar player who could also sing.

Hensley was friendly with a guitar player from Marion, Virginia, who had moved to Baltimore and was "one of the finest pure bluegrass singers" around and "had hands like bear paws and could really pull the tone out of a guitar."[31] With those impressive credentials the man from Marion was an easy choice to replace Porky.

Jim McCall was born April 30, 1930, in Marion, Virginia, in the southwest part of the state, not far from where Taylor and Hensley were originally from. McCall was the oldest of six kids, having four younger brothers and one sister. His father was disabled, and McCall had to quit school in the ninth grade to start working full time to help support the family. He first worked on a farm before getting a full-time job driving a bus. Like so many others down South, steady work was scarce and McCall eventually moved north to Baltimore to find better opportunities for work. His hardscrabble upbringing left a lasting impression on him, as he always stressed to his children how hard it was growing up in the Great Depression and instilled his limitless work ethic in them.

Like the man he was replacing in the band, Porky Hutchins, McCall had started out playing the banjo; but after meeting and starting to play with Hensley, he realized that, like Porky, the quiet banjo picker was a special talent and he switched to guitar. McCall and Taylor had first met through an introduction from Hensley sometime in the late 1950s before the Stoney Mountain Boys' famous appearance at Carnegie Hall. They most likely had played together already in Baltimore prior to McCall's joining the band. Hensley, always a man of few words, summed up McCall's musical abilities: "His guitar playing was great. He had that drive. He was very smooth. He didn't play rough."[32] It was those traits that would go on to define McCall and make him a highly respected player. Much like his bandmates, Hensley and Taylor, McCall would resonant strongly with West Coast bluegrass icon Sandy Rothman:

> Jim McCall was a very important person for me for sure. His expert bluegrass rhythm guitar sounded as confident as Walt on the banjo. I think of him as an exact vocal cross between Lester Flatt and Jimmy Martin. He could do it just about as well as either of them. He was one of the most incredible, wonderful, honey-voiced bluegrass singers there ever was. And like Earl not parlaying himself into wider recognition, he was very regional. He had a good following and fan base in the mid–Atlantic and Ohio areas. If you talk to J.D. Crowe he would tell you that Jim McCall was a fabulous guitar player and singer, but few beyond the region really know about Jim. I think it's one of the great crimes in bluegrass that Jim isn't more well known.[33]

In bluegrass the core trio in a band has often been the defining characteristic of a great group. If you have three strong vocalists and instrumentalists, then you can add a bass and fiddler from that point and create a really strong band. Many a classic bluegrass band has been formed around this template, with Jimmy Martin, Paul Williams, J.D. Crowe, and Bill Monroe, Lester Flatt, and Earl Scruggs being some of the more important and better known trios. With the addition of McCall, Taylor and Hensley solidified one of the most underrated core trios ever in bluegrass, one much admired and emulated by many. Again Rothman expresses his admiration for the three musicians from Baltimore: "The vocal trio has always been a very important thing, and that particular trio you cannot say enough about. There just wasn't anything better than that. They were as good as any others. They were a top-flight, totally together unit."[34]

The long relationship between McCall and Taylor, while productive and successful musically, would grow to become one of the most complex and frustrating of both the men's lives. While they clearly had an undeniable musical chemistry, it was off the stage and in matters of business that the two would butt heads, coming to blows many a time. They were both stubborn and hard-drinking and that can be a volatile combination. For these two men it was. Rothman played with the pair in the early seventies after they had over a decade of battles between them and could sense this in their relationship: "Jim and Earl were cordial, but you could feel a history of tension between them."[35] McCall's son, Dwight—who would gain fame first as a member of J.D. Crowe's band and later as part of his own band, American Drive—

recalls the contemptuous "love, hate" relationship the pair had. He says, "They loved each other like brothers, but were not without disruptions from time to time."[36] Much like brothers they would argue the whole day long, but if one was threatened or needed help the other was there for him. A story Dwight relates perfectly encapsulates this.

While the pair was working a show in Middletown, Ohio, in the sixties, Taylor and McCall began arguing before the show. Dwight said that Taylor had been drinking heavily and carried the argument to the stage. At some point during the show McCall, who "was stout as an ox, and had hands like a gorilla,"[37] had enough and turned around and using those gorilla-like hands for more than strumming his guitar, punched Taylor, knocking him out cold on the stage. McCall felt bad about what he had done and decided to help carry Taylor out to the car. While he was doing so, some of Taylor's friends who were in attendance and had taken offense to what McCall had done in knocking their friend out headed out to the parking lot to confront him. As Taylor lay in the back of the car, McCall and Taylor's friends got into a heated exchange. Taylor slowly regained his senses, saw his bandmate about to get in a fight with his friends, leapt out of the car yelling, "Let's get 'em, Jim," and helped McCall run them off. There may have been a lot of animosity between the two, but they always felt close to each other. It was exactly this brotherly relationship that would define the pair's long partnership. Dwight says, "Dad was kind of the bodyguard of the band. Whenever someone messed with Earl, they dealt with Dad. I think Earl liked that security."[38] But at that time, before any of these complexities in their relationship had begun to fester, the pair were simply trying to come together as a band with Hensley, Boatwhistle, and Cody to prepare for the tour dates Lomax had planned for Europe. As mentioned the tour never happened.

Shortly after McCall joined the band, and for reasons that are unclear, Lomax cancelled the European tour he had planned for them. Del McCoury said that in conversations he had with Taylor, Taylor told him Lomax had warned that if the next time he worked with the band and it was not the same one he hired to play Carnegie Hall he would drop them and cancel any plans he had for them. He emphasized this to Taylor, by drawing his hand across his throat in a slashing manner.[39] It is not clear why Lomax took such a rigid stance on the band's lineup and did not want to see any changes to it. It's curious given that Porky's replacement, McCall, was arguably a more talented singer and guitarist. For reasons unclear to everyone but Lomax, he seemed to have a complete negative reaction to McCall's addition to the Stoney Mountain Boys and never bothered to give him a chance in the band.[40] It has been speculated that Lomax did not feel McCall was as authentic as Porky. He made clear in the liner notes to their album, *Folk Songs from the Blue Grass*—in which he stated, "The Stoneys are sure enough country boys from way up the crick"—that he valued the straight-out-of-the-cabin feel the band possessed. But given McCall's rural upbringing in Southwest Virginia, similar to the rest of the band, and the comparisons of his singing to Lester Flatt and Jimmy Martin, it is a mystery how Lomax could make the conclusion that McCall was not authentic enough. Regardless of Lomax's reasons, his cancelling of the tour and the severing of his relationship with the band effectively ended the band's brief flirtation with the folk-revival world.

While this was a big blow to the band's opportunities, they had built up a big enough cache of recognition that they should have been able to parlay it into bigger things and a better payday. While this was not the end of Taylor and the Stoney Mountain Boys—they would all go on to find varying degrees of success after the Carnegie Hall show—they would never truly turn that event into the life-altering opportunity it should have been. There is only one band that can lay claim to being the first bluegrass band to grace the hallowed stage at Carnegie Hall and it is not Bill Monroe, or Flatt and Scruggs, or Jimmy Martin, or any other legendary figure. No, the only band that can wear that title is Earl Taylor and the Stoney Mountain Boys from Baltimore. It's a title they should have used the rest of their careers to their benefit, but, unfortunately, for a multitude of reasons they did not. "I think the lack of education played into it," explains Sandy Rothman, who played with both Monroe and Taylor in the sixties. "Earl had common sense—it wasn't like he didn't know how to exist in the world—but in terms of the larger picture, he really didn't take the opportunities he'd had earlier when Alan Lomax found him in the late fifties and put on that show at Carnegie Hall. It seems like he could've have done more to build on that history-making experience."[41]

The opportunity laid out before Taylor and the Stoney Mountain Boys after their appearance at Folksong '59 was massive. It should have been a life-changing moment, but, as what seemed to happen so often with Taylor and so many other great musicians from Baltimore, opportunities were missed and chances were squandered. For a seeming laundry list of reasons, those bands would end up back in the bars of Baltimore playing to the same crowds they always had.

Some of them had no choice and were never able to move beyond the run-down bars in Baltimore. Many others made the pragmatic decision they would have arrived at through lives that included the Great Depression: hold a steady job at the expense of their music and play only when possible, despite the monetary windfall that could come from a successful music career. Chris Warner was a young, ambitious banjo player who started out in Baltimore in

1963 before finding and taking advantage of his big break when he was asked
to join Jimmy Martin's band, the Sunny Mountain Boys, in 1968, which helped
catapult him out of Baltimore and on to bigger things. He saw this struggle
for many Baltimore musicians up close: "They had to make a living.... I think
it was just safer for them to play on the weekends, do their jobs during the
week and pay the bills."[42] Dobro pioneer Russ Hooper fell squarely into this
category. He was a highly in-demand session player at the time and considered by many to be the heir to the legacy of Dobro and resonator-guitar master Josh Graves. No less an authority than Del McCoury would declare, "He
was the first guy that could play anything that Josh Graves did.... I never
knew anyone who could play all that stuff that Josh did, but Russ could."[43]
Despite these accolades Hooper would spurn multiple offers to join their
bands from the legendary Flatt and Scruggs and the County Gentleman
throughout the sixties. Hooper, who had a good-paying, steady job, famously
told Charlie Waller from the Country Gentlemen when offered the job, "I
got to turn the job down. I know when I get old I want to have a roof over
my head and food on the table."[44] And while he might have been able to have
that playing music, Hooper knew he could guarantee he would have it if he
stayed with his job.

For some, like Taylor and the Stoney Mountain Boys, that lucky break
showed its face and the band did try to pursue it, only to find they could not
take advantage of its full potential. Jim McCall's son Dwight thinks that for
his father, Taylor and Hensley it was something else: "I actually think they
thought playing in the bars was a lifetime job. They had so many other opportunities to do so many big things from Carnegie Hall. I finally realized later
why they drank the way they did in the later years was because they were not
comfortable playing anywhere but the barrooms. When they would play a
big festival somewhere they were so nervous they almost couldn't play. Everybody loves you in a bar and that is where they were most comfortable."[45] The
opportunity to play Carnegie Hall and gain exposure to a whole new audience
was one originally offered to Monroe, who was already established as a known
commodity. Taylor and the Stoney Mountain Boys were still mostly unknown
outside of Baltimore at the time and this was a chance for them to be discovered by a large audience eager to be introduced to new music like theirs. It
is a question worth pondering; what could have been if Taylor and the Stoney
Mountain Boys had been able to fully capitalize on the enormous opportunities Lomax had presented to them after the Folksong '59 concert? Perhaps
it would have changed the history of bluegrass as we know it. Perhaps that
modest bar band from Baltimore would have been regarded like the other
heavyweights of the genre and considered truly legendary. The Stoneys' career

did not end after Carnegie Hall. Quite the contrary, they would all still gain a good sense of success and fame and they would all, collectively and individually, release well-received and important albums that influenced a slew of pickers who followed. But it was not the success that could have been— that should have been.

5

Not Even Gunfights
Could Stop the Music

Recommended Listening: Rebel Records' sprawling, four-album box set *35 Years of the Best in Bluegrass*, provides an aural journey through the years that includes much of what was going on in Baltimore and the surrounding area. The four albums are sequenced chronologically and bring to the forefront the subtle changes that Baltimore—like so many other cities—experienced as the bluegrass played evolved from straight-from-the-mountain pickers to younger musicians with more traditional backgrounds.

"I will never forget her name if I live to be nine thousand years old," says Russ Hooper. "Ollie Boggs. How do you miss that?"[1]

It was 1961 and Hooper was a twenty-one-year-old mainstay of the bluegrass scene in Baltimore. He had spent the better part of the previous six years developing a reputation as one of the hottest young musicians in town. During that time he played some shows with an emerging new band called the Country Gentlemen, which was just starting out and would go on to become one of the most influential bluegrass bands of all time, but not quite yet. When not sitting in with the Country Gentlemen, Hooper was spending the majority of his time as a regular member of Bob Baker's band, the Pike County Boys.

Since their formation in 1954, the Pike County Boys had become one of the top bluegrass bands in Baltimore. The band had gone through many lineup changes since Baker, Mike Seeger, and Hazel Dickens had first gotten together, but they continued to be a favorite in the city. A few years after first forming, Seeger and Dickens moved on to different musical endeavors. Seeger had relocated to Washington, D.C., and was in the process of starting the folk-revivalist band New Lost City Ramblers, with Tom Paley and John Cohen. Dickens was still active in the Baltimore house-party scene, mostly playing as a duo with Alice Gerrard. Dickens and Gerrard were still a few

Bob Baker and the Pike County Boys onstage at the Sykesville Carnival in 1960 (from left): Kimball Blair (fiddle), Ronnie Ninkovich (banjo), Russ Hooper (Dobro), Bob Baker (guitar), Dickie Rittler (mandolin), and Billy Ray Baker (bass) (courtesy Russ Hooper).

years away from their groundbreaking debut album, *Who's That Knocking?*, which would be released in 1965, but they were starting to build quite an impressive buzz through their performances. After the departure of Seeger and Dickens, the Pike County Boys' lineup had solidified around Bob Baker, with his brother Billy Ray on bass, Hooper on Dobro, and the band's latest additions, fiddler Kimball Blair and banjoist Ronnie Ninkovich. As with all the bands in Baltimore at the time, members were constantly shuffling around playing with multiple bands, which served to blur the lines and distinctions between the different groups. Hooper recalled this fondly, though, saying that despite the tensions that could arise as bands competed for the better-paying jobs in the city and the occasional fight that might ensue, there was generally no animosity among groups. They "just helped each other out when we had too."[2] Of course, there wouldn't have been the willingness to help out if there hadn't been the potential for some monetary return on that help. It was exactly this constant shuffling of lineups and the potential monetary return that prompted Hooper to mention Ollie Boggs, the woman with the unforgettable name who owned and ran the 79 Club on Cross Street.

In 1961 Bob Baker began to struggle to find work. Musical jobs were plentiful for him and the band, as they were one of the most in-demand bluegrass bands in the mid–Atlantic region, playing seven nights a week and appearing regularly on a radio show on local station WDMD. But real work was growing scarce and Baker could no longer support himself and his family, so he decided to move back home to Blacksburg, Virginia. The band regularly played local music parks like New River Ranch and Sunset Park and had recently taken over the residency at the 79 Club from Earl Taylor and the Stoney Mountain Boys, who had moved away from Baltimore in search of bigger paydays. The Pike County Boys had been playing their new residency for a couple of months when Baker informed the rest of the band he would be heading back to Blacksburg. On the band's final night at the 79 Club an acquaintance of Hooper's, Marvin Howell, was there with friend Roy Cole watching their set. Howell and Cole were both also bluegrass musicians and a regular part of the Baltimore scene. Howell had been establishing himself as one of the new leaders in this scene and had been playing with some of the heavyweights of the area including, Earl Taylor, Red Allen, and Bill Harrell. During one of the band's set breaks, Hooper informed Howell that this was Baker's last night and their spot at the club would be open. Howell was not one to miss an opportunity to play and make some money, so he marched upstairs to talk with Boggs about the opening. Twenty minutes later Howell came back downstairs and announced to Hooper, "I got the job, now I need a band, do you want to play with me?" Hooper instantly agreed to join him.[3]

Marvin Howell was born in 1936 in Shooting Creek, Franklin County, Virginia, an area often referred to as the moonshine capital of the world. Howell's family would move north to Baltimore in 1941 when Howell was still a young boy. He and Hooper first met, a few years prior to Baker's last gig at the 79 Club, on the set of a local Baltimore TV show called *The Collegians*. *The Collegians* was a variety show that mostly featured school-age acts and bands that were just starting out. It had everything from dancers to acrobats to singers to bands and musicians. It was unintentionally hilarious at times, with a house band made up entirely of accordions, and the deadpan delivery of charisma-challenged host T. Oliver Hughes only adding to the overall weirdness of the show. Hughes had no background in television and it was plainly evident by his awkward presence on-screen. His role on the show came about because he owned a lumberyard on Reisterstown Road, which was the main sponsor of the show. Unsurprisingly, film director John Waters, a Baltimore native known for his quirky and off-beat movies, was a fan of the show growing up. "I remember *The Collegians* as being the most staggering show in the history of Maryland television," Waters said. "I keep a tape of the shows in my collection." The show aired Sundays on WMAR from noon until 2:00 p.m. It was on the set of *The Collegians* in 1955 that Howell and Hooper would first meet. Hooper was sixteen at the time and playing occasionally with Bob Shanklin and Shanklin's brother Ricky, in addition to appearing on *The Collegians*, which he did for about a year and half. Howell also played on the show during this same time and the two bluegrass pickers became friendly. After Hooper left the show he did not see Howell for the next five years, until their paths crossed at New River Ranch Music Park one Sunday afternoon. They rekindled their friendship and Hooper invited Howell to an upcoming gig he had at the 79 Club with Bob Baker. This gig would turn out to be Baker's last show in Baltimore before he headed back to Blacksburg, Virginia.

Howell played banjo and, while his picking would never be confused with Walt Hensley's dynamic work on the five-string, he knew how to make what he did enhance the sound of any band he worked with. Roy Cole says he was never impressed with Howell's musical skills but believed that he used his loud, oversized personality to "make people think he could play banjo."[4] It was this oversized personality that would make him such a desirable bandmate, as he was recognized as an exceptional singer and an engaging front man. Longtime Baltimore musician Dean Sapp thought of Howell as a "real showman."[5] Carroll Swam played with Howell during the sixties and referred to him as an "intelligent musician who always knew how to put on a good show."[6] In addition to his singing, Howell's other desirable trait was his ability to get gigs for whatever band he fronted. He was "a good salesman," says Cole, "who could get the work."[7] This unmatched ability to "get the work" and score gigs kept his band's busy and making money, and in turn made for happy bandmates.

To fill the void left by Baker, Hooper and Howell added Cole on mandolin, Joe Hales on bass, and Kimball Blair from the Pike County Boys on fiddle. The band settled on the name Marvin Howell and the Franklin County Boys and took over the residency at the 79 Club. Howell was so committed to this new band he quit his day job as a machinist and focused all his efforts on getting gigs. With the number of opportunities available to bands to play at bars, music parks, halls, or radio stations, some bands in a number of cities such as Baltimore, Cincinnati, Dayton, and Boston were able to actually make a fairly decent living playing primarily as a local or regional band. These bands would garner a nice-size following in their local area and would be able to secure enough gigs and shows to be able to support themselves without having to travel outside of that area. Howell was one of those musicians whose primary income came from the high number of shows he would schedule for the Franklin County Boys. Hooper estimates that at the band's peak in the mid-sixties they were working around 300 shows a year. Many of those shows would come on the weekends and they would work five or six shows throughout the day and into the night on Saturday. They would start out playing an afternoon set for a local radio station and then bounce from club to radio station to club all day and night. Sundays would often be booked affairs and the band would play multiple sets at one of the nearby music parks.

The Franklin County Boys endured throughout the sixties as one of the more popular bluegrass bands in the Maryland, Virginia, and southern Pennsylvania region. The core of Hooper and Howell would remain intact throughout the band's run. Shortly after forming they picked up Hooper's close friend Danny Curtis, on mandolin, who would remain with the band until just about the end of its nine-year run. The addition of Frank Joyner on guitar gave the band the all-important core vocal trio that solidified the lineup. The rest of the band would feature a rotating cast of the some of the more prominent players in the Baltimore area. The first change to the band's lineup came two months after forming, when Cole was drafted into the service and had to leave. Following Cole's departure they saw a rotating procession of players file through the band, Frankie Short, Ronnie Ninkovich, and Carroll Swam all taking a turn in the band. For a three-month stretch in 1962 the band even added Del McCoury on banjo and his brother Jerry on bass. Despite the turnover in the band they found great success playing live

(From left) Earl Taylor, Walt Hensley, Jim McCall, and Boatwhistle play at the 79 Club in 1960 (author's collection).

throughout the decade, though they did not venture into the studio much. In 1962 they recorded four songs that would appear on Rebel Records' sprawling *70 Song Bluegrass Spectacular*, including the Hooper/Howell original "This Heart of Mine," the Hooper instrumental "Dobro on the Ridge," and the Mac Wiseman-penned tune "Bluebirds Are Singing for Me," which the Franklin County Boys were the first group to record.

Starting in June of 1968 the band played a regular half-hour television spot every Tuesday night from 8:30 to 9:00 p.m. on the now-defunct station WMET-TV in Baltimore. In 2001, *Live Bluegrass from WMET-TV, 1968*, a collection of twenty-three of the band's performances from the show, was released. The album was highlighted by the musical prowess of Hooper, Curtis, and Joyner and showed that despite Howell's limitations as a banjo player, his singing and ability to entertain a crowd were never in question. Hooper says, "When Marvin was going full tilt I don't think there was any band that could compete with him."[8] Unfortunately Howell was not exposed to as wide an audience as he could have been. With his unmatched ability to score gigs the band was making good money working locally and Howell felt he had no need to travel any further when work was so plentiful for the band in the immediate area. As the years wore on Howell became increasing difficult to work with. He developed a bad drinking problem that at times left him unreliable to perform shows and eventually led to the demise of his band.

As the 1960s dawned in Baltimore, Bob Baker was not the only prominent bluegrass musician from the city on the move. Following their brush with the big time after their appearance at the Folksong '59 concert, Earl Taylor and the Stoney Mountain Boys attempted to expand their horizons beyond Baltimore and the East Coast. They found themselves managed for a short time by local rockabilly star Stinson Barth, who was able to secure the band high-profile spots opening for local DJ and sometime performer Don Owens and country singer Roy Clark.[9] With thoughts of the big time and audiences beyond Baltimore guiding them, the band gave up their residency at the 79 Club (allowing first Baker and then Howell the opportunity to take over their residency) and hit the road. Generally the four core Stoneys, Taylor, Boatwhistle, Walt Hensley, and Jim McCall, were along on the trip, with a rotating roster of fiddle players and sidemen, including Tom Hall, Jimmy Grier, Leon Morris, and Billy Baker, joining when they were available, the two most prominent of that group being Morris and Baker.[10]

Morris was a regular in the Washington, D.C., area at the time as part of Buzz Busby's band and would remain a solid figure there over the years. Born in Pound, Virginia, in 1936 Billy Baker was the cousin of fiddle legend Kenny Baker. Billy would become a rock-solid part of the Baltimore scene for the next decade as one of the premier fiddle players in the area. Del McCoury called him one of the "best breakdown fiddlers"[11] he ever heard or had the pleasure to play with. Noted bluegrass historian Neil Rosenberg called Baker "one of the most soulful fiddlers in bluegrass."[12] Baker would go on to log many years as a part of McCoury's band and the two would create a formidable musical partnership.

The core four Stoney Mountain Boys and whatever sideman was with the band at the time bounced from city to city in hopes of a better-paying job. They made stops in many cities along the way, including Boston, Chicago, Kansas City, and St. Louis. Jobs were not always plentiful for the band as they traveled from city to city. Hensley says that when things got really desperate and money very tight while on the road, the band would subsist on nothing but baloney and crackers.[13] During these times they would resort to pawning their overcoats and tape recorders they had brought along with them. Once they even covered up a crack in the neck of a broken guitar with brown shoe polish and sold it for $150.[14]

While on a trip to St. Louis during the winter in fiddler Billy Baker's old beat-up Cadillac, the band was out of money and forced to sleep in the car. The Cadillac, which had no heater and holes in the floorboards the band tried to plug with spare clothes, was no match for the unrelenting Midwest cold. While the band was shivering the night away in the car one evening, a policeman came by and rapped on the window and asked what they were up to. They told him they were a band in town looking for work and even opened the trunk to show him their instruments. The policeman was unable to help them in finding any gigs, but he did inform them they were in one of St. Louis's worst neighborhoods and if they wanted to keep those instruments they had better move along.[15]

While the Stoneys did have some success while on the road, even finding steady work in Kansas City for a stretch, the various road trips were generally unsuccessful for them, forcing them first back to Baltimore and then later to relocate to Cincinnati. The Stoneys would often find that their return to either Baltimore or Cincinnati equaled better financial security. They were a well-known commodity in both of those areas and could consistently count on procuring regular gigs in either city. The band found that some of their greatest success throughout the sixties did not involve their travel and tour schedule but instead their time in the studio and the albums they made.

The exodus of Bob Baker and the Stoneys out of Baltimore was not the only change happening in the city's bluegrass scene at the time. The folk-revival scene that Mike Seeger and Alan Lomax had tapped into with their recordings and concerts was not confined to New York City. The bluegrass scene in Baltimore started to see the influx of non-hillbilly, non–Appalachian-bred musicians into its ranks. The musicians were usually younger and college educated or still in college and had an interest in acoustic and folk music that soon would develop into a love of bluegrass. "The result of the folk influx was you had different kinds of folks coming out to see the music," explains Carroll Swam, who was part of this new generation of younger musicians in Baltimore at the time. "You had college kids, professional or college-educated people, along with the local blue-collar people who had moved up from the South. So in the 1960s you had a transition, so to speak."[16]

Another one of those younger musicians was Chris Warner, who was born in 1946 in Red Lion, Pennsylvania, about an hour's drive north of Baltimore. Unlike the majority of bluegrass pickers in the area at the time, Warner had no background or connection to bluegrass until one day in 1962 when a couple of his friends, Ray King and Dick Laird, got onstage at a high school assembly and picked a couple of bluegrass tunes for the gathered students. Warner, who did not even know his friends played bluegrass at the time, was instantly infatuated with the sound of the banjo. He immediately began to search out bluegrass music and it did not take him long to "zero in on Lester Flatt, Earl Scruggs, Jimmy Martin, the early Stanley Brothers, and Bill Monroe."[17] Anything that had a good banjo in it drew his rapt attention. Within a year and half Warner was making the fifty-mile trip down to Baltimore, at first just to watch and listen. But soon he was a part of the exciting Baltimore scene, playing regularly with Kimball Blair, Jack Cooke, Del McCoury, Jerry McCoury, Frankie Short, Hoppy Ledford, and even, for a time, Boatwhistle. These formative years helped shaped Warner as a musician, especially his time with Del McCoury's experienced band. Warner said his time with McCoury "gave me the opportunity to hear some of those little details, those things I would have never have heard just playing with some local pickers who would have never played like those guys [McCoury's band]."[18] Those little details would serve Warner well, as just a few short years after first picking up the banjo he would be asked to join Jimmy Martin's band, the Sunny Mountain Boys, in 1968. His time with Martin would establish Warner as a "local legend" who "is considered one of the best banjo players in Jimmy Martin's opinion and a lot of other people's opinions."[19]

Like Warner, Carroll Swam was younger then the already-established musicians in Baltimore. He was originally from the surrounding Baltimore area, having grown up in the nearby town of Parkton. While he would not go on to the same success on a national level as Warner, he would establish himself as an important figure in the Baltimore area. He was a multi-instrumentalist who found success with a number of bands, including Bob

Arney, Jack Cooke, and Al Jones' various groups. He went on to play bass in the latter half of the sixties with Russ Hooper and Marvin Howell in the Franklin County Boys. Over the years Swam would become known for his passionate and powerful singing, which "did not sound like anybody else."[20] He would play with a variety of bands over the ensuing decades before starting the band Bluestone in 1990. Swam formed that band with one of those pickers who first inspired Warner to pick up a banjo at his high school assembly, Dick Laird. They would add Tom Neal on banjo, a well-respected musician from the area who played bass on Del McCoury's first solo album. Swam would later ask his former Franklin County Boy bandmate Russ Hooper to join him in Bluestone.

While growing up Swam had no real connection to the culture of Appalachia, but like Warner he would discover bluegrass as a teenager. Swam had first been exposed to acoustic music at the age of four when he was visiting a barbershop for a haircut. After his haircut he recalled that all the men in the shop broke out instruments and started playing, which really impressed the young Swam. He also heard some picking around the house from his dad, who played a little guitar and as a young man played in a string band. But it was not until Swam was a little older and got his first radio that he really discovered country and bluegrass music. Much like others of his generation who benefited from long-range AM radio that broadcast this growing type of music, Swam was heavily influenced by the sounds he discovered on the radio dial. "I would hook the antenna up to a bedspring or hang it out the window," remembers Swam. "I was fascinated by the music you could pick up on an AM radio. You could pick up stations from all over the country at night. I was particularly drawn to acoustic stuff, bluegrass, country, and early blues stuff. As a young kid I would listen to it all." Like guitar legend Carl Perkins, Swam was influenced by Elvis Presley's version of Bill Monroe's "Blue Moon of Kentucky." Unlike his friends, Swam connected more to Monroe than Presley. "My friends gravitated towards rock 'n' roll, so I couldn't tell them I was into bluegrass," joked Swam.[21] His interest in bluegrass grew upon his entry into Towson College in the fall of 1959, which gave him access to many of the bars in Baltimore. He saw the Stanley Brothers play a show at Overlea Hall on Bel Air Road while he was attending Towson, which had a huge impact on the budding bluegrass picker in him. The show was hosted by a local DJ, Ray Davis, whose bluegrass radio show on station WDMB was also having a big impact on young Swam.

Ray Davis was a local Baltimore DJ who broadcast a regular bluegrass show on radio station WDMB from the little studio above the automobile showroom at Johnny's Used Cars. Many young, second-generation bluegrass

(From left) Brian Charlton, Carroll Swam, Eleanor Arney, Bob Arney, and Tom Neal tune up before starting their set at the Manchester Inn in Manchester, Maryland, in 1966 (courtesy Russ Hooper).

pickers in the area got their first regular taste of bluegrass from that radio show.

Johnny's Used Cars was owned and run by Johnny Wilbanks. Wilbanks had lost both his legs in 1945 while working as a brakemen for the Baltimore and Ohio Railroad. This did not slow him down, as the outgoing Wilbanks used his insurance check from the accident to help open his first car lot. Johnny's Used Cars was originally at 900 East Fayette, where Baltimore's main post office is located now, but later moved a few miles north to 4801 Harford Road. In addition to the car lot and the radio show broadcast from there, Wilbanks sponsored many local sports teams, including an amateur baseball team that was one of the elite teams in the area. Despite all that he did and accomplished, for many Wilbanks would be best known for the bluegrass radio show broadcast from his car lot and hosted by Davis.

Davis's deep, booming voice has been introducing generations of music fans to bluegrass in the mid–Atlantic region since he first started broadcasting from Johnny's Used Car Lot in the late fifties. His influential show would have a thirty-eight-year run, over which time everyone from the most established of bluegrass stars to local pickers would find air time. "Ray would book many of the bluegrass bands from Nashville or from the barn dances in Richmond or from the Saturday barn jamborees in Wheeling," says Del McCoury. "When those bands came to town, he was the man to know. He was part of the reason the music was so big in [Baltimore] and the surrounding area."[22] Davis would branch out from radio with the start of his own record label, Wango (named after his Maryland hometown), which would record and release albums by many of the artists who appeared each week on his show. He has seen this music he loves so much go through many peaks and valleys,

A typical scene in downtown Baltimore as (from left) Kimball Blair, Chris Warner, Frankie Short, Sr., and Hoppy Ledford play the All Vue Inn, May 14, 1966 (courtesy Chris Warner).

watching it go from a time when people "would turn down their radios at traffic lights so nobody would know they were listening to bluegrass" to seeing it become a part of "pop culture."[23] Davis's impact on the spread of bluegrass is immeasurable. "Ray Davis is a legend in music broadcasting. He has helped define bluegrass music on-air since its earliest days as a discrete genre, and has placed a lasting imprint on it with his dedication to playing, promoting, and recording its musicians," writes Richard Thompson for *Bluegrass Today*.[24] Davis's motivation for his life's work is simple: his unyielding love of bluegrass, a genre he says "gets to people's heart and soul."[25] Davis continued to broadcast his radio show regularly on Washington, D.C., station WAMU until he retired in September 2013. After a long battle with cancer the influential DJ passed away in December 2014.

Despite the departure of some of the biggest names in the Baltimore bluegrass scene and the changing face of the makeup of the players with the addition of younger folkies into the fold, two things remained constant. First was the continued high level of excellence among all the musicians who played in Baltimore; even as Taylor, Hensley, Boatwhistle, McCall, and Baker had moved away, a whole new wave of pickers rose up to carry the mantle of Baltimore bluegrass forward. For many of those early pickers who had moved away, the pull of Charm City would prove too strong to resist and they ended up back in the city to live and play throughout the rest of their lives.

This second wave of pickers from Baltimore, many of whom had been around as youngsters for years, would go on to become some of the biggest names to emerge from the city. Del McCoury and his brother Jerry, Jack Cooke, Billy Baker, Bobby Diamond, Chris Warner, Bill Harrell, Kenny Haddock, and Hoppy Ledford were just a few of the leaders to emerge from this second crop of bluegrass musicians out of the Baltimore area during the sixties. Mandolin wizard Frank Wakefield even spent some time in Baltimore during this period. He came to the city at the insistence of Dobro player Haddock, whom Wakefield had met while touring with Jimmy Martin a few years earlier. Haddock convinced Wakefield to come to Baltimore, as there was more work and better pay. Upon his arrival in Baltimore, Wakefield would join Howell and Hooper in the Franklin County Boys for three months in 1960. When he informed Hooper he had no place to stay on his arrival, Hooper offered up a room in his house, not knowing that Wakefield had his wife and four children with him, and was surprised to find out he would be hosting the entire Wakefield family.[26] Wakefield lasted only eight months in the Baltimore area, and he and Haddock left for Washington to start playing with Red Allen.[27]

Many of the Baltimore musicians at this time would find their greatest success as sidemen for bigger acts. Some of the better-known sidemen to emerge during this time were Warner, who would play banjo with Jimmy Martin in the Sunny Mountain Boys, and Jack Cooke, who first played with Bill Monroe and his Blue Grass Boys and later served as the bass player for Ralph Stanley and the Clinch Mountain Boys, a spot he held until his death in 2009. Even Earl Taylor found success working as a sideman. He first worked briefly with the Stanley Brothers in 1964, before rejoining Jimmy Martin in 1965 for a couple of months. He left Martin in August of '65 and started working with Flatt and Scruggs playing mandolin and harmonica and remained with them for the next year and a half, appearing on the albums *When the Saints Go Marching In* in 1966 and 1967's *Strictly Instrumental.*

The second constant in Baltimore was the notoriously rough scene in the bars, dives, and honky-tonks where most of the bluegrass music in the city and its surrounding areas was played. From the earliest days, hillbilly music and bluegrass found a home in the working-class bars tucked into side streets and perched on the corners in hillbilly ghetto neighborhoods across Baltimore. Russ Hooper was a regular at these places and remembers the low pay and long hours you could expect working in these joints: "Bluegrass at the time was synonymous with drinking establishments. That seemed to be where you had to go to catch the music. And I'll tell you, when you told people you were playing these bars and you started at nine and were done at quarter to two and you were making $5 or $6 a night, people had a hard time understanding that."[28] In addition to the low pay, if there was any pay at all, musicians and patrons could expect a healthy amount of violence when they ventured to these places. Roy Cole recalls the Manor Inn, where the bartender tried to keep the peace with a bat he kept behind the bar. He says the bartender "would point his bat at your head if there was a problem to remind you to think about what you were doing."[29] It can probably be safely said that while the bartender was imploring rowdy patrons to think about their actions he was also reminding them if they kept it up they could expect to catch his Louisville Slugger across their heads. With a clientele built upon the working-class Appalachian migrants who populated these neighborhoods and who exuded a rough, rowdy demeanor amplified by large amounts of alcohol, fights were commonplace occurrences, and they would break out and start with no regard to the band on the stage. To those that wanted to fight, the band onstage was simply a backdrop. Tom Mindte grew up in the area in the sixties and seventies and fell in love with bluegrass music as a young man and eventually started a record label, Patuxent Records, that specialized in this type of music. The unsavory atmosphere at those bars where he first went to watch the music left a lasting impression him. "These were tough places full of tough people," he says. "I remember going to those bluegrass bars in East Baltimore—the Sandpiper Inn, Club Ranchero, Cub Hill Inn, the 79 Club. When you walked in the door, you walked onto a floor of sticky beer and into a cloud of cigarette smoke. I thought it was great—this was how it was supposed to be. Bluegrass wasn't meant to be sterile and healthy."[30] Every bluegrass musician in Baltimore at that time has his own stories about the violent fights at those tough places. Many of those stories happened at the infamous Stonewall Inn.

The Stonewall Inn on Pulaski Highway was a hole in the wall that was one of the leading places to see bluegrass in the Baltimore area. "The pickin' was hot. The beer was cold," explains longtime Baltimore bluegrass musician Dean Sapp about the Stonewall Inn. "But the place was known for fights. Rough as they came back then, a biker bar without the bikers. What a dive, but a great place to be. When you went there you felt like the circus was in town. Some of the craziest rednecks went there."[31] Del McCoury would hold a steady gig there throughout the middle half of the 1960s, and it was not uncommon to see some big-name bluegrass star playing there or stopping by when in the area, to check out what was going at the Stonewall. Nor was it uncommon for the music to continue when last call closed the bar at two a.m. A local motel up the street from the Stonewall called the Clarkson would give the band playing the Stonewall that night a free room, and all the musicians would "congregate there and jam until daybreak."[32] You never knew who would show up at these late-night picking sessions. Chris Warner remembers both famed picker Red Allen and bassist and comedian Chick Stripling stopping by to join in the late-night festivities. Warner says the appearance of Stripling, though, was not always a welcome one, as he would often be "pretty inebriated"[33] when he showed up and trouble would frequently ensue. While the late-night parties would occasionally get rowdy, it was at the Stonewall Inn itself that you could count on seeing a violent altercation while the band played on.

The Stonewall had a large oval bar in the middle of the room, with the stage at one end of the bar, which provided a nice perch for the band to see some pretty violent events in front of them. At a Bob Paisley and Ted Lundy show in 1970, the pair leaned into the microphone and were just about to start their next number when a man and woman walked in. The woman's husband was sitting at the bar waiting for them, clearly not pleased they were together. As they entered, the man at the bar pulled out a pistol and took aim at the couple. Someone sitting nearby saw what was about to happen and bumped the man's arm just as he was about to shoot, causing his arm to move and to shoot towards the stage instead. The bullet flew between Paisley and

Lundy and lodged into in the wall behind them, barely missing the pair. At the sound of gunfire, the place quickly cleared out. It would be a relief to say this shooting was an isolated incident, but unfortunately it was not the only case of some hot picking being interrupted by a blast of gunfire at the raucous Stonewall Inn.

One night during a Del McCoury show, McCoury heard a "big ole pop!" that "sounded like a .22 pistol." He saw a man duck behind the bar while another man across the bar from him with a pistol was firing at him. The man without the gun would duck behind the bar and run a bit then pop his head up to see where the other guy was. Every time the man popped his head up the guy with the gun would squeeze off another shot. McCoury just kept on playing. "Club owners did not want you to stop playing if a fight happened, even if it was a gunfight," he says.[34]

Russ Hooper was playing a show at the Stonewall when he heard the all-too-familiar loud "pow-pow-pow" of gunfire while he was onstage. He looked around and "apparently there was a guy who caught his wife cheating on him and he came into the bar and shot both of them." While the Stonewall might have been the place to catch some of the best bluegrass in Baltimore, it was definitely not the best place for a cheating spouse to go. Of course, if this was Hooper's only brush with cold-blood killing while performing it could easily be chalked up to bad luck. Unfortunately it was not. In addition to seeing the couple shot at the Stonewall, Hooper was onstage at the 79 Club working a gig with Bob Baker in the late fifties when he saw two men get into an argument near the stage. One of the men walked out and returned fifteen minutes later with a gun and shot and killed the other man right in front of Hooper. Another time, while working with Marvin Howell in 1968 at the Shangri-La Club, Hooper saw a man stabbed to death while he himself continued to play onstage. Hooper thought he was extremely lucky to have avoided a potentially stray bullet whizzing his way, but his best friend Danny Curtis had a different take on it. With a laugh he used to ask Hooper, "You ever stop to think maybe they were aiming at you and they kept missing?"[35]

Maybe it was simpler than that. In a scene known for a very violent atmosphere in the bars where bluegrass was played, chances were if you spent any time in those bars you were bound to see something, and very few people can claim to have spent as much time in those bars as Hooper. Since first starting as a teenager in 1954, Hooper has been regularly playing in them for over fifty years and has just about seen it all. Sometimes it was not the place or fights that would stick out so clearly; often it would be the unique patrons who inhabited these Baltimore bars. There was a pair of guys who used to come out to watch when Hooper played out at Johnny's on Reisterstown

Road. Their unforgettable features were burned forever into Hooper's memory. "There were two guys that use to come in and would stand near the stage and watch. One guy had an arm missing on the right side; the other guy had an arm missing on the left side," Hooper laughs at the thought. "We used to call them the bookends." They were a much safer pair than the duo Hooper recalled who would come in every weekend and "try their darndest to start a fight with somebody inside the place. If they couldn't find anybody inside to fight they would go out in the parking lot and beat the hell out of each other."[36]

Not all of the memorable patrons Hooper saw were missing limbs or tried to fight everyone. While working at the Cub Hill Inn in the 1970s he saw a different clientele start attending shows there. Doctors, lawyers and professional people started coming to shows because bluegrass music became the trendy and hip thing to do for a while in Baltimore. Among those professional people who stopped by the Cub Hill Inn were local celebrity and longtime Baltimore TV weatherman Bob Turk. Hooper says that on at least one occasion Turk brought a young news anchor from WJZ-TV who had just moved to the city for one of her first big jobs in TV. She would go on to become one of the biggest names in all television. The young news anchor's name was Oprah Winfrey.

In the late fifties and early sixties Alice Gerrard was regularly in Baltimore and becoming a presence in the bars, though mostly just to watch and listen. She was still very young at the time, and all the fights she saw at those bars "impressed [her] big time." Gerrard was at a Benny and Vallie Cain show when, she said, you "could sense that a fight was about to break out. Before the first blow was landed they [Benny and Vallie Cain] grabbed their instruments and ran offstage into the back room. Bottles were flying and people were hiding under tables."[37] Making a beeline for the safety of the kitchen or back room was sometimes the best action for the musicians. Hooper said when things started flying he would often head back to the kitchen and stay "there until I didn't hear tables getting turned over or chairs getting thrown anymore."[38]

In conversation Hooper will rattle off a seemingly endless list of bars and clubs in Baltimore and the surrounding area, with details about each that only serve to enhance the notoriously dangerous reputation these places had. There was Oleta's and Marty's Bar KY on South Charles Street, which had the stage set up in the front window. The odd placement of the stage, though, was the not the most unique feature of the bar. That would have been the chicken wire that covered the stage. Hooper admits with a laugh the chicken wire did "help a little." There was the Beltsville Tavern outside the city in nearby Laurel that Hooper said should have been called the "Bloody Bucket," due to the number of fights he saw there.[39]

Despite the rough, unsavory nature of the places they played and the bars they inhabited, the majority of the musicians did not live the up-all-night, hard-partying lifestyle so common among musicians and many of the patrons of these places. Most were hard-working family men who played all night in this dangerous environment to make a couple of bucks or simply for the love of the music. While some were hard-drinking men who saw the downside of such a tough lifestyle, many were completely abstinent from drugs and alcohol and highly intolerant of those who were not. Chris Warner says he "wasn't a drinker or smoker, so I went in those places just to play or listen."[40] Roy Cole was well known for asking fellow musicians who wanted to smoke a little dope around him to take it somewhere else.

Some of these rough bars and venues were remembered less for the violence that ensued there than for the quality and amount of music played there. Jazz City, located on Pratt Street, was a large club that featured music continuously throughout the night. Sets would alternate between a country band and a bluegrass band all evening. Many of Baltimore's best pickers played there throughout the years. Before they started their residency at the 79 Club, Earl Taylor and the Stoney Mountain Boys played at Jazz City. Another club just around the corner from Jazz City called the Blue Jay was a smaller venue by the water in Fells Point where many bands got their start. Taylor and the Stoney Mountain Boys played some of their earliest shows at the club. The Blue Jay was also the bar that Baker, Seeger, and Dickens had first played in when they started the Pike County Boys in 1954. Another musician who regularly played at both Jazz City and the Blue Jay was Jack Cooke. Cooke had spent some time playing a regular gig with Taylor at Jazz City but would soon form his own band and begin a residency at another local club.

Jack Cooke was born Vernon Crawford Cooke in 1936 in Norton, Virginia, in the southwestern part of the state. Southwest Virginia would serve as the cradle of Baltimore pickers, with Taylor, Hensley, Howell, and McCall, among many others, emerging from the area. Cooke played around the local Virginia area as both a bassist and guitarist until he got his big break when he was hired to play bass with the Stanley Brothers. He had played with the Stanleys for only a year when the opportunity to join Bill Monroe's Blue Grass Boys presented itself. Cooke worked for three years playing guitar and singing with Monroe. He was living in Nashville during this time and grew homesick for Norton. He quit Monroe and headed back to Norton, but the pull of music was too strong and shortly after returning home he headed north, first to Washington and then to Baltimore. Upon his arrival he began playing with

Taylor at Jazz City. When Taylor left to begin the Stoneys residency at the 79 Club, Cooke approached the owner of another club just up the street from Jazz City about playing there. The owner agreed and Cooke started playing at the Chapel Café, located on Chapel Street, a small side street located off of Pratt Street just south of Johns Hopkins Hospital.

In a town full of violent bars and dangerous honky-tonks, the Chapel Café was one of the most notorious in Baltimore. Chris Warner, who played the Chapel many times over the years with Cooke, remembered it as a "rough joint."[41] It was smaller than its close neighbor Jazz City and featured bluegrass exclusively. A young Carroll Swam stopped by the Chapel Café in 1965 and was impressed by the "driving traditional bluegrass" emulating from the band onstage, the band at the time consisting of Jack Cooke, Jerry McCoury on bass, Bobby Diamond on banjo, and Billy Baker on fiddle.[42]

The bar was run by a man named Parker, whose full name has been forgotten over time and who was known to take charge in his own unique way. Jerry McCoury recalled that when someone "would get a little rowdy he [Parker] would grab the rowdy patron by the hands and feet and use their head and body as a battering ram to open the door. Then he would throw them right out of the bar and slam the door shut and go on about his business."[43] This unique way of dealing with rowdy customers was a common occurrence and a distraction the musicians onstage learned to ignore while they played there.

When Cooke started playing the Chapel, he began to find and hire some of the most talented musicians in Baltimore and the surrounding area to play in his band, the Virginia Mountain Boys. Many of those young musicians would graduate from the dingy atmosphere of the Chapel Café and move on to bigger bands and better paydays. A handful of them would go on to play with the master himself, Bill Monroe. The most famous of these was destined to become one of the biggest names in bluegrass and one of its most iconic figures and voices, Del McCoury.

6

"Getting out there and playing for nothing"

Recommended Listening: For someone with as much history as Del McCoury it is preferable to dig into as much of his rich discography as possible. The five-disc box set *Celebrating 50 Years of Del McCoury* is the ideal companion for just such an undertaking. Each 10-song disc is organized by decade, so a listen straight through provides an auditory tour of Del's long life in music.

It was a gorgeous late–May evening at the 5th Annual DelFest in Cumberland, Maryland. The sun had finally set behind the mountains that stood guard around the festival grounds, which helped release some of the heat of the day, giving way to a comfortable, cool mountain breeze. Jam-grass stalwarts Yonder Mountain String Band were onstage headlining the day's festivities. Yonder Mountain String Band is one of the leaders of the modern jam-grass movement. They are a band that can just as easily slip into a lengthy, jam-filled take on the Grateful Dead's "Althea" as they can blast through a perfect rendition of the Jimmy Martin classic "Hit Parade of Love." And on this perfect mountain evening they were doing just that. The first half of their set was dominated by a near thirty-minute exploratory workout that flowed seamlessly from their own "Dawn's Early Light" into a spirited take on Talking Heads' "Girlfriend Is Better" before wrapping up neatly with a glorious rendition of John Hartford and the Dillards' (both of whom can rightly claim to be godfathers of the jam-grass movement) "Two Hits and the Joint Turned Brown."

Yonder Mountain String Band has become a regular part of DelFest, an annual festival named for its founder, Del McCoury. The four-day festival has become one of the premier bluegrass festivals in the country, with its namesake and host, McCoury, serving as the musical anchor over the weekend as he and his band play a minimum of four main stage sets over the

Jeff Austin (right) thanks Del McCoury for sitting in with Yonder Mountain String Band at the 2012 Delfest in Cumberland, Maryland (photograph by Jordan August).

course of the festival. One can easily expect to find McCoury gracing the stage with any number of bands throughout the weekend. He is an omnipresent figure all weekend. If spotting McCoury around the festival was turned into a drinking game, one would be mighty drunk pretty quickly, whether it's seeing a blurred version of his immaculate white pompadour zipping around on a golf cart or spotting him hanging by the merch tent or looking away and turning back only to find that he has somehow jumped onstage with yet another band. The elder statesman of string music makes the rounds at the festival.

The band lineup for the festival each year runs the gamut from traditional bluegrass stars and living legends such as J.D. Crowe, Jesse McReynolds, Sam Bush, and Bobby Osborne to new, younger bands like the Infamous Stringdusters, Greensky Bluegrass, Railroad Earth, and Leftover Salmon who, like Yonder Mountain String Band, are easily tagged with a jam-grass label but who—just like the living legends they share the stage with at DelFest— are keeping the spirit of bluegrass alive. Despite the stellar lineups that have become the norm at the festival year in and year out, the real star every year is without a doubt Del McCoury, whose long-lasting impact and influence can be seen in every band that graces one of the three stages over the course of the festival.

Yonder used to be led by hyperactive mandolin player Jeff Austin, and midway through his band's set on that gorgeous May evening, he paused to talk about his musical influences:

> Well, one of the great joys of getting to play this is festival is that I have a lot of people I admire in the music world, and the top two, one was Jerry Garcia who—I never got to meet him. I admired him from afar for a long, long time. He really inspired everything that I do, and the other one is about to walk onstage and sing some songs with us, and that is just awesome in so many ways. Please welcome to the stage the one, the only, we are so blessed to know and have him, Del McCoury.[1]

McCoury then strolled onto the stage with Yonder Mountain String Band, a band whose career did not even start until nearly forty years after McCoury first played the Chapel Café with Jack Cooke. Despite the large generational gap, McCoury fits in flawlessly with Yonder on this night as they team up for a take on the classic "Feast Here Tonight (Rabbit in a Log)" and

Trey Anastasio and Del McCoury play together at the 2013 Delfest in Cumberland, Maryland (from left): Ronnie McCoury (Del's son), Anastasio, and McCoury (photograph by the author).

the McCoury murder ballad "Eli Renfro." That ability to fit in flawlessly is what has become one of the genius qualities of McCoury. While many of his aging contemporaries seem to be resistant to seeing bluegrass music change and evolve, McCoury is perfectly comfortable sharing the stage with anyone from Jesse McReynolds to David Grisman to Leftover Salmon to the String Cheese Incident to Yonder Mountain String Band, which he has done at DelFest. It is this quality that has set him apart from so many of his aging bluegrass contemporaries.

The following year, 2013, at DelFest another longtime McCoury fan and admirer, Phish guitarist and front man Trey Anastasio, was headlining the festival with his solo band. Just like Jeff Austin the year before, Anastasio was onstage between songs rambling in his trademark way as only he can about the virtues of McCoury and how long he himself has been a fan. He began telling a story about being on tour with Phish in 1992 with Aquarium Rescue Unit. The guys in Aquarium Rescue Unit passed on a copy of McCoury's 1992 album, *Blue Side of Town*, to Anastasio and the rest of Phish, and they were all immediately smitten with it. Anastasio says the album became a constant presence in the van while on tour, and they must have listened to it "fifty million times" while driving. From that moment, Phish "just dreamed of getting to meet or see Del McCoury. And in 1999 we asked Del to come to one of our Phish festivals in Oswego, and he came, the whole family came in the bus." He adds, "We were just so thrilled he came and we got to get on stage and sing together.... So today we get to be at Del's festival, we are so honored and we are going to bring him out here and sing a song on his stage."[2] As he did with Jeff Austin and Yonder Mountain String Band, McCoury and his entire band hopped onstage and ripped through a couple of numbers with Anastasio's band. The first, "I'm Blue, I'm Lonesome," shows that even at seventy-four years old McCoury can still hit a spine-tingling, high note that immediately finds the crowd roaring its approval every time he climbs up the vocal register. It is a note that very few people have ever been able to hit, let alone with the polished style and grace of McCoury. The second number they played together was the longtime McCoury classic "Beauty of My Dreams," a song that has crossed over from the bluegrass realm into the jam-band world, thanks to Phish's regular inclusion of it in their ever-changing set list.

At the New Orleans Jazz Fest in 2008 McCoury joked from stage about the positive impact that Phish's playing of "Beauty of My Dreams" has had on his wallet. "This is a song I wrote a long time ago and I put it on a record and then a band named Phish recorded it," McCoury says. "And I was really tickled when they did that because every time I go to the mailbox there is a lot of money there."[3] This mixing and crossing of musical styles is precisely the beauty of DelFest: the ability to blend the traditional bluegrass of McCoury's past and meld it with the younger bands who are keeping that old-timey sound alive in their own unique way. It is this ability that has helped define McCoury's long-lasting, genre-crossing, and highly influential career.

There is no definitive answer as to why younger musicians across a broad range of genres have seemed to gravitate towards McCoury so much as opposed to some of the other legends of bluegrass. It may be as simple as that he has taken the time to embrace them. Not shying away from the chance to take the stage with Phish at one of their massive annual summer festivals, covering folk-icon Richard Thompson's "1952 Vincent Black Lighting" and turning it into the 2002 IBMA song of the year, or recording an album with outlaw songwriter Steve Earle has allowed Del to be discovered by a multitude of diverse fans. "Del is one of the best examples of how eclectic an artist can be," explains Chris Pandolfi of the Infamous Stringdusters, one of those younger bands McCoury has not only influenced but played with at DelFest. "Del pretty much does one thing—he plays rhythm guitar and he sings. But he is able to take that art into so many different meaningful styles with his collaborations, from the Lee Boys, or Preservation Hall Jazz Band, or the first time I saw Del McCoury with Phish in western New York at [Camp Oswego]."[4]

McCoury is one of the only musicians who can truly say he has reached the upper echelon of both the bluegrass world and the jam-band world. He finds himself equally accepted by an aging bluegrass traditionalist who believes the music should be unamplified, have no drums, and never veer from what Monroe and Scruggs started as much as he can be loved by a dreadlocked, tie-dye wearing hippie-kid who emerges from his car in a haze of blue smoke before each show. According to McCoury's son Ronnie, who is regarded as one of the premiere mandolin players in the world, "He [McCoury] just wants to be involved with whatever is good. He has no requirements or aesthetic standards or certain sounds to preserve or adhere to. He just wants to make great music with other musicians."[5] It is not surprising to see someone like McCoury, with his never-ending talent and overflowing charisma, come along and say his door is open to everyone and then get exposed to an audience like Phish's, which is fanatical about music, and see great things blossom and explode from the pairing. He is truly unique in that he represents both the qualities of traditional bluegrass and the open-mindedness of today's music. It's a short list of people who can say they have played at the Grand Ole Opry and the annual Bonnaroo music festival or have shared a stage with both Bill Monroe and Trey Anastasio. Del McCoury is one of the select few on both those lists.

McCoury's upbringing was not much different from the majority of musicians he would encounter and play with in Baltimore. He was born in 1939 in Bakersville, North Carolina, and like many others at the time his family would move north. The McCourys moved shortly after Del's birth, to York County, Pennsylvania, and settled in Glen Rock, just over the state line from Maryland and a little more than forty miles from Baltimore. Del discovered music at age nine, when his older brother, G.C., taught him how to play guitar. His musical path was sealed in 1950 when he first heard an album by Flatt and Scruggs and discovered bluegrass. "All the other kids were listening to Elvis Presley because that's the way it was all over the world then," says McCoury. "But it didn't faze me because I had already been turned on to Earl Scruggs."[6] Scruggs' playing on "Roll in My Sweet Baby's Arms" greatly inspired the young McCoury to take up the banjo. While McCoury had family mem-

Keith Daniels and the Blue Ridge Ramblers play radio station WLBR in Lebanon, Pennsylvania, in the late 1950s. From left, Sterling Sauble, Frank Campbell, Keith Daniels, Lloyd Herring, and Del McCoury (courtesy Chris Warner).

bers who could play the banjo, none of them could play like Earl Scruggs. That is what McCoury really wanted to do, so he taught himself to play by listening to Flatt and Scruggs records over and over. The banjo became his primary instrument for the next ten years, until he switched to guitar at the insistence of Bill Monroe.

McCoury graduated from high school in 1957 and his music career began in earnest shortly after that. He had purchased a brand-new Gibson banjo a few years earlier, but he would soon purchase another banjo, which had been used by a Baltimore picker McCoury admired at the time, Walt Hensley. "He was a great banjo player," says McCoury. "He was a great guy to play lead and back up the singer. He was just really good."[7] McCoury had first seen Hensley play with Earl Taylor and the Stoney Mountain Boys at the Blue Jay on Broadway in the Fells Point neighborhood of Baltimore. He had made the trip down from Pennsylvania with a fellow musician, Keith Daniels, whom McCoury had recently become acquainted with. Daniels was a transplanted North Carolinian who was living near McCoury. A fiddler who played in a local band, the Stevens Brothers, Daniels had been encouraging the younger McCoury to show up with his banjo whenever the Stevens Brothers were playing and sit in when possible. This eventually led to a full-time spot in the band for McCoury. The Stevens Brothers gained a small bit of local fame, as they performed regularly as part of a Saturday morning live music show on local radio station WCBG broadcast out of Chambersburg, Pennsylvania.

Daniels and McCoury lasted about a year with the Stevens Brothers before deciding to start their own band, Keith Daniels and the Blue Ridge Ramblers. The Blue Ridge Ramblers worked steadily, making trips down South to appear on the long-running New Dominion Barn Dance radio show broadcast out of Richmond, Virginia, as well as regularly playing in Baltimore. The band's lineup, much like those of other bands at the time, was always in constant flux, a steady stream of musicians flowing through the ranks. Frank Campbell, Billy Sage, Sterling Sauble, and even fresh-from-Virginia Jim McCall spent time with the Blue Ridge Ramblers.

Daniels was fairly well known in the Baltimore and Washington areas and introduced the recent high school graduate McCoury to many of the top players in both cities, including Buzz Busby, John Duffey, Bill Emerson, Earl Taylor, and Charlie Waller. While with Daniels McCoury would also first cross paths with another young Baltimore picker who would go on to become a titan of the scene as well, Russ Hooper. Hooper remembers that first encounter with Del. "Keith called me one night and said, 'I am doing an album in Mechanicsburg, Pennsylvania, at Alexander's Studio' and he asked if I would come up and do it with him," says Hooper. "I said sure. He came over and picked me up. On that session there was a fella named Frank Campbell playing guitar, Keith Daniels playing mandolin, Billy Sage playing fiddle, I played Dobro, Del played banjo. We might have done nine or ten tracks." With a laugh, Hooper continues: "Last time I saw Del I gave him a copy [of the session recording]. I said, 'Do me favor. Don't listen to this until it's two in the morning and no one else is around.'"[8] Despite Hooper's apparent lack of enthusiasm for how the session turned out, two of the tracks were eventually released as a 45 for Rebel Records, "Live and Let Live," with "I've Been Working on the Railroad" on the flip side.[9]

McCoury would go onto play for almost four years with Daniels in the Blue Ridge Ramblers. McCoury's time with the band came to an end when he was drafted into the army in 1962. Right before he was drafted, the band recorded a couple of original Daniels songs for Empire Records (a small label associated with Empire Recording Studios in Tacoma Park, Maryland, near Washington). The two songs, "Mocking Mandolin" and "You're My Everything," featured McCoury on banjo and came out as a 45 in 1962 shortly after he was drafted.[10]

McCoury was in the service for only a couple months before receiving a medical discharge. Upon his return home he found that Daniels had ended the band and gotten out of music. Daniels' brothers all owned restaurants and he had gotten into the same business while McCoury was away, opening a small carry-out joint in Glen Burnie, just south of the Baltimore city limits. His newly opened place was very small, almost like a long hallway, and Hooper used to joke, "If you wanted to rob the place you had to go outside to draw your gun."[11]

With Daniels out of the music business, McCoury started looking for a new band to play with. He hooked up for a while, along with his younger brother Jerry, who played bass, with Marvin Howell and Russ Hooper in the Franklin County Boys, who were in the middle of one of their numerous lineup changes that plagued the early years of the band. McCoury lasted only three months with Howell and Hooper before he began playing with Jack Cooke.

Cooke had recently begun to work at the Chapel Café. Since his time in Monroe's band, Cooke had established himself as one of the leading bluegrass figures in the city. Over his lengthy career, which would find him joining Ralph Stanley and the Clinch Mountain Boys in 1970 and remaining with them until his death in 2009, Cooke became known as one of the most versatile bluegrass singers and a rock-solid musician who could be counted on to be proficient at any number of instruments. He had recently secured a three nights a week spot at the Chapel Café when he and McCoury crossed paths. Cooke was assembling a band and asked McCoury if he would like to join. McCoury agreed and brought along his younger brother Jerry to play bass. They added local fiddler Kimball Blair and began playing under the name Virginia Mountain Boys.

Fiddler Blair, originally from Harlan County, Kentucky, had been making the rounds in the city. He had played with both Bob Baker and Marvin Howell previously, and was a highly valued addition to any band because of his skill with the bow. Blair worked full time as a house painter and never was able to commit to music only; therefore he never received much recognition outside of the Baltimore/Washington area. But those in the area knew of his immense talents and reveled in the luxury of having such a skilled player always at their disposal. He would become one of the most respected and sought-after fiddlers in the city, with a long and distinguished career. His son, Warren, has carried on his father's legacy, as he has also become a highly respected fiddler in the area. The younger Blair has carved out a long, successful career like his father, starting in the late seventies with his work with the Bluegrass Cardinals.[12]

With the addition of Blair, Cooke's new band started playing three nights a week—Friday, Saturday, and Sunday—at the Chapel Café shortly after McCoury returned from his short stint in the army. The Sunday night shows made for difficult Monday mornings for the band's young bassist, Jerry McCoury. "In '62 I would have been fourteen or fifteen. I was just in high school, so it made going to school Monday morning kind of hard," explains Jerry. "At the time, I didn't know if it was the right thing to do as a young kid, even though I was getting a lot of experience with good musicians."[13] Despite the bleary-eyed Mondays Jerry struggled through in high school, his time as a teenager spent in the clubs of Baltimore would clearly pay off for him, as he, like his older brother, would find a long and successful career in music. Since his time as a teenager playing with Cooke at the Chapel Café, Jerry has gone on to become an in-demand bassist and to play with Don Reno, Bill Harrell, Red Smiley, Red Allen, and David Grisman.

Del also relished his time with Cooke. In conversation he mentions Cooke many times, always with extreme fondness. Despite all the success Del has achieved and all the legendary bands and musicians that he has had the opportunity to grace the stage with and record albums with, he admits with a palpable sense of longing in his voice, "I didn't get to play with Jack as long as I wanted."[14]

Del's short time with Cooke would come to an end on a cold early-February night in 1963. As he did most nights before a show, Del got to the Chapel Café "with just enough time to tune up and walk out on stage." Del was still playing the banjo that had been previously owned by Hensley. Everything was going as it normally did during the first set until Del "saw a guy walk through the side door and sit down pretty close to the stage." The man had a big hat on, which Del though was "pretty strange, because it was kind of dark in the club. I thought that he looked like Bill Monroe, but thought, *What would he be doing here?*"[15] After the first set the band headed back to their small dressing room and the man in the big hat followed. Once back there Del realized it was Monroe, and he was in complete awe. Cooke introduced his former bandmate Monroe to the star-struck members of his current band, who could not figure out what he was doing there. They found out later Monroe had talked with Cooke previously and told him he would be stopping by. Cooke had failed to inform the rest of the band of this. Monroe was on his way to a gig he had a few days later, on February 8, in New York City at New York University. He needed a couple of players to fill out his band, which currently consisted of fiddler Kenny Baker and bassist Bessie Lee Mauldin, and he thought Cooke might be able to help him out. Cooke agreed to go to New York to play guitar and sing and suggested that since he needed a banjo player as well they take Del along. Del agreed to go and the five musicians piled into Monroe's 1959 Oldsmobile Super 88 station wagon and headed north through the February cold to New York City.

Monroe was famous for his huge repertoire of songs and the large number of audience requests he would take during the course of a show, but Del was confident he could handle whatever might come his way musically. "I had been playing quite a while and wasn't afraid to try anything. I was at a point where I thought I could play 'Rawhide' or any of those real fast numbers," he said. Fortunately, Del was not only confidant in his skills but extremely competent in them as well. Expecting to rehearse before playing the show, he was surprised when they wound up playing without any rehearsal for their show on February 8, 1963, at New York University. The lack of rehearsal was common for Monroe and what Del would come to call the "Monroe Way."[16]

In attendance at the show were many of the elite of New York's folk and bluegrass scene. Mike Seeger's good friend Ralph Rinzler was there that night. Rinzler had been playing with his own bluegrass band, the Greenbriar Boys, and was finding fame in the folk circles in New York. (His fame would soon become eclipsed by the incomparable talents of one of the Greenbriar Boys' opening acts. A young, unknown folk singer named Bob Dylan would open for the Greenbriar Boys over a string of shows between September 25, 1961, and October 8, 1961. A review of the September 29 show by Robert Shelton for the *New York Times* would help launch the then-unknown Dylan into the

David Grisman and Jerry McCoury onstage together at the 2010 Delfest in Cumberland, Maryland (photograph by the author).

folk stratosphere.)[17] Rinzler had also recently become Monroe's manager after the two had bonded during the course of a lengthy interview Rinzler had conducted with Monroe. The resulting article published in *Sing Out!* magazine was one of the most detailed interviews Monroe had given to that point in his career. It helped to set the historical record straight concerning Monroe's place as the Father of Bluegrass. The folk revival was in full swing and legions of fans began discovering bluegrass through the sweet sounds of Flatt and Scruggs, but many were blissfully unaware of who Monroe was and his place in the development of bluegrass. Rinzler's article placed Monroe in the proper context he rightly deserved as the bandleader of the group whose name had become the accepted term for this new style of music.

About a third of the way through the evening's show at New York University, Monroe stated to the crowd, "I know you folks in this part of the country play with Ralph Rinzler, and we are going to get him to come out and help out with a couple of numbers tonight." Rinzler, with mandolin in tow, took the stage and much to the approval of his hometown crowd sat in for a couple of hymns, with Monroe and his Blue Grass Boys helping out on "I Am a Pilgrim," and "Life's Railway to Heaven."[18]

Another young mandolin player, David Grisman, was also at the show that night. Grisman had been studying the instrument under Rinzler's knowledgeable eye and was excited to see Monroe up close. Del says he cannot recall for sure if he met Grisman that night, but Grisman says he is positive he and Del first crossed paths at that show. "I met Del the day he played his very first gig (on banjo) with Bill Monroe and his Blue Grass Boys. It was at NYU (where I was a student) early in 1963," remembers Grisman.[19] Regardless of whose memory is more accurate about their initial meeting, a deep friendship would eventually develop between the two. They played their first show together a few years later in 1966 at Rensselaer Polytechnic Institute in Troy, New York. Del's brother Jerry was in Grisman's band at the time, and Grisman asked Jerry to talk Del into coming and playing with them. Del agreed and made the trip north in his 1965 Plymouth. Grisman and Del went on to share the stage and studio countless times together over the following decades. It is a friendship and musical partnership that exists to this day. Grisman has played DelFest multiple times, and whenever he does it is a guarantee you will see the two longtime friends share the stage together at some point.

Also in attendance at the New York University show was Pete Wernick, the future banjo master and cofounder of influential bluegrass group Hot Rize. At the time, he was just a seventeen-year-old Columbia College freshman who had discovered the banjo a few years earlier. He was excited about the chance to see Monroe in person, but even more excited for the chance to check out the banjo player, McCoury, and see what he could learn from "a real pro." Wernick watched Del intently during the show and when he heard Del play a particular Earl Scruggs lick that had been mystifying him he knew he had to get backstage after the show and meet him. "Of course I was intimidated when I went looking for him," recalls Wernick, "but my first memory of spotting him sitting in the dressing room with his banjo was that great friendly smile. When I asked him about the lick, he knew which one I meant and showed it to me. He was quite friendly. That made my day of course."[20]

Throughout their show at New York University Monroe kept calling Del "Dale" whenever he mentioned him on stage. Del has said that this mix-up was common. The whole time they worked together, Monroe always called him "Dale," never Del. Monroe was not the only person who would mispronounce Del's name over the years. Mandolin player extraordinaire Sam Bush said when he first heard people talk about the new singer in Monroe's band he thought his name was "Delmar Coury," telling people "I really like that Delmar guy."[21] It was not until years later Bush realized his name was Del

McCoury, not Delmar Coury. Regardless of what Monroe called him, Bush recognized real talent when he saw it and he knew that Del was real talent. When they arrived back in Baltimore after their drive from New York City, Monroe walked Del backed to his car, which was parked near the Chapel Café. Monroe, always a man of few words, simply said to Del before going their separate ways, "I need a banjo. If you want to come down to Nashville call me up and I'll come see you."[22]

Del pondered Monroe's offer for some time. He knew it was a great opportunity, but, he said, "I was kind of afraid to go, and I really enjoyed playing with Jack."[23] Del's good friend Robert Rook, better known as bluegrass musician Bobby Diamond, stepped in to set Del straight. "Some people would kill for that job," he told Del, adding that he would drive him down to Nashville in his Cadillac if Del would agree to go on the audition.[24] Del agreed it was the best move to make and after a few months eventually headed down to Nashville. Upon his arrival he checked into the Clarkston Hotel next door to the National Life and Accident Insurance Building, the sponsor of the *Grand Ole Opry*. Monroe had told Del to meet him in the lobby for breakfast the following morning. When Del got to the lobby with his banjo in hand, he was surprised to see another man down there with a banjo in hand as well. Monroe showed up and told both banjo players to follow him. They went to a nearby restaurant for breakfast, during which there was very little conversation among the three. Monroe then led the pair next door to a rehearsal space at the National Life and Accident Insurance Building, where they were going to audition.

When they got there, Monroe told Del he was going to audition on guitar, which Del thought was odd until he heard the other banjoist in the room play. "I had never heard anyone play like him," says Del. "Everybody up to that point had tried to play with Bill like Scruggs or Don Reno or someone like that, which included me. It's what I would have done."[25] But the other banjo player in the room did not try and mimic those previous pickers; instead he played like no one else had ever done before. Del realized Monroe needed a player like this in his band.

That other banjo player was Bill Keith, a Boston-born, Amherst College–educated, highly inventive musician who had developed his own unique style of playing born from his desire to play two fiddle-like melodies at once. His approach to the instrument would come to be known as "Keith" picking style. Keith's style was very modern, highly progressive, and would impact how a generation of banjo pickers who followed approached the instrument. For Monroe it was an easy decision to add Keith to his band; his unparalleled talent and inventive approach took care of that. The only decision concerning

Keith for Monroe was the issue of his name. "There is not room for two Bill's in this band," announced Monroe. He began to refer to Keith as Brad, from his middle name, Bradford.[26]

With Keith settled upon as the new banjo player in Monroe's band, the issue of what would happen to Del had to be settled. When Monroe asked Del to audition on guitar Del was reluctant, as he thought of himself as strictly a banjo player. But after seeing Keith play, and some reassurance from Monroe, who told him, "You will like this job better than playing banjo,"[27] Del agreed and picked up the guitar. Monroe then informed Del that in addition to guitar he would be the band's lead singer. Despite his initial reluctance to switch to guitar, Del was confident he could handle the musical side of the job. What did worry him was the large number of songs he now had to learn the lyrics to. "Me being the lead singer I had to learn to do some solo stuff on the verses. It was a big learning thing for me because I had to learn all his [Monroe] songs," says Del. "If I had just went in as the banjo player it would have been a lot easier—just to have to remember the changes in the choruses."[28] Del would admit later that at first he did not think Monroe was right to move him to guitar and lead vocals, but that at the end of the day the Father of Bluegrass proved to be right in asking Del to make the switch.

Del's addition to the Blue Grass Boys also proved to be beneficial for his younger brother Jerry. Jerry joined his older brother on the road with Monroe when his school schedule allowed; and he would help bassist Bessie Lee Mauldin take care of her bass. Before shows as the band was tuning up off-stage, the teenaged Jerry would "tune Bessie's bass and play along with him [Monroe] and the band. [He] thought it was the neatest thing to get to play with Bill Monroe, and then when it was time for the band to hit the stage [he] would give her the bass and they would walk out."[29]

Del stayed with Monroe for only about a year, during which time they toured extensively. On a trip to California shortly after Del joined the band, they were playing a residency at the famous Ash Grove in Los Angeles. A young Chris Hillman made the 150-mile trip from his home in San Diego to catch Monroe in person. The teenaged Hillman was just a budding bluegrass fanatic and aspiring folkie at the time and still a few years away from his groundbreaking work with the Byrds and the Flying Burrito Brothers, but he was already becoming a well-respected picker in the Southern California bluegrass scene. The long drive to see Monroe and his Blue Grass Boys was well worth it to Hillman and he remembers the show as being "great and inspiring." He was very impressed with a young Del, who sang an extremely memorable version of "Dark Hollow" that night. Hillman said that even then Del was "as good as he is today."[30]

Also in attendance at the Ash Grove residency was another young guitarist who hailed from San Francisco. Del would later have a chance to talk with the guitarist years later at a Grateful Dead show at Merriweather Post Pavilion in Columbia, Maryland. The young guitarist, Jerry Garcia, would tell Del when they chatted backstage at Merriweather, "Man, I was in the audience every night, watching that. I wanted to be a blue grass boy!"[31]

Shortly after the Blue Grass Boys returned from California, fiddler Kenny Baker informed Monroe he would be quitting the band to take a job working at the coal mines in eastern Kentucky. It was a job above ground at the mines and was well-paying and steady work. Over the years Baker would go on to spend more time as a Blue Grass Boy with Monroe than any other musician; but when his children were still young, in the fifties and sixties, he often joined up with Monroe only to quit when the chance at a better job presented itself. After his children had grown up and left home, Baker rejoined the band and spent nearly twenty years with Monroe as his fiddler. When Baker departed the band in 1963, it was taking a break from the road and Del had gone back to Pennsylvania to see family and friends. While home he also went down to Baltimore to see his good buddy Jack Cooke at the Chapel Café. Fiddler Billy Baker, who was Kenny Baker's cousin, was playing with Cooke, and at some point during the night Del approached Billy Baker about the fiddle vacancy in Monroe's band. Billy, like his cousin, was a highly seasoned fiddler. Most recently he had been playing with Cooke, but before that he had spent time playing with Earl Taylor and the Stoney Mountain Boys, including a brutal trip to St. Louis in his car in the dead of winter. Baker also had already played with Monroe for a short time in 1961. His time with Monroe as a Blue Grass Boy had come about from his friendship with Cooke. Billy agreed to join Monroe's band and left with Del to go back to Nashville. Del and Billy would play with Monroe for about a year, during which time they were with Monroe when he made his first ever appearance at the legendary Newport Folk Festival in Rhode Island on June 26 and 27, 1963.

During his tenure with Monroe, Del played on one recording session on January 28, 1964. This session yielded three songs: "One of God's Sheep," released on 1964's *I'll Meet You in Church Sunday Morning*, "Legend of the Blue Ridge Mountains," and the classic "Roll On Buddy Roll On," which was not released until 1967 on *Bluegrass Time*. Del was scheduled for another recording session with Monroe the day before, but due to a scheduling mix-up he and Billy had accepted a gig in Knoxville, Tennessee, to play on the Cas Walker show and had to miss it.[32] Del and Billy ended up lasting only a few more months with Monroe after their recording session. They would leave to follow up an opportunity Del had in California to play with a band out there.

The Golden State Boys were one of the leading bluegrass bands in Southern California. Their roster over the years was a who's who of Southern California pickers and musicians: Herb Rice (Tony Rice's father), Hal Poindexter, Vern Gosdin, Don Parmely, and Chris Hillman all spent time with the Golden State Boys during the early sixties. The band had a regular TV spot at the time, playing every Sunday afternoon as part of *Cal's Corral*, a live show broadcast from the Huntington Park Ballroom. Del had crossed paths and become friendly with the Golden State Boys while on tour with Monroe during their trip to California. When an opening in the band for a banjo player came up they called Del and asked if he would be interested in joining the band. Del took a few months to think about the offer and in early 1964, after he and Billy had left Monroe, he called back and said he was interested in the spot but he had a fiddler friend who wanted to come as well. The band did not have a fiddler and agreed to take Billy on as well. Del and Billy moved out West and spent a couple of months playing with the Golden State Boys. The band's lineup was in constant flux while they were there, and Del ended up switching back to guitar, which he has played ever since. Despite having a regular spot on a TV show the work was not as plentiful as back East and Del and Billy soon headed back to the bustling, busy scene in Baltimore.

Upon their arrival in Baltimore Del would settle into a pretty steady routine that found him balancing a real job with his music career. He found work with his wife's uncle doing logging, which gave him the flexibility to still be able play music and travel to play festivals and shows. He would work in the woods all week, play Friday through Sunday, and often have to drive all night to get back to work Monday morning. He would continue working as a logger until the early eighties, when he finally made the full-time commitment to music. Even with a regular day job, Del and Billy found the time to put together a new band and began playing as the Shady Valley Boys. The Shady Valley Boys, like seemingly every other band in Baltimore at the time, saw a constant rotation of players file through the lineup. In an early version of the band they recruited former Stoney Mountain Boy Boatwhistle on bass, Del's brother Jerry on mandolin, and a young hotshot picker who had discovered bluegrass only a few years earlier, named Chris Warner, on banjo. The band played steadily in and around Baltimore over the next few years, even making the occasional trip to play festivals around the country. Very few part-time bands got the chance to play festivals, but Del was developing an impressive reputation and the Shady Valley Boys was one of the first part-time bands to be invited to play at some of these larger festivals.

The Shady Valley Boys and Del were a regular part of the Baltimore scene, though they were generally viewed as a group effort as Del had not fully developed his front-man persona yet. He took his first big steps on to the national scene and in establishing his credentials as a bona-fide superstar front man with the formation of Del McCoury and the Dixie Pals a few years after his return to Baltimore. Del explained the impetus of the formation of the new band. "I loved to play music and I'm not even sure I thought about leading a band. So I started playing all these little places on my own, just calling up guys that I knew to play. And still, I got thinking I'm going to have to do the emceeing because these guys won't say nothing, and I got to do all the singing because they can't sing good, and I got to do all the rhythm playing, you know, so that's when I started thinking, if I am doing all this, I might as well have my own band."[33] The name Dixie Pals came from Del's longtime friend and occasional musical cohort Bobby Diamond, who was playing a show one evening in Baltimore in 1967 with him. The band had yet to be named, and someone shouted from the audience asking what the name of the band was. Diamond yelled back, "The Dixie Pals." The name stuck and it was Del McCoury and the Dixie Pals from then on.

In 1968 Del released his first album, *I Wonder Where You Are Tonight*. The Dixie Pals at the time included Del's longtime accomplice Billy Baker on fiddle, Bill Emerson on banjo, Wayne Yates on mandolin, and Tom Neal and Dewey Renfro on bass. Emerson was well established at the time, having already served stints with both the Country Gentleman and Jimmy Martin. Still relatively new to the scene, Neal would likewise establish himself as a strong presence in Baltimore, eventually playing in Bluestone with Russ Hooper and Carroll Swam.

Starting with the release of *I Wonder Where You Are Tonight*, Del would begin establishing himself as one of the leading voices in bluegrass. He would release eight albums between 1968 and 1988, all while still working full time as a logger. He later immortalized his time spent as a logger on his 1996 album, *Cold Hard Facts*, with the track "Loggin' Man." With each release Del's stature continued to grow. The Dixie Pals lineup would solidify in the eighties with the addition of his sons Ronnie on mandolin and Rob on banjo who both helped invigorate their dad musically and pushed him to listen to different music and try different things. With the addition of Del's sons, the band changed the name from Dixie Pals to simply the Del McCoury Band. Del would eventually quit logging and commit to music full time, after which he had a seemingly meteoric rise to top of the bluegrass game. He won nineteen International Bluegrass Music Association awards between 1990 and 2004, as well as a pair of Grammy awards for bluegrass album of the year, in

The addition of his sons Ronnie and Rob helped solidify the Del McCoury Band lineup. Ronnie would go onto become one of the leading mandolin players in the world. Ronnie (left) and Del harmonize together at the 2013 Delfest in Cumberland, Maryland (photograph by the author).

2006 and 2014. Banjo great and longtime McCoury fan Tony Trischka was relieved Del finally got his due: "Thank goodness people recognized the talent he had from the very beginning."[34] Russ Hooper, who played with Del in the early sixties in Baltimore, was also glad to see his longtime friend get the accolades he was due. "Anything Del gets, he deserves," says Hooper.[35] To some people, with the success of his albums and the constant winning of awards, it seemed like overnight success. Hooper sets those people straight: "It amazes me when you are in a conversation with somebody and you can tell they don't know what's going on, when they say about Del, 'Here's a new guy on the scene,' when he has been there for so long. Del has paid his dues. He has done what we all have done, getting out there and playing for nothing."[36] To Del it is clear that he owes much of his success to Baltimore, the city where Hooper said he paid his dues and was able to hone his craft night after night in those rowdy, rough bars. "It was a learning thing to me. It was like going to school," states Del. "I owe a lot to Baltimore. I really do."[37]

Del McCoury (right) and brother Jerry onstage at the 2013 Delfest during the Masters of Bluegrass set (photograph by Melissa Varanko).

Amazingly, for all the accolades Del has received for his unmatched musical talents and ability, he is praised even more and universally revered more for his personality. Writer Chris Stuart argues in an article for *Bluegrass Unlimited* that "Del is possibly the most admired and most liked person in bluegrass and country music. He commands a quiet respect, love, and admiration from almost everyone. But he also remains true to his vision of his music, to himself and his family, and to those business associates around him."[38] Banjo legend Trischka easily sums up Del's amiable nature: "[He] is the sweetest guy in the world."[39] Dean Sapp has played in Baltimore since he was a teenager in the mid-sixties and first met Del through his uncle, Sonny Miller, who played with the Dixie Pals in the late seventies and early eighties. Sapp, like Trischka, has nothing but praise for Del: "No matter how many times he has won an award, been called the best of his time, Del has never been anything but humble. He is the most approachable person you will ever meet. If you walk up to him with your hand stuck out he will greet you with a smile and say it's good to see. And he means it."[40]

Pete Wernick, from Hot Rize, who first met Del in 1963 at the New York University show he played with Monroe, calls him "an amazing guy" and says he is a "good-hearted, sincere person who really knows and loves bluegrass music." Wernick experienced this good-hearted nature firsthand when Wernick was still a young, struggling musician. Ken Irwin and the people at Rounder Records, which was based in Ithaca, New York, at the time, had booked Del and his band for a show there in 1971. Wernick lived in Ithaca as well and was friends with the folks at Rounder Records, who asked him and his then girlfriend and now his wife, Joan, if they would host the after-party for the show since their home was a little more "bluegrass-friendly" than the commune where the Rounder Record folks lived with their Che Guevera posters on the wall. Wernick had written his first ever song after catching a Bill Monroe show in late 1963 in New York City after Del had joined the band full time. When Wernick wrote the song he said he always imagined it being sung as a duet between Del and Monroe. It was a traveling song he called "It's in My Mind to Ramble." Eight years after writing the song, Del was sitting in Wernick's house after his show in Ithaca and the two were casually chatting. Del was showing off pictures of his new baby boy, Ronnie, when Wernick told him he had written a song a few years before with Del's voice in mind. Del asked to hear it and Wernick played him "It's in My Mind to Ramble." Del liked it so much he asked if could record it and wound up including it on his 1972 album, *High on a Mountain*. The first song Wernick had written was recorded and released, and it "meant a lot for a Bronx banjo player!"[41]

Del's good nature is evident every time he takes the stage. He plays every show with a big, broad, beaming smile on his face, and that "smile on his face is very real," says Infamous Stringdusters banjo player Chris Pandolfi.[42] "He demands as much musically from himself as he does those around him," explains Del's wife, Jean. "He understands that fans are spending their hard earned money to see the band's shows, so he makes sure to always show his appreciation and respect for the fans and tries to keep the music fresh every night. That's why he never uses a set list and always takes requests."[43] Del's penchant for taking crowd requests was one of the many things he learned from his short time with Monroe. While Del claims he first learned about managing a band from his earliest days with Keith Daniels and the Blue Ridge Ramblers, he says he learned about the hard life on the road for a musician from Monroe and adopted many of the professional habits and traits of the demanding band leader. Del says the large number of requests he takes during his live shows is directly related to his time with Monroe, who used to do shows that were nothing but audience requests. Del appreciated the way it required the band to be on their toes musically for the entire night.

Del's interaction with an audience is on display every year at his annual DelFest. His sets are relaxed, casual affairs that find Del chatting with the crowd between songs and taking requests yelled out from the audience. At each DelFest Del is helping carry on the tradition of bluegrass started years before by Bill Monroe and birthed in hard-working cities throughout the fifties and sixties. Del patterned his festival after many of the festivals he played as a young musician. He remembered the festivals Carlton Hanney held in the sixties, where he would have Bill Monroe play on the final day and all the musicians that were present at the festival that had played with Monroe would take a turn onstage with him singing one of the songs they had done together.

At the 2013 edition of DelFest, Del found his own unique way to connect to those first-generation bluegrass superstars. Recruiting some of the most legendary bluegrass musicians of all time, musicians who can trace their roots back to the earliest days of the genre, Del formed the Masters of Bluegrass band. In addition to Del, the band consisted of first-generation mandolin pioneer Bobby Osborne, banjo icon J.D. Crowe, hall of fame fiddler Bobby Hicks, and Del's brother Jerry on bass. Their multiple sets throughout the weekend highlighted the quintet's unmatched abilities and allowed them to showcase the history of bluegrass. Their set also highlighted an interesting change taking place in bluegrass music. With only a handful of first-generation bluegrass performers still alive in 2013, new fans to the music will no longer have access to any of those influential players. Many hard-core fans of the genre pride themselves on this ability to connect to the past and not change or evolve. But Del is unique among many of the old-time performers in that he is open and willing to accept new music and try new things while still remaining true to his bluegrass roots. It is the ability to embrace the past but change with the times over his long career that has made Del such an important figure, and as the few remaining first generation players die, Del's stature will only increase. "In ten years Del will be the absolute royalty of bluegrass and in thirty years his sons will be the biggest things ever," says Chris Pandolfi. "They will be the last link, that authentic link to that early generation."[44]

At DelFest in 2012 on that gorgeous evening—right before Yonder Mountain String Band's set during which Jeff Austin shared his feelings about Del and how much he admired him—Del was onstage with his own band, which includes sons Ronnie and Rob, fiddler Jason Carter, and bassist Alan Bartram. They were doing what they have always done, delivering an energetic set that showcases Del's amazing talents. Del does not use a set list when he plays, and the music they choose to perform can reflect the mind-set or mood of the band. As the Western Maryland sun set behind the mountains, giving way to dusk and the cool evening air of Cumberland, it seemed Del and the boys were in a reflective mood. His set included many subtle nods to his past in Baltimore, a spirited take on "White House Blues," a tune he undoubtedly heard Earl Taylor and the Stoney Mountain Boys play numerous times at the 79 Club or Jazz City when he was a young man in Baltimore, the instrumental "Baltimore Johnny," written by son Ronnie about Baltimore fiddle legend Jon Glik, who played with Del and was a mentor and inspiration to Ronnie. The band's encore of "High on a Mountain" was another nod to the power of bluegrass in Baltimore and the surrounding area. Since the 1970s the song has emerged as one of the most well-known bluegrass and country songs of all time. It was first popularized by Del and the Dixie Pals after it appeared on his 1972 album of the same name and has since gone on to be covered by countless artists, eventually earning gold album status for country superstar Marty Stuart's version of the song, which appeared on his 1992 album, *This One's Gonna Hurt*.

"High on a Mountain" was originally written by Ola Belle Reed, who was a resident of Cecil County, which is just a short trip north up I-95 from Baltimore. Reed was a mainstay at New River Ranch Music Park, which her husband and brother owned, and Sunset Park, where the Reed Family Band served as the house band for many years. Reed authored over 200 songs and is one of the most influential female bluegrass musicians of all time. She was a songwriter, singer, banjo player, all-around amazing person, and the living embodiment of Appalachian life and traditions. Despite residing fifty miles to the north of Baltimore, she was a huge influence on the music made in that city.

7

"High on a Mountain"

Recommended Listening: Ola Belle Reed's 1976 autobiographical album, *My Epitaph*, is the ideal accompaniment for Chapter 7. Reed's straightforward, bold songwriting—which is interspersed with snippets of interviews recounting her childhood in the mountains and her later life in Maryland—brings to life those experiences which shaped her unique life. The sparse backing instrumentation of her son David on banjo and guitar and the simple splashes of color from her husband, Bud, on harmonica only serve to highlight the power and truth with which Ola Belle sings.

The sounds of fiddle and guitar mingle with the quiet calm of an unseasonably cool mid–August day that would normally be filled with unrelenting heat and stifling humidity but today is filled with the sweet sounds of an afternoon pickin' session. Those sounds are interrupted by the occasional rumble of a car going past the wide-open front door, which allows the cool breeze to filter in and cool down the hot pickin' between two musicians taking place in the back of the store. The name of the store is Childs, located in Childs, Maryland, fifty miles north of Baltimore. With its rustic exterior and old-timey furniture on sale, the inside looks as if it has been untouched by the hands of time.

The two musicians are seated across from each other. The older man with the grey handle bar mustache is seated on a large, well-worn couch and picking away at his guitar he had proudly showed earlier with Hazel Dickens' autograph on it. The tall, lanky, bearded, younger man across from him has been alternating between guitar and fiddle. The pair have been trading off songs, each playing a couple of tunes they have recently written as well honoring the requests for some personal favorites from their music-playing buddy. They are both powerful singers who write rich, dynamic songs of simple pleasures like "mom's homemade bread" and "Vienna sausages." The songs spring to life as they roll off of the tongues of the two musicians in this quaint, personal setting.

Caleb Stine (standing) and Hugh Campbell (seated) play at the back of Childs Store, August 18, 2013 (photograph by the author).

The younger man is Caleb Stine, a transplanted musician from Colorado who has spent the past decade living in Baltimore. Stine is the soul of the current Baltimore music scene. He finds himself equally comfortable and accepted in any realm he chooses to play. He glides easily from shows at the hipster-haven Ottobar with indie bands and alt-rockers, to his powerful and compelling album (2008's *Outgrow These Walls*) he recorded with Baltimore rapper Saleem, to regular shows at run-down honky-tonk joints like 1919 on Fleet Street, where his sets reflect the past tradition of bluegrass and hillbilly music so common in similar Baltimore bars years before. *Honest Tune* magazine declares about Stine, "His music falls somewhere between the renegade cowboy-poetry of Townes Van Zandt and the sweet rough and tumble sound of Neil Young's Harvest. The power in his music comes not from overwhelming volume or violent guitars, but from simple strums and carefully measured words that together carry an army of unmatched strength."[1] Stine is deeply woven into the fabric of the city and has released six albums that reflect the vibrant, troubled passion that is Baltimore. "He embodies what music is all about. He is the real deal as an honest, pure songwriting musician. He doesn't do it for anything but the artistry of it and the expression," says another young Baltimore musician, Cris Jacobs, who himself has been an integral part of the city's musical personality since he started his first band in high school.[2]

The older man is Hugh Campbell, a songwriter who resides above the store in which he and Stine are playing music. Like Stine, Campbell is a songwriter who dives deep into the heart of every song he sings, weaving stories and narratives that echo the world around him. He seems most comfortable playing in simple settings such as the one at the back of Childs Store, but his songs have a wide appeal. In 2003 his song "Shape of a Tear" was recorded by the Lynn Morris Band and nominated for song of the year by the International Bluegrass Music Association. He was selected in 2013 as one of only ten songwriters from across the country to play at the IBMA songwriter showcase at the World of Bluegrass Convention.

The store where the pair are playing is owned by Hugh's cousin Jerimy and features handcrafted wood items made by Hugh and custom painted by his brother Zane. Zane, like Hugh, is a singer/songwriter. The sign out front of the store advertises their work as "Fancy Hillbilly Folk-Art."[3] Childs Store keeps alive the long tradition the Campbell family has not only in owning stores in the northeast corner of Maryland, but also their deep musical roots in the region, roots that stretch back almost 100 years. Stine, Hugh, Zane and other like musicians congregate in the back of Childs Store on those wellworn couches surrounded by walls adorned with music memorabilia that reflects the Campbell family's long, distinguished history in music.

The Campbell family was originally from Ashe County, North Carolina, near the southern musical hotbed of Galax, Virginia. Arthur and Ella May Campbell had thirteen children and they all learned the power and beauty of music at a young age from their parents and relatives. Like many southern families at the time, they were isolated and access to luxuries like radios, record players, and phonographs was something they could not afford. Instead they relied on each other for entertainment, with the entire family learning how to sing and play an instrument.

The area where the Campbells were from near the North Carolina and Virginia border was a musical hot-bed, with many famous musical families emerging from the area over the years. The epicenter of this musical area was the town of Galax, Virginia, which has been hosting the annual Old Fiddlers' Convention every year since 1935. The Old Fiddlers' Convention was regularly visited by many of the musicians in Baltimore and Mike Seeger, Alice Gerrard, Hazel Dickens, and many in their circle of friends made the trip down each year. Their good friend Lisa Chiera would document the festival on the 1964 album *Galax, VA: Old Fiddlers' Convention* released by the Smithsonian Folkways label.

Like many other depression-era families the Campbells moved north in 1934 in search of work. They settled fifty miles north of Baltimore, right over the Pennsylvania line in Chester County. Among the Campbells' thirteen children were older brothers R.J., born in 1913 (Hugh and Zane's father), Herbert, born in 1918 (Jerimy's father), sister Ola Wave, born in 1916 (who would add Belle to her name in the mid–1930s when she started playing music professionally), and her younger brother Alex, who was born in 1923. Upon their arrival up north Ola Belle found work as a housekeeper and Alex fell in with the local music community made up mostly of southern transplants. In 1936 Ola Belle—who had learned how to play clawhammer style of banjo from her Uncle Dockery Campbell when she was young and the family was still living in North Carolina—found her way into the local music scene as well. Local guitarist Arthur "Shorty" Woods was looking for a singer for his band, the North Carolina Ridge Runners, and asked Ola Belle to join. Ola Belle agreed and joined as the band's singer and banjo player. It was at this time that Ola Belle added the "Belle" to her name, "perhaps drawing on the example of other established 'hillbilly' singers such as Lulu Belle, from the WLS Barn Dance, and Maybelle Carter."[4]

The Ridge Runners were composed mostly of musicians whose families had migrated from Ashe County in North Carolina, much like Alex and Ola Belle's family. In addition to Olla Belle and Woods the band featured Johnny Miller on steel guitar, his cousin Lester "Slick" Miller on fiddler, Inky Pierson on banjo, and Deacon Brumfield on Dobro. They played regularly at the various regional music parks that dotted the area and made frequent appearances on the local radio stations that played hillbilly type music. The band was one of the first hillbilly bands in the Maryland-Delaware area and became quite popular among the local transplanted Appalachian population. The Ridge Runners' popularity allowed them to cut a pair of 78 RPM records. The first consisted of "Orange Blossom Special" on side A with "You Were Only Teasing Me" on the flip side. Their second 78 was "Remember Me" with a John Miller original, "Ridge Runner Boogie," on the B side.[5]

As the band became more popular Ola Belle in particular began to garner a well-deserved reputation as a performer. "Alex pushed her out front and center and once she got there people instantly flocked to her, especially the women," explains her nephew Hugh. "She had that freedom onstage, she was always moving around. She was not just standing there; she was flinging her dress around and having a good time. People were digging it. She brought that wild mountain performing part to the stage."[6] It was this honest approach to music that really drew people to Ola Belle. She believed music and singing was something special that had to come from within one and that it relied on the singer's personality and daily life to bring the meaning of the song across. "I can sing a song today and sing the same song tomorrow and it's going to be a little different because I'm not the same person every day," she explained. "Singin's not something you do by the push-buttons. You have to have a feeling for what you're doing."[7] Her wild, uninhibited performing style not only was a hit with the locals, but also caught the attention of some of the biggest names in country music.

In 1945, after a show where the Ridge Runners had shared the bill with country legend Roy Acuff, he was so impressed with Ola Belle that he offered her $100 a week to join his band. Acuff was a star of the Grand Ole Opry and one of the biggest names in country music, and a $100 was a lot of money for the time. It was a great opportunity for Ola Belle to be exposed to a wide audience and establish herself in Nashville. Despite the money and unlimited potential, Ola Belle turned Acuff down. "She always said the reason was she was not going to take orders from a man," explained Hugh. "She said, 'I don't take orders from anybody. It was not a sexist thing. She was just saying I am not taking orders from No Man, from anybody.'"[8] Despite the extraordinary opportunity presented and the great unknown potential and financial windfall Ola Belle could have found from going to work with Acuff, Hugh says that Ola Belle never regretted turning down Acuff's offer. It is unknown what might have been had she left to work with him, but it can be said that by staying true to herself and refusing to answer to anyone Ola Belle achieved a different success and found fame on her own terms. It was those terms that would make her such a special force in the history of music.

Ola Belle continued to play with the Ridge Runners through the forties and soon her brother Alex would join the band as well. He joined upon his return from Germany in 1945 after he had served in the army during World War II. Alex had played in various bands before heading overseas and was able to continue his musical endeavors while in Germany. He served in the same unit as Louis Marshall Jones, who would become better known as country music star Grandpa Jones. The two bonded over their musical passions and became good friends. While Alex and Jones were in Germany, Allied forces captured a 100,000-watt radio station and soon began broadcasting radio shows from it. Alex and Jones got a regular spot on the captured radio station and performed for eight months as the Munich Mountaineers.[9] Jones recalled how Alex had told him of his future musical plans while the two were still in Germany: "In our room in Munich we always had a crowd of boys because I carried a guitar with me and we sang a lot.... Alex Campbell played guitar; he told me when he got home he and his sister Ola Belle were going to start a band."[10] True to his word, Alex played with Ola Belle in the Ridge Runners until 1948, when the two left to form their own band, the New River Boys and Girls. The band was named in honor of their father's band he had formed with family members while still living in North Carolina. Joining Alex and Ola Belle in the new band were Ridge Runner bandmates Slick and Johnny Miller and Deacon Brumfield. Ted Lundy, another local banjo player, was recruited to complete the lineup. This lineup would stay intact for many years, though like most bands of the time there was always some turnover. For a short stretch in 1965 and 1966 they would even add Jerry McCoury on bass.

Much like the Campbell family, the Miller family was a key part of the country-hillbilly-bluegrass music scene that sprouted in northeast Maryland and southern Pennsylvania. Like the Campbells, the Millers were from North Carolina and had moved north in 1943 in search of work. The entire family was known throughout the North Carolina mountains as some of the finest pickers and players around, and they brought that musical background with them when they moved north. Johnny and his cousin Lester, who was better known as "Slick," had first played with Ola Belle and Alex in the Ridge Runners. When Alex and Ola Belle left to start the New River Boys and Girls Johnny and Slick followed them. Upon joining the new band, they added Johnny's brother Sonny on fiddle. Sonny proved to be a special talent who would spend a few years honing his craft playing with Ola Belle and Alex as part of the New River band before embarking on a career that saw him become a highly regarded traditional fiddler. He was old enough to have learned the Appalachia traditional fiddle music repertoire firsthand but young enough to have been part of the generation of pickers who gained fame in the seventies and eighties. One of his earliest recorded appearances was on the Lisa Chiera-produced 1964 album *Galax, VA: Old Fiddlers' Convention*. After a few years of playing with the New River Boys and Girls Sonny would leave to join up with Boston bluegrass pioneer Joe Val's band. He would play with Val throughout the seventies before he was offered a spot by Del McCoury to join the Dixie Pals. While with McCoury he appeared on the 1981 album *Take Me to the Mountain*. Like other bluegrass journeymen players, Sonny would find work with many different bands over the years, including a stretch with another group from northeast Maryland, Bob Paisley and the Southern Grass.

Paisley had been a longtime player in the area who found his greatest success in the sixties and seventies when he teamed with former New River band member Ted Lundy. The Paisleys had also moved from Ashe County,

North Carolina. Paisley's uncle, Wiley, played with Ola Belle's dad in North Carolina. Upon their arrival in southeastern Pennsylvania, the Paisleys jumped into the burgeoning scene developing around the Campbell family. Paisley died in 2004, but his son Danny has carried on his dad's legacy, as he now fronts Southern Grass. Danny is one of the best modern representations of the classic high lonesome bluegrass sound. He has been nominated for many IBMA awards over his career including Emerging Artist of the Year, Male Vocalist of the Year, and Album of the Year. His song "Don't Throw Mama's Flowers Away" was named the 2009 IBMA Song of the Year. Danny kept alive the Paisley family tradition when his teenaged son Ryan joined Southern Grass on mandolin in 2012.

Like the Paisleys, the Miller family would see a younger member of their family carry on the family's long musical legacy. Their nephew Dean Sapp was always around while Johnny, Sonny, and Slick were playing at New River Ranch and he seemed to absorb the music that came off the stage. He became proficient on banjo, guitar, mandolin, Dobro, and bass, and would first grace the stage at the fabled music park as a precocious thirteen-year-old on banjo with a two-song set in 1963. He would go on to become a regular player in the downtown Baltimore bluegrass scene. Since then he has released sixteen

Russ Hooper (far right) plays his first show at New River Ranch with Don Owens (center with guitar) in 1952 (courtesy Russ Hooper).

albums and steadily toured with his band, the Harford Express (named after a county in the northeast corner of Maryland). Like that of most musicians from the Baltimore area, his music is rooted in the traditional hard-driving style so common in the area. He credits his musical family for much of his success: "Dedication is the key. I learned that from my Uncles Johnny Miller and his brother the late Sonny Miller. They taught me that if you really, really want to do it, don't give up." He also learned valuable lessons from Ola Belle, a woman he said was like a grandmother to him. "She told me, 'young man, don't ever put anything on a record you can't reproduce on stage.' That has stuck with me more than anything anyone else has ever told me."[11]

With the Campbell and Miller families dominating the lineup the New River Boys and Girls would become a vital part of the music scene built around the various outdoor music parks scattered around the northeast corner of Maryland and the southern tip of Pennsylvania. These parks were in close proximity to Baltimore and many of the pickers from the city would make the trip up to them on the weekends to perform and watch the other bands at the weekly shows that featured hillbilly, bluegrass, and country music. Russ Hooper made his first trip to New River Ranch as a fifteen-year-old with best friend Danny Curtis and local country-music comedian Luke Knucklehead. He played his first show there the following year, in 1952, when he turned sixteen, backing up local DJ and country crooner Don Owens. Later at that same show he also played with the day's headliners the Browns. He remembers the excitement that surrounded these music parks:

> When the summertime rolled around everybody just looked forward to going, because they were the only country music parks that were within a short driving distance. Most people would bring their families. They would pack a lunch and go there and spend the day. It only cost one dollar apiece to get in. The main headliners would play three shows, and all the other bands would play three times as well. You would be there from eleven a.m. to eleven p.m. You got your money's worth. It was a lot of fun and everyone always enjoyed themselves.[12]

In addition to the musicians from Baltimore who played there regularly, these parks attracted many of the biggest stars of the era. Folks would travel from across the country to get a taste of this music up close, and these music parks were the ideal setting. One of the oldest and most important of the music parks was Sunset Park in Jennersville, Pennsylvania, just over the Pennsylvania line in Chester County. It was opened in 1940 by "Uncle" Roy Waltman, who owned the land and thought that a music park would be a nice way to supplement his income as a dairy farmer. Sunset Park hosted live music every Sunday from the time it first opened until it closed for good in 1995.

In addition to Sunset Park, the other dominant music park of the era was New River Ranch. New River Ranch was built, run, and owned by Alex, Ola Belle and her husband, Ralph "Bud" Reed, near their home in Rising Sun, Maryland. Originally the Campbell-Reed family helped run the Rainbow Music Park in Lancaster, Pennsylvania, but after a couple years of that and steady touring to play music with the New River Boys and Girls, Bud had tired of the road. He still wanted to play live music and thought, *Instead of taking music to the people why not bring the people to the music.* "We're traveling too far," he remarked. "Why don't we just open our own park?"[13]

The family rented a plot of land forty miles north of Baltimore just north of the Conowingo Dam on Route 1. Frances Riale played bass in the New River Boys and Girls at the time and remembers how all their friends and family pitched in to help get the park built and ready for its first show. "We, and I mean everyone they could get to work, helped clear the land and build the stage, seats, stands and all the buildings needed for the Park," she said. "Ola Belle and I would put our babies to sleep on heavy quilts and blankets and we would rake leaves, bring food or go get food for the workers, or do whatever was needed to help."[14] The property had only one preexisting cabin when they began work, but they cleared twenty acres of land and added a kitchen, concession stands, spaces to host carnival-style games, a set of toilets, and a parking lot. Bud designed the layout of the park and decided on the location of all the new buildings. "I built the stage down at the bottom ... and lined all the seats up the hill so everybody could see. I hung the speakers up in the trees so they wouldn't blast right up at the people, and they had one mike and they'd all gather around the mike—it was wonderful, just wonderful."[15] Primitive seats were made of wooden planks laid across concrete blocks. Directly above the stage was a sign declaring "Uncle Alex's New River Ranch—For the Finest Entertainment." Surrounding that sign were ads for the various local business that supported the park, including Akers Upholstering Shop, KeeSee and Web Dry Cleaners, Edwards Motor Company, and Huber Baking Company, among others. With the help of their friends and family, the family opened New River Ranch in May 1951 with a show headlined by Lester Flatt and Earl Scruggs. As would become the norm, much of the rest of the bill would be filled out with local talent, much of it drawn from the wealth of talent just a short drive south to Baltimore. Popular Baltimore radio DJ Ray Davis was hired to serve as the emcee each weekend. The hiring of Davis helped assure the presence of big-name acts, as Davis would use his vast connections and influence to help lure the most popular bands to New River Ranch. The chance to see some of the biggest and most popular country and bluegrass acts each week and the hiring of Davis and the inclusion of so many bands with ties to Baltimore helped make the Sunday shows at New River Ranch regular weekly events for the folks from Baltimore.

New River Ranch also became well known for their annual July 4 banjo contests started by Alex. The annual banjo contest was a crowd-pleasing event that allowed professional musicians and amateurs alike to compete against each other for the chance to win a brand-new Gibson Mastertone five-string banjo. Despite the inclusion of professionals such as Mike Seeger, Smitty Irwin, Larry Richardson, Porky Hutchins, Sonny Miller, and seasoned folkies like Eric Weissberg and Carl Chatzky, the amateurs had just as much a chance, if not more, to win, as the winner was chosen through audience applause. Porky Hutchins, who played with Earl Taylor in the Stoney Mountain Boys, won a hotly contested competition in 1958 at Sunset Park when he narrowly

Earl Scruggs (3rd from right in dark jacket) enjoys lunch with fans after his show at New River Ranch in 1958 (courtesy Russ Hooper).

beat out a local picker who played a rocking version of "Milk Cow Blues."[16] But often the crowd tended to side with the underdog, or in some cases the local favorite would pack the audience with their own cheering section, increasing the difficulty for the professionals of winning. Russ Hooper remembers a sailor from the U.S. Navy training center in Bainbridge, Maryland, winning at New River Ranch. "Some of the banjo players that the guy beat out were great banjo players," he said. After winning and accepting his brand-new Gibson five-string, the sailor, who played a tenor banjo during the competition, announced to the crowd, "I don't know how to play this, but I guarantee you I'll be back next year and I'll show you what I have learned."[17] Hooper jokes the sailor was never seen again at New River Ranch.

New River Ranch and Sunset Park were important destinations for fan and performer alike. For many musical acts of the time, the two parks were the farthest north they would travel and perform. So for many northeast fans, the Sundays at New River Ranch and Sunset Park were often their only chance to see stars of Nashville in a live setting. The atmosphere at the park was extremely open, with fans having a great deal of access to the bands. Hooper says that it was almost expected of the bands to spend time with the fans who had come to the park. "You could touch base with the artists there," he says. "There was no distance between fan and the performer. If you were a performer or a local act and had a following, after your show was done people would set up a table and bring food and they would expect you to sit with them and have lunch."[18] Like some of the larger and more famous parks in the South like Galax, Virginia, and Union Grove, North Carolina, Sunset Park and New River Ranch helped keep alive the tradition of live music so pervasive in the South. For many musicians living up North the parks provided them a way to stay in contact with those musicians who were based in the South and Nashville. Hooper used his many trips and appearances at the music park to stay in touch with his musical peers and friends from the south. They also served to connect many a rural migrant to an old home place, as well as provide a meeting ground for many of the younger, educated city folk who were just starting to discover this rural sound.

These parks not only helped many of the transplanted hillbillies stay in touch with their rural upbringing, they also allowed many of the suburban hillbillies who were so prevalent in Baltimore experience this music up close. For many of these folkies and suburban hillbillies this opportunity proved to be a highly beneficial learning experience for them. The mixed scene of people in Baltimore that flourished in Willie Foshag and Alyse Taubman's house regularly made the trip north on Sunday afternoons. Mike Seeger's good friend Ralph Rinzler had first become enamored with old-timey traditional music when he saw Mike's half-brother Pete Seeger play at Swarthmore College and regularly began making trips to Sunset and New River. "There were a few of us from the city who were following Bill [Monroe]—Mike Seeger, myself, Willie Foshag, Jerry and Alice Foster [Gerrard]," says Rinzler. "Mike and I would go to the various parks sorting out who we liked...."[19] The inclusion of Rinzler and others, like Eric Weissberg, David Grisman, and Andy Statman, who all had deep ties to the New York City folk revival scene, helped to strengthen the bond between them and the more traditional bluegrass-orientated scene flourishing in Baltimore and Washington.

The weekly trips to the various music parks for the Baltimore crew that was centered around Foshag and Taubman's house regularly included Seeger, Gerrard, Hazel Dickens and her brothers, Carl Chatzky, Lisa Chiera, and Myron Edleman. "There were the trips up from Baltimore to the country music parks, New River Ranch and Sunset Park on Sundays," remembers Gerrard. "We would come up from Washington and stop off in Baltimore. Alyse and Hazel would make these big fancy picnics with fried chicken and deviled eggs and we would pack into the car and drive north on Route 1, and go to New River Ranch or Sunset Park and spend the afternoon there."[20] Gerrard says they would sometimes stop at both New River Ranch and Sunset Park on the same day, as they were separated by less than thirty miles. "We'd share our picnic with Ralph and Carter Stanley or Bill Monroe during the dinner breaks," Gerrard says. "In those days two bands started playing about one p.m. and alternated shows until maybe nine o'clock. You could take your time listening, and the musicians could take their time."[21]

Oftentimes the crew from Baltimore would all pile into Seeger's Chevrolet Carryall for these weekend road trips. For Seeger the trips were all about the music and the opportunity to not only see the music played up close, but also to record it on his large Magnecorder M-33 reel-to-reel tape recorder. With his laser-like focus and single-minded intensity, Seeger became irritated when his trip was interrupted so that Hazel's brother Robert could stop to pick up a six-pack of beer. For the teetotaler Seeger, who took his music very seriously, it was a source of constant annoyance that his arrival at the music park would be delayed because of the stop for beer.[22]

While Appalachian migrants and suburban hillbillies had been mingling and playing together in Baltimore for years, outside of the city the interaction between the two types of people was rare. Carroll Swam was one of the suburban hillbillies from Baltimore and had been playing in and around the city since graduating from Towson College in 1963. He played a few shows with Jack Cooke before joining Marvin Howell and the Franklin County Boys. He had begun going to Sunset Park in the early sixties to see shows, and then

Bill "Brad" Keith (banjo) and Russ Hooper (Dobro) jam in the parking lot at Sunset Park in 1964 as fans gather to watch (courtesy Russ Hooper).

started playing there when he joined Howell. "I was up there quite a few times to see some of the greatest bluegrass bands and they had some pretty great shows packed with people everywhere," Swam says. "It was an interesting cross section of humanity. You had these people like David Grisman coming down from New York City and you had these very blue-collar people who had moved up the Route 1 corridor from the South and they were the prime audience for Sunset Park."[23] Both New River Ranch and Sunset Park provided a place where the suburban hillbillies and college-educated folkies could see and hear this music played by those who did it best and in a setting more akin to its rural roots as opposed to the bars in the cities. John Cohen played with Mike Seeger in the New Lost City Ramblers. Cohen was an acclaimed photographer and documentarian, the inspiration for the Grateful Dead's song "Uncle John's Band,"[24] and a regular at both parks throughout the sixties. The unique atmosphere so prevalent at the music parks had a big impact on Cohen. "The ambiance was just amazing," he says. "It was one of the first times that city people and country people were really meeting on the country people's terms, and that was a big adventure."[25]

The music played onstage was not the only important music being made at the parks. In between sets band members and park patrons would gather in the surrounding woods, picnic areas, and parking lots and informal picking sessions would erupt. These informal sessions recalled the long evenings many of those with Appalachian ties were familiar with from their lives in the South and the mountains. "There was music all over the park, until it was time for the next act to begin," explained Ola Belle's son David, an accomplished musician in his own right who played at New River Ranch as a child and as a part of those informal pickin' sessions later as a teenager.[26]

Over the years Sunset Park and New River Ranch took on an almost mythical status, a status reserved for the most revered of music venues. Country music superstar Marty Stuart first performed at Sunset Park as a thirteen-year-old guitar prodigy in Lester Flatt's band and would return to play at the hallowed park almost every year until it closed in 1995. On a trip to New Orleans Stuart caught a show at the legendary Preservation Hall and the importance and similarities between the two venues struck him: "I sat there on the floor listening to that real deep Dixieland jazz, and I thought 'Sunset Park is the Preservation Hall of Country Music.'"[27]

After eight years of ownership the Campbell-Reed family was forced to sell New River Ranch after it was destroyed in the blizzard of 1958 when snow fell for 28 hours straight. It snowed so hard that the roof caved in and many of the structural facilities were completely demolished due to the weight of the snow. The family was never able to afford to reopen the park. Don Owens, an influential DJ in the Baltimore/Washington took over the park after the Campbell-Reed family. Owens was very familiar with the park, as he had occasionally performed at the ranch over the years and had helped book many a band there. Owens ran New River for a couple of years until another Baltimore DJ, Bobby Brown, took it over. Brown would keep it open until 1963, when it was finally closed for good.[28]

After the blizzard forced them to sell New River Ranch, the Campbell-Reed family began to regularly perform at their general store, Campbell's Corner, which they owned and operated in Oxford, Pennsylvania. The store had a music studio and a small stage and many country and bluegrass stars would stop by to play when they were passing through the area. Starting in 1949 Alex hosted a regular radio show called *Campbell's Corner*, broadcast from the studio in the store. Jerry McCoury played in the New River Ranch band with Alex and Ole Belle in 1965 and '66 and was part of many of the radio performances at the store. "It was a grocery store and in the back there was a stage," he says. "Every Saturday night people would crowd in. At eleven he [Alex] would flip a switch and we would be broadcast on WWVA for a half-hour."[29] The radio show was picked up by larger radio stations and broadcast around the country and lasted through the 1970s. Customers lucky enough to be shopping in the store when shows were being taped might get the opportunity to catch an intimate set from Bill Monroe, Grandpa Jones or some other big act from Nashville. When Alex could not get a big-name act for his show he would rely on some of the bands from Baltimore. Russ Hooper says that throughout the years he played with Marvin Howell and the Franklin County Boys they often played the radio show broadcast from Campbell's Corner.

The New River Boys and Girls Band, which was still headed by Alex and Ola Belle, found a new regular gig as the house band at nearby Sunset Park and would remain there for the next twenty-six years. Alex became an integral part of Sunset Park beyond his role with the band. He would often serve as the emcee and started broadcasting a radio show each Sunday from a small setup near the stage. He also opened a small record store on the premises where the performers could sell their latest albums. Alex was usually too busy with other areas of the park to run the record store so for a couple of summers that responsibility fell to Alex's nephew Jerimy. Those summers working for Alex were memorable ones for the teenaged Jerimy, who met some of the biggest country stars. One in particular left a long-lasting impression on him. "I met Reba McEntire at Sunset Park and she was beautiful," remembers Jerimy. "She had just come out. I was young and I was watching her perform and she was wearing the tightest pair of designer jeans I have ever seen. They were the tightest pair of Jordache I had ever seen. I will never forget it. When she came down off stage she changed into a big pair of baggy Levis and, I was like, 'Why don't you put the other jeans on.'"[30]

Through not only their music but their lifestyle as well, Ola Belle and her family helped develop a deep connection with both the folk revival people and a younger generation more in-tune with a hippie lifestyle. "Late sixties, early seventies she was exactly what people were looking for, that idea of communal living, living clean, and growing your own vegetables," says her nephew Hugh. "That's what the hippies were doing, but she was doing it for real. These college students were getting up and saying, 'Real? I'll take you to Rising Sun and show you Real.' She had a lot of professors and upper-crust people who were visiting her. She was doing the college circuit."[31] As Ola Belle began to gain fame with the folk-revival scene more and more visitors found their way to Sunset Park and the Reeds' home in Rising Sun. One of the most prominent was folklorist Henry Glassie, who helped expose Ola Belle to an even wider audience with his recordings of her. Glassie's recordings of her in January 1966 were the first professional solo recordings she had ever done.

Ola Belle Reed at the Brandywine Mountain Music Convention, Concordville, Pennsylvania, July 1974 (photograph by Carl Fleischhauer).

Through Glassie, Ola Belle was introduced to Ralph Rinzler, who by the late 1960s was working as a folklorist at the Smithsonian Institute. Rinzler invited Ola Belle to play at the annual Smithsonian Folklife Festival in 1969, '72, and '76, helping expose her music to a brand-new audience. Up until that time Ola Belle's audience had mostly been country folk much like herself.

But through the work of Glassie and Ola Belle's appearance at festivals like the Smithsonian Folklife Festival she began to find acceptance among those in those in the folk-revival world. "She was a discovery—the genuine article, the kind commercial performers, whether they realized it or not, were imitating," declared the *Baltimore Sun*. This discovery and recognition of her as a "national cultural treasure"[32] was acknowledged by the awarding of an honorary doctorate from the University of Maryland Baltimore County (UMBC) in 1978 for her contributions to Maryland's culture.

Ola Belle Reed's acceptance as a true national treasure and cultural icon reached its pinnacle in 1977 when she was invited to play at the White House for President Jimmy Carter.[33] In 1996 she was awarded the Heritage Award from the National Endowment for the Arts for her longtime contributions: "authenticity, excellence, and significance in keeping Appalachia music traditions alive."[34] This acceptance by a different musical community, which came much later in her life, saw the demand for her increase greatly and was the start of a whole other career for Ola Belle, one that found her new audience as interested in her and her lifestyle as they were her music. "She was playing up this mountain woman role. It was her second career as this folk artist. Her first career was with the band with Alex. Two very distinct careers," says nephew Hugh.[35]

Ola Belle also saw her popularity grow as other artists and musicians began to discover her intensely personal songwriting and started to cover her songs on their albums. Del McCoury got the ball rolling in 1972 when he covered the Ola Belle standard "High on a Mountain" for his album of the same name. McCoury's version helped introduce the song to a brand-new audience who may not have heard of Ola Belle at the time, as she was just beginning to be discovered by the folk-music world. Progressive bluegrass group Hot Rize would also record "High on a Mountain" for their debut album, *Hot Rize*, released in 1979. Even much younger bands at the start of the 21st century are discovering the power and beauty of "High on a Mountain," as it has become a regular part of the live sets of such jam-grass bands as the String Cheese Incident and Cabinet. The song would go on to become a staple of the bluegrass and country world and is arguably Ola Belle's best-known song. She included it on her autobiographical 1976 album, *My Epitaph*.

"High on a Mountain" was a powerful statement from Ola Belle. She described this powerful nature in the liner notes to *My Epitaph*: "You cannot separate your lifestyle, your religion, your politics from your music. It's a part of life. And that's what our music was in the mountains. It was a part of our life."[36] Her husband, Bud, elaborated on his wife's thoughts, "I was with Ola

Belle when she wrote that 'High on a Mountain.' You know where she wrote that at? At her mother's graveyard. That was about her people. A lot of people thought it was a love song, but it was about her people."[37] The song and Ola Belle would gain their greatest notoriety in 1992 when country music superstar Marty Stuart recorded "High on a Mountain" for his album *This One's Gonna Hurt.* The album was a huge success, and Stuart's country-rock version of "High on a Mountain" (renamed "High on a Mountaintop") was a hit, climbing into the top twenty-five on the country music charts. Ola Belle's son David was especially thrilled by the new attention his mom's song was getting. "I flipped my lid over it," he said. "This guy [Stuart] has taken this song and turned it into something else here, in another field of music. The next thing you know my Mom's song was being played across the whole world in the mainstream country music."[38]

While some of Ola Belle's other songs and compositions have gone on to be covered by a wide range of musicians—most notably "I've Endured," which like "High on a Mountain" has become a staple in the bluegrass community—she has seen her legacy carried forward in other ways as well. Alt-folk rockers Olabelle named their band in honor of Ola Belle. They felt a kindred spirit with her and respected what she stood for musically. Olabelle features The Band drummer Levon Helm's daughter Amy and also included their namesake's "High on a Mountain" on their 2004 album, *Riverside Battle Songs.*

In addition to her songwriting and musicianship Ola Belle was almost as well known for her never-ending generosity. She freely gave her time to those who needed help. Ola Belle was always quick to open her door and provide a place to stay for someone in need. She also served as a mentor and inspiration to younger musicians, especially those of similar backgrounds. Her nephew Hugh says she had a special kinship with Hazel Dickens and Alice Gerrard, with whom she shared the distinction of being a pioneer of female musicians in the male-dominated bluegrass movement. She also shared a special bond with Dolly Parton, who played at Sunset Park many times at the start of her career. "Her and Ola Belle were very close. Every time she came they talked for as long they could get away with it," recalls her nephew Jerimy.[39]

Ola Belle's home was an open place to stay and she would serve breakfast in the morning for all the bands and musicians that traveled through. "During those years at Ola Belle's house everyone would stop by because they were playing the radio show or New River or Sunset Park," remembers Hugh. "Ola Belle, being all-inclusive, would always say, 'You can stay my house.'"[40] Heather Coffey spent a lot of time at the Reed household as a child with her mother, Betsy Rutherford, who was a prominent Baltimore musician who played with the New Ruby Tonic Entertainers and who, with her husband John Coffey, recorded with Ola Belle throughout the 1970s. Heather remembers "the whole family as being very nice, very welcoming"[41] during the times she spent there. Ola Belle's son David admits that his mom's generous nature and willingness to open their house caused friction between his parents occasionally. But his dad, Bud, did recognize the positive side to Ola Belle's open-door policy. "The burn factor is always present when working with so many, but the percentages of success stories were well worth the investment."[42]

One particular story of her generous nature had a long-lasting impact on her nephew Hugh. Growing up, Hugh and his brother Zane did not see Ola Belle as much as some of his other cousins did because they lived in a different part of Maryland and his father did not want "his kids coming up in the music scene for various reasons." As Hugh and Zane got older, the pair were already writing their own music and were intrigued by their aunt Ola Belle and wanted to find out more about her. When they were old enough to drive in the early seventies they began making the trip to visit her. There was an immediate connection. "She saw us as different because we were writing songs," says Hugh.

Despite the encouragement and help that Ola Belle gave him, Hugh did not devote himself to his music fully until years later. In the mid-eighties Hugh called up Ola Belle and said to her, "I have been writing these songs and would like to get out and play with you somewhere before you get any older." Ola Belle answered as if she had been waiting for the call: "Don't say anymore. We are going to be playing in Raleigh, North Carolina and if you find your way down there I will get you on stage. I want folks to hear you, especially that song you wrote about my brother [Hugh's father]." Hugh found his way to Raleigh and to the show, which also featured Alice Gerrard. Unsure of what would happen, he waited patiently off to the side of the stage. Ola Belle as was her norm was "just working it, telling funny stories and everything." While sitting on the well-worn couch at the back of Childs Store Hugh recalled the rest of that memorable show: "She knew my limitations as a musician. She had finished the bulk of her show and then introduced me to do a couple of songs. The crowd loved us. We then closed the show with one of the old gospel songs. She kinda took a risk doing that [having Hugh play]. She didn't know how the audience was going to react and how people were going to respond. This was a prestigious function at one of the colleges down there. There were a lot of people there."[43]

For Hugh the positive reaction he received was a life-changing experience: "When people in that kind of setting give you that kind of positive feedback it gives you the sense that I may need to keep doing this." This life-changing show for Hugh would turn out to be one of the last shows Ola Belle would ever play. Shortly after that show in 1987 Ola Belle suffered a debilitating stroke. She was confined to a wheelchair and bedridden for the next fifteen years, until her death in 2002, only one day before her eighty-sixth birthday.

8

"Imprinted on my musical DNA"

Recommended Listening: The trio of albums released by Baltimore stalwarts Earl Taylor and Walt Hensley in the 1960s perfectly accentuates Chapter 8. Unfortunately, all three albums, Taylor's *Bluegrass Taylor-Made* and Hensley's pair of progressive releases, *5-String Banjo Today* and *Pickin' on New Grass*, are long out of print and extremely hard to find, though the occasional vinyl copy turns up. Instead the Earl Taylor and Jim McCall album *20 Bluegrass Favorites* provides much the same flavor as the aforementioned trio (though with not quite the same spice).

"If we like you, we'll keep you," responded Earl Scruggs to Russ Hooper when asked what would happen if Josh "Buck" Graves returned and wanted his job back playing Dobro with Flatt and Scruggs in the Foggy Mountain Boys. It was January of 1963 and Graves had decided to take leave from that band. When he first joined the Foggy Mountain Boys in 1955 the Dobro, or resonator guitar, was an afterthought and had fallen completely out of favor with bluegrass and country musicians. Graves, with his elegant, bluesy style, helped change that and revolutionize the role of the Dobro in bluegrass music. When Graves quit the Foggy Mountain Boys, Scruggs reached out to the only person that many felt could truly fill Graves' role in the band, Russ Hooper. Graves' style was so far ahead of his time that he left all other resonator guitar players in his considerable wake. But Hooper "was the first guy who could play all the stuff that Josh did," says Del McCoury.[1]

When Scruggs reached out to Hooper, Hooper expressed reservations about taking the job. Foremost on his mind was his young son at home, whom he did want to leave for long stretches of hard time on the road. He also had a steady, good-paying job he could not afford to leave. There was also the worry about what would happen if Graves changed his mind and wanted his job in the band back. Scruggs' answer concerning Graves' possible return did not instill faith in Hooper. Scruggs response was evasive. Instead of giving a direct answer he told Hooper if he wanted the job to meet the band at the

Denison Square Theater in Cleveland in two weeks. Hooper told Scruggs, "If you don't hear from me in a week that means I am not coming."[2] Hooper never called Scruggs back. Scruggs ended up replacing Graves with another Baltimore Dobro player, Kenny Haddock. Haddock had been making the rounds in Baltimore playing with Earl Taylor, Billy Baker, Frank Wakefield, and the Country Gentlemen. Hooper's worry about a returning Graves proved true, as Haddock lasted only a few months with the Foggy Mountain Boys before Graves returned and was given his spot in the band back. Years later, in 2006, Hooper went to see Scruggs play a show at the Birchmere Theatre near Washington, D.C. After the show Hooper went backstage with fellow Baltimore musician Mike Munford to talk with Scruggs. Hooper had not spoken to Scruggs since their phone conversation over forty years earlier. As introductions and greetings were shared Scruggs stuck out his hand to Hooper. Hooper shook it and asked Scruggs, "How come you never returned my phone call?" After a few uncomfortable moments and a look on Scruggs' face that Hooper called "priceless," Hooper finally let Scruggs know he was just "yanking his chain."[3]

In 1966, a few short years after the offer from Scruggs, Hooper was approached to join the Country Gentleman, who were well on their way to establishing themselves as one of the preeminent bluegrass bands of the last fifty years. Charlie Waller, lead singer and guitarist of the Country Gentlemen, called Hooper to inquire if he was interested in joining. Waller and Hooper knew each other from back in the early days in Baltimore, where they had played together a few times. While Hooper was intrigued by the opportunity, he turned it down. "I told Charlie, 'I got to turn the job down.' When I get to the age I am now I wanted to have a roof over my head and food on the table," Hooper said in 2013.[4] In addition to the financial security he was afforded by his job, family was very important to Hooper and he was not about to head out on the road for long stretches and leave them alone. Hooper would turn down Waller two more times when asked to join the Country Gentlemen again in 1969 and 1971. He agreed to help out the Seldom Scene in 1971 and joined the band briefly as a fill-in for Mike Auldrige. He later said he never had an interest in joining the band full time. Hooper's decision to stay close to home and value a steady job over the hard life of touring musician begs the question of what might have been for Hooper if he had taken his immense talents on the road and been exposed to a wider audience. It is a question Hooper has never asked himself. "You have to look at your priorities, and family's always been a priority for me," says Hooper. "Don't get me wrong. I appreciate all the accolades, I really do. All the honors mean a lot to me. It makes me feel all the years I have worked to do what I've done, it's been appreciated by people. But my family comes first and that's the way I look at it."[5]

Another Baltimore picker, Hooper's longtime friend Walt Hensley, was also asked to join the Country Gentlemen. He was approached a few years before Hooper was and actually took the job in September of 1961. He replaced the band's regular banjo player, Eddie Adcock, who had taken a brief leave of absence. Hensley had recently returned to Baltimore after time on the road with Earl Taylor and the Stoney Mountain Boys when they had been looking for gigs and steady work in St. Louis and Cincinnati.

After accepting the job offer from Waller, Hensley relocated to Washington and moved in with Waller and his family while he was in the band. In typical Hensley fashion, he grew homesick for Baltimore and the comfort and familiarity of the small bars he regularly played. After only a month with the band Hensley quietly bowed out and returned to Baltimore, allowing Adcock to rejoin the band. Upon his return to Baltimore Hensley fell into familiar routines: he rejoined Taylor, who was back in the area, and resumed playing the same dingy corner bars he knew so well. He also began working a "real" day job and soon was limiting the amount of time he was playing music in public.

This was common for many of the musicians from Baltimore. While some of the factories in the area, most notably Bethlehem Steel, were starting to experience a slow decline in production that began at the dawn of the sixties, opportunities for well-paying nonmusical jobs were still fairly plentiful. Many of the musicians in the area decided it made more financial sense for them to hold a high-paying steady job throughout the week and to play only on weekends or when time allowed. This would limit the amount of touring they could do and their exposure to potential new fans. Instead they would focus their energies on increasing their profile locally and making as much money as they could from playing regionally at the various music parks and carnivals. Within the city there were also still many opportunities for bands to regularly play; but to be able to make a full-time living as a bluegrass musician was still very hard at the time. For many of the bluegrass musicians who had lived through the Great Depression or whose parents had lived through it the decision to hold a steady job and support their families was an easy one.

Tom Neal had first started playing in Baltimore in 1966 while still in high school and would become one of the most versatile players in Baltimore. He got his start playing bass with Del McCoury and Jack Cooke (appearing on McCoury's first solo album in 1967), before becoming a highly regarded banjo picker. Like most young musicians, Neal wished to make a living playing music, but he knew that it was likely not a realistic option. He was married with two young children and started working as a union heavy-equipment operator in 1969. "I had health and welfare benefits, dental and eye coverage for the whole family," says Neal. "You weren't going to get that playing music anywhere. I did play as much as I could and work a forty-hour job. I was playing in Baltimore Wednesday through Sunday night and working a forty-hour job Monday through Friday."[6]

Baltimore afforded many musicians the opportunity to hold a regular job and a chance to play music and make some extra money in the process. "They had to make a living. They had families and of course there were not very many people back then that were really making a living playing bluegrass," says Chris Warner. "So I think they just hung around where they knew it was safe. They could play on the weekends and still work a day job."[7] While their families surely appreciated the prudent decision to stay close to home and to work, the rest of the bluegrass world lost out on the opportunity to discover the abundance of talent that inhabited Baltimore.

The hard life on the road was another deterrent for many working musicians. "People don't know how rough a life that is to live. You are constantly on the go," says Hooper. "There are times you leave a show at ten o'clock at night and, let's say you are in Maryland, you may then drive seven, eight, ten hours to get to Ohio and you drive all night to get there. By the time you get there it is time to get cleaned up and hit the stage." Along with the brutal grind that was the life of a bluegrass band on the road, the lack of steady pay at home and being forced to always be on the road to make money took its toll on many a road-weary bluegrass musician. Hooper counts himself lucky he was not one of them and recognizes the damage the road caused to so many of his peers. "I've been around long enough and I've seen it all go downhill for some," he says. "I've watched guys in the business who've drank themselves to death. And I see a lot of the other guys that have to keep working to bring money in because they don't know how to do anything else."[8]

While staying close to Baltimore may have helped them hold steady jobs and raise families, it definitely limited their growth on the national bluegrass scene. And that, to some extent, is what defines the bluegrass scene in Baltimore throughout the sixties: missed opportunities and denied chances. At the same time Baltimore was beginning to see some of its fortunes in the bluegrass world dry up, Washington, D.C., began to draw more attention with a pair of highly inventive bands, the Country Gentlemen and the Seldom Scene, who were both discovering how to bring bluegrass to a wider audience. "What happened is you had John Duffey and the Country Gentleman, and they just reached across into a broader market," explains longtime Baltimore musician Carroll Swam. "They really took the folk thing and ran with it at a time when folk music was very popular and they kind of helped bring bluegrass out of the shadows and the clubs to a wider audience."[9]

This highlighted another distinct difference between the two cities. Whereas Washington saw the Country Gentlemen and the Seldom Scene push the envelope of what was thought possible in bluegrass as they began to incorporate elements of rock, pop and folk, Baltimore's music stayed closer to the genre's earliest roots. Through the large influx of Appalachian migrants into Baltimore, the city kept stronger ties to the genre's country music origins. "The early players [in Baltimore], Frankie Short, Earl Taylor, and Walt Hensley, were almost always a traditional-style band," says Warner, who first played in Baltimore in 1962. "Washington, D.C., was more progressive in the form of the Country Gentlemen and the Seldom Scene. I can't think of any bluegrass band at that time in Baltimore that was not traditional orientated."[10] This hard-driving Baltimore sound, while being eclipsed by the progressive sound emanating from D.C., flourished on a trio of albums released by two of Baltimore's top musicians during the sixties.

After his short stint with the Country Gentlemen, Hensley rejoined Taylor in late 1961, and they, along with Jim McCall, resumed playing as the Stoney Mountain Boys. During this time the band seemed to be in constant flux, shuttling back and forth between Baltimore and Cincinnati. The band still had a little bit of name recognition from their brief foray into the folk world with Alan Lomax. On this little bit of recognition Taylor was approached by Country Music hall of famer Ken Nelson, a longtime producer and A&R man for Capitol Records, about recording an album for Capitol. Since 1951 Nelson had been the head of the Country Artist division at Capitol and had helped launch the careers of such country artists as Buck Owens, Merle Haggard, Gene Vincent, and Wanda Jackson. In Taylor, Nelson thought he spotted similar star potential.

In January of 1963 Taylor, Boatwhistle, Hensley, and McCall, along with master fiddler Benny Martin, headed to Nashville, Tennessee, to record a new album. The well-seasoned band completed twelve tracks in one high-speed session in less than four hours.[11] The resulting album was a collection of covers that had already been recorded and released by others. Among the album's twelve tracks there were four songs by Bill Monroe, two by Earl Scruggs, and a version of country singer Gentleman Jim Reeves' "I've Lived a Lot in My Time." It was a version that bluegrass musician and writer Tom Ewing called "the most original inclusion" on the album. Delivered in Taylor's straightforward, true-to-its roots, hard-drivin' style, the album found great appeal, with its reliance on already established songs that were familiar to many bluegrass and folk-music fans at the time. Ewing, who was just a seventeen-year-old budding bluegrass novice when the album was released in 1963, called it "a great album for a beginner like me."[12]

Shortly before the album was due to be released Taylor and McCall, as was there norm, had begun arguing again. Tensions had been rising between the two for some time, as McCall was feeling he was being treated more like a hired player in the band than an equal partner. McCall had joined the band after the Carnegie Hall show when he replaced Porky Hutchins. McCall's son Dwight says that, despite having joined later, his dad felt he carried just as much of the responsibility in the band as Earl did and it really bothered him that "Earl's name was out front" and his was not. Dwight says his dad always thought "he [McCall] actually led the band, but Earl got all the credit."[13]

These simmering, underlying tensions finally reached a head while the band was in the studio rehearsing for the album. McCall and the rest of the band were off to one side practicing and asked Taylor to join them. Taylor responded, "You boys go ahead, I have my part." Dwight says this perceived disrespectful slight "ate at my Dad worse than anything up to that time."[14] The end result was that McCall left the band right before the release of the album. In a further blow to his pride, when the album was released McCall's name was nowhere to be found on it despite his contributions to it. Instead, Frankie Short, another musician from Baltimore, who had replaced McCall in the band but not played on the album, was listed in the album's credits as singing lead and playing guitar. In addition to Short, the album's credits also included another musician who had not contributed to the album, Boatwhistle's son, Vernon McIntyre Jr. McIntyre had joined the band on banjo when Hensley left the group shortly after McCall. The liner notes also failed to credit fiddler Martin for his contributions, which, given his status as one of the legendary members of the Flatt and Scruggs band, was a surprising omission.

In addition to listing two musicians who did not contribute to the recording of the album and leaving off some who did, upon its release by Capitol Records in 1963 the album was oddly titled *Earl Taylor and His Bluegrass Mountaineers: Bluegrass Taylor-Made*. This led to some confusion. Calling the band the Bluegrass Mountaineers led many to believe that Taylor was playing with a new band, when in fact it was basically the same Stoney Mountain Boys lineup that had been together for years. The name Bluegrass Mountaineers came from someone at Capitol Records and the mistake was not caught until the album was pressed and the covers printed.

McCall would find some resolution to his resentment a few years later when he and Taylor reunited and began playing together. This time there would be equal billing, with the band being called Earl Taylor and Jim McCall and the Stoney Mountain Boys. The differences and tension between the two would still rise from time to time and they would occasionally end their partnership only to restart it again. Their union would be solid enough that over the ensuing years they would record a trio of solid albums for the Rural Rhythm label.

Despite the tensions that clouded the recording of the *Bluegrass Taylor-Made* album, the final result was extremely well received, catching many fans off guard when it was released. At the time, in that pre–Internet age, there was little prerelease publicity for many musical acts, especially smaller, less-established acts that played bluegrass and country music. Unless one subscribed to professional trade magazines or worked at a music store or as a music teacher it would be very likely the first encounter with a new album was by chance when it was stumbled across in a record shop. West Coast bluegrass icon Sandy Rothman attributes the surprise of the album to another factor as well: "Capitol [Records] had a country series but wasn't known at all for bluegrass releases. Thus it was an enormous surprise to us out here on the West Coast and probably most everybody else following bluegrass to see and hear the incredible *Bluegrass Taylor-Made* album, complete with its erroneous band name." Rothman praised the musicianship on the album: "Walter Hensley's precision-spaced banjo notes never sounded better in a straight bluegrass context and the rest of Earl's boys turned in stellar performances, undoubtedly inspired by the high-octane combination of Earl Taylor and 'Big Tige' Benny Martin." For the young, developing bluegrass musician in Rothman the album left an indelible mark, with him declaring, "*Bluegrass Taylor-Made* is imprinted on my musical DNA."[15]

A few short years after the album's release Rothman would find himself face to face with Taylor and soon a part of his band. Taylor and Boatwhistle along with their families had relocated to California in hopes of a better payday and more opportunities. "They had this bluegrass Gold Rush fantasy in their minds," Rothman says. "You know, head out West and find all kind of pickers, jobs, and work."[16] Rothman heard through friends that Taylor was living near Los Angeles. Not wanting to miss the opportunity to meet the man whose album was so important to him, Rothman headed south from San Francisco to try to find him. He eventually tracked the pair down living in a ramshackle house in a remote part of Orange County outside of Los Angeles. Rothman drove out and introduced himself and for a few short months he was part of a West Coast version of the Stoney Mountain Boys. Taylor and Boatwhistle lasted only a couple of months on the West Coast before realizing their vision of life out there did not match the reality. They

Sandy Rothman as a member of the Stoney Mountain Boys in 1970 at the Terrace (later Aunt Maudie's) in Cincinnati, Ohio. Onstage are (from left) Rothman (banjo), David McCall (obscured by Rothman), Taylor, McCall, and Boatwhistle (hidden by McCall). Note poster on far right wall advertising the band (photograph by Carl Fleischhauer).

soon fled back to Cincinnati. Rothman would join them again in Cincinnati a couple of months later and continue to play with them. During his time with the Stoney Mountain Boys, he would record one album with the band, 1973's *The Bluegrass Touch*.

After the release of *Bluegrass Taylor-Made*, Capitol Records A&R man Nelson—who was impressed with Hensley's playing and perhaps hoping to "ride the wave of banjo popularity across the country (and the world) in the wake of Pete Seeger and the Weavers, Flatt and Scruggs, and their [Capitol Records] own *Bluegrass Taylor-Made*"[17]—asked Hensley if he would be interested in recording an album of his own. Hensley agreed and traveled to Nashville for three sessions spread out over two weekends in 1963. The first session took place September 12, during which the band completed nine tracks. The second was on September 27 and the band finished five songs. The final session was the following day, when the band completed the remaining three tracks.[18]

Russ Hooper says that when Hensley arrived at the studio he had no idea who was going to be playing on the album with him, as Nelson had arranged for the band. One familiar face did join Hensley in Nashville to record the album. His bandmate McCall came along to play guitar, though his contributions to the album would be minimal. McCall would appear on only two tracks, as Nelson instead chose to use a couple of Nashville session aces, guitarist Ray Eddington and fiddler Tommy Jackson. Nelson also hired famed second-generation traditional bluegrass mandolinist Red Rector to play on the record. Nelson, who was hoping to capitalize on the folk-music craze and possibly make the album a bit more appealing to a mainstream audience, reached outside the box and normal bluegrass realm for the remainder of the band he hired. These outside-the-box additions along with Hensley's unique playing would really provide the album with its unconventional sound.

Nelson brought in a famed vocal quartet, the Jordanaires, to sing on the album. The Jordanaires were best known at the time for their work with Elvis Presley, as they had provided background vocals on some of his earliest recordings. This helped establish them as the go-to vocal harmony group for many country music recording sessions. Their harmonies and gospel-flavored style brought a brand-new element generally not associated with bluegrass to Hensley's album. The other unique sound Nelson brought in to work on the album was legendary saxophonist Boots Randolph, who was best known for his 1964 hit "Yakety Sax" (more commonly referred to as "The Benny Hill Theme Song"). Hensley made it very clear that despite the popularity of Randolph's sax on the album that addition was Nelson's and Hensley did not especially care for it. He says he went along with it because he did not want to blow his opportunity to record a solo album. Despite Hensley's stated aversion to the addition of Randolph's saxophone to the album the odd pairing worked spectacularly. Longtime Hensley fan Rothman is not surprised that Hensley was able to mesh so well with the nontraditional bluegrass accompaniment of Randolph's saxophone. "I think of Walter Hensley as a real forward-thinking traditionalist," he says. "He cut his teeth on real traditional bluegrass, loved it the most and played it the most. But on his solo banjo outings he had a lot of modern ideas."[19]

The recording process got off to a "shaky" start, with Hensley admitting to Hooper years later that he was extremely nervous about being in the studio with such seasoned professionals as Randolph and the Jordanaires. After a couple of disastrous attempts to get started, one of the Jordanaires pulled Hensley aside and took him for a walk around the building to help calm his nerves.[20] Eventually Hensley settled down and got to work. The resulting album, 5-String Banjo Today, with its odd lineup, was a sonically adventurous success. The liner notes to the album attempted to describe the odd band configuration: "Backing up Walt in a program that's about half old favorites and half new surprises, is an unusual group—a solid rhythm section, a characteristic clutch of fiddles, those wonderful singers, The Jordanaires, who sing both with and without words, and a where-did-he-come-from saxophone, that fits in like an ace to a king-high-four-card-straight."[21] The album also continued Hensley's impressive streak of firsts. He could already lay claim to being part of the first bluegrass band to play at famed Carnegie Hall in 1959 with the Stoney Mountain Boys at Alan Lomax's Folksong '59 Concert. He was part of the Stoney Mountain Boys' appearance on Mike Seeger's 1959 album, *Mountain Music Bluegrass Style*, one of the first full-length bluegrass albums. And with the release of his *5-String Banjo Today*, Hensley released the first solo banjo album on a major label.

The album was composed of a handful of Hensley compositions: "Walt's Breakdown," "Kickin' Mule," and "Long Way from Home," a couple of traditional tunes and bluegrass standards, including "Bear Tracks," "Rose Conlee," and "Chokin' the String," and a mix of pop songs, including "The World Is Waiting for the Sunrise," and "When You're Smiling." It was Hensley's reading of the pop standards that really showed off his innovative style. They subtly mixed Hensley's banjo and bluegrass with the more modern sound of Randolph's saxophone. When delivered with Hensley's forward-thinking picking an album was created that longtime bluegrass radio DJ Peter Thompson called "pretty progressive sounding."[22] Rothman agrees the combination of Randolph's saxophone with Hensley's dynamic banjo playing was something special and wholly unique. He says that, with this combination and the resulting album, "Walt made the very clear statement that he wasn't playing by the old rules."[23] Russ Hooper thinks the album represents the pinnacle of Hensley's playing. "When he [Hensley] did the Capitol session I would have put him up against anybody—even Scruggs—and Scruggs was the epitome of playing banjo. That's how good Walt was."[24] Despite his natural shyness and lack of belief in his immense talent, Hensley recognized the power and popularity of the album, with its unique instrumentation, and added a saxophone to his own band, the Dukes of Bluegrass, for a short stretch after the album's release to try to replicate its sound live.

Upon its release in 1964 *5-String Banjo Today* began to sell fairly well. The combination of Hensley's banjo, the Jordanaires, and Randolph's saxophone proved to be a captivating sound. It also helped that much of the material was made up of songs that would be familiar to a broad audience. Hooper says the album was promoted to "a lot of those middle-of-the-road stations and they played the living hell out of that thing."[25] Due to a lack of accurate record keeping it is hard to determine exactly how many copies of *5-String Banjo Today* were sold, though it seems generally accepted that it was somewhere in the realm of 50,000.

Unfortunately for Hensley, at the same time as his album was released another band, made up of four mop-topped lads from Liverpool, England, had just exploded in their home country. As the onslaught of Beatlemania reached American shores the demand for their albums reached epic propor-

Marvin Howell and the Franklin County Boys on the set of their weekly TV show on WMET (from left): Danny Curtis, Russ Hooper, Carroll Swam, Howell, and Frank Joyner (courtesy Russ Hooper).

The Franklin County Boys at the Manor Inn in Baltimore in 1962 (from left): Bobby Diamond, Marvin Howell, Russ Hooper, Roy Cole, and Joe Hales (courtesy Russ Hooper).

tions. Capitol Records was unable to keep up with the demand and began devoting more of their resources to the Beatles. "By the time our albums came out, the Beatles had just hit," says Hensley, "and they were so hot that Capitol stopped pressing anyone else's albums. They even had other labels help press Beatles albums."[26] As Capitol's focus—and more important, the record-buying public's attention—shifted towards the Beatles, many artists, especially those who played country and bluegrass, found that Capitol was no longer interested in their albums and the small markets they would attract, instead putting all the manufacturing efforts into Beatles albums. "When that happened that put a hurting on everything," Hooper says. "It wasn't just Walter's stuff. It was everything else that Capitol had in the can."[27]

Interestingly, it seems that when Hensley's album was swallowed up by the demand for the Beatles, Capitol lost all record of Hensley having ever recorded for them. Years after the album's release Hensley called Capitol Records to inquire about using a couple of tracks from it as part of a compilation album he was putting together. After being transferred from department to department, Hensley finally got a hold of someone who told him that Capitol Records had no record of anything he had ever done for them. Hensley figured that meant it was okay for him to use whatever he wanted.[28]

Initially Ken Nelson had approached Hensley about doing a follow up to *5-String Banjo Today*, but as the album got lost in the shuffle of Beatlemania and time went by, the idea of another album eventually fell by the wayside. Hensley returned to Baltimore and resumed his regular routine of driving a truck for work and playing in the bars. Disillusioned with his experience with a major label and the big-time atmosphere of Capitol, Hensley slowly began to pull back from playing music live, playing only on the occasional weekend. For a stretch he even stopped performing completely. After a couple of years away from the stage Hensley got the itch to return to music. He started casting around for new players to fill out his band, the Dukes of Bluegrass. At the same time, Hooper's time with Marvin Howell and the Franklin County Boys was coming to an end.

The Franklin County Boys had become one of the most popular bands in the mid–Atlantic region throughout the 1960s. Howell kept them continually working a marathon schedule, which exposed the band to a large audience. They regularly played New River Ranch and Sunset Park as well as holding down weekly residencies at a number of bars in Baltimore and the surrounding area. They had also secured a spot on local Baltimore TV station WMET and played a weekly show every Tuesday night from 8:30 to 9:00 p.m. Baltimore has a long history of televised music shows including *The Collegians* and *The Buddy Deane Show* (the inspiration for the movie *Hairspray*), and the Franklin County Boys helped carry on that tradition.

Over the years, Howell had developed a bad drinking problem that could make him at times difficult to work with. This led to some tensions within the band. Roy Cole had played with Howell and Hooper in the Franklin County Boys off and on for a decade and had seen Howell's problem grow. As it did, Cole said, "he [Howell] went to hell. When he got to drinking you couldn't depend on him."[29] Hooper had twice quit the band when Howell, angry from too much drink and perhaps a bit of jealousy of Hooper's steady work as a session musician, had begun lashing out at him. Hooper was always the consummate professional and found Howell's actions completely offensive. Each time Hooper had quit the band, Howell, recognizing his importance to the music they made, had rushed to Hooper's house and talked him into coming back. Upon his return the second time Hooper warned Howell: "I am going to record with who I want. It's as simple as that. If you can't handle that its best we part now as friends." Hooper, like the rest of the band, had grown tired of Howell's antics when he had been drinking and could not be counted on to perform. He added, "If I ever quit you again I ain't coming back."[30]

The end came on a Tuesday night in August of 1969. As Hooper prepared to go into the studio for the band's weekly TV show he got a call from Frankie Short, who was playing with the band at the time, saying he was not going to be able to make it to that night's taping. When Hooper got to the studio he told Howell that Short would have to miss that evening's show. Hooper could tell Howell had already been drinking and that he was not pleased with Short's absence. The show started and Howell began to lash out to the rest of the band about the absent Short. In between each number Howell spent the time criticizing Short and bad-mouthing him. His attacks grew more vicious and personal as the show wore on. Howell's actions were so offensive to Hooper that at the end of the show he told Howell, as he was leaving the studio, "Marvin, you have absolutely no class. A man wasn't here to defend himself. I quit, don't ever call me again."[31] Hooper's longtime friend Danny Curtis was in the band at the time and was just as disgusted at Howell's behavior. He lasted another week with Howell before he quit as well. Curtis's quitting marked the end of the Franklin County Boys and the band would never play together again.

Hooper would not see Howell again until three years later, when he bumped into him at a bluegrass festival in Carmel, Maryland. The pair exchanged pleasantries. Then Howell said he was thinking about "getting the old guys together, do you want to play?" Hooper told Howell, "You must have a short memory," and ended the conversation. Howell would continue his hard living and die at the age of 48 in 1984 after suffering a heart attack while waiting in the car for a friend who had gone into a liquor store. Despite his personal demons, Howell was for a time a giant of the Baltimore scene, but one who unfortunately outside of the Mid-Atlantic region was mostly unknown. He could be hard to work with; some of the difficulties could be attributed to his belief in his talents as a bandleader and the skill of the bands he assembled. In a scene like Baltimore's, where band members came and went constantly and freely worked with many bands at one time, Howell believed in the power of a band, the strength of a tight musical unit, and he expected his bands to believe the same. This led to tension with his bandmates. As Hooper said about Howell, "Marvin had this idea that you were committed only to his band and that was it."[32]

The demise of the Franklin County Boys freed Hooper up to begin playing with Hensley and the Dukes of Bluegrass full time in September of 1969. Also in the band at that time was Hensley's brother Jim on guitar and ex–Franklin County Boy Short on mandolin. The bass spot was filled by a rotating cast of players, which even included someone remembered only as Sam the bass man. As the tumultuous sixties came to an end—with rock 'n' roll and Woodstock changing a generation, Neil Armstrong becoming the first man to walk on the moon, and the Vietnam war swirling out of control—Hensley and the Dukes of Bluegrass continued to do what they had done for the previous decade, play high-quality, hard-driving, traditional bluegrass in some of the worst bars in Baltimore. Despite the changes that were taking place around them, bluegrass musicians in Baltimore went about business as usual. Built around the undeniable talents of Hensley and the rock-solid foundation of Hooper and Short, the new Dukes of Bluegrass lineup was regularly playing six or seven nights a week at Pete's Lounge, with a matinee on Sunday from three to eight. At the urging of Rebel Records

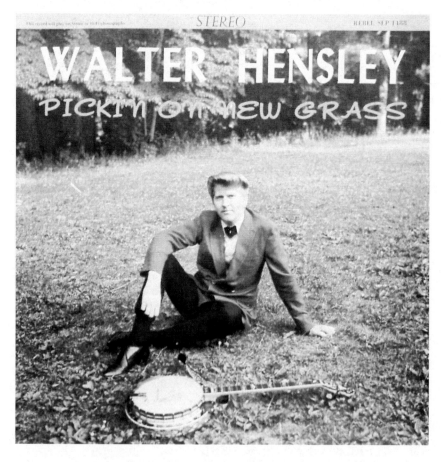

Walt Hensley's *Pickin' on New Grass* (author's collection).

owner Dick Freeland, the band soon entered the studio to begin work on a new Hensley album.

Freeland had booked them time at Recordings Incorporated Studios on Cold Spring Lane in Baltimore on Sunday nights after they finished up their weekly matinee show. The first night they showed up at the studio, Freeland had brought in an adman from an agency in New York City who wanted the band to play a jingle for a new commercial he was putting together. Hooper says they wasted two hours working on the jingle the adman insisted had to be exactly sixty seconds long. The only bright spot for the band was that they were paid for their time, which Hooper says was unlike the time they would put in working on Hensley's album, for which no one was paid.

The band returned to Recordings Incorporated the next couple of weeks to work on the album each evening after their matinee show. The recording process went smoothly, with the only hiccup coming after the first session when they realized the bass player they had "wasn't that good."[33] They hired session player extraordinaire Ed Ferris to fill in. Ferris was a longtime integral cog of the Washington-Baltimore bluegrass scene. Over the years, he would record and play with the Country Gentlemen, Ralph Stanley, Bill Harrell, and the Johnson Mountain Boys, among many others. Through his regular studio work with Rebel Records Ferris would become one of the most recorded bluegrass bassists of all time.[34] They also brought in Danny Curtis to add a mandolin break on the track "Running Bear." The veteran band was able to complete the album fairly quickly over a couple of Sunday evening sessions. On their final night in the studio, when they had eleven tracks in the can, album engineer George Massenberg asked if the band could do one more song. Hensley asked Hooper what he wanted to play. Hooper told Hensley, "It's your album. It's not what I want to do. It's what you want to do."[35] The band had recently added Jimmie Rodgers' contemporary pop hit "It's Over" to their set list and it was already a fan favorite in their live show. Hensley suggested they do that one. He had completely reimagined the arrangement of the song and turned it into a dreamy, lilting waltz highlighted by Hooper's conversational Dobro lines.

The finished album, *Pickin' on New Grass*, was released by Rebel Records in 1969 and "displayed a dizzying wellspring of ideas on many new tunes and some rooted in tradition."[36] With its focus on Hensley and the lack of added instrumentation that had populated his previous album, *Pickin' on New Grass* was the banjo master's most personal statement. *Bluegrass Unlimited* proclaimed, "There is a fine, controlled, almost lyrical quality of playing.... [T]his album is the peak of the art."[37]

Hensley was long recognized for his inventive techniques and inspired playing. The album was the perfect culmination of his career to that point, highlighting all the elements that made him so great. The album flowed easily from the simple dreamy note-perfect picking on "It's Over" to the hyper-grass speed of "Foggy Mountain Chimes" to the reinvented take on "America" to the haunting barreling drive of "Ghost Riders." It was a widely diverse palate, but one that Hensley and his veteran band dexterously wove into a grand, groundbreaking statement. "His mastery of Scruggs' tuners, special mechanical banjo pegs allowing pedal-like effects, on his own 'Edsel Break-down' and Scruggs' 'Foggy Mountain Chimes' is mind-bending," explains Rothman. "*Pickin on New Grass*—with its cover photo of Walt and his banjo literally sitting on a grassy field—has something for everybody ... no saxo-phone, just pure drive and unparalleled creativity."[38] Tom Neal spent a lot of time practicing and playing the banjo with Hensley over the years, and he said the music Hensley made on both *Pickin' on New Grass* and *5-String Banjo* was "really out there."[39] Despite the universal praise *Pickin' on New Grass* was receiving, one of the musicians who played on the album did find a flaw with it. While there was no saxophone this time around there was a drummer named John Warren playing a snare drum with brushes. It was an addition to the music that Hooper said he "detested."[40]

Despite the drumming Hooper detested on the album, *Pickin' on New Grass* seemed to break the traditional mold of bluegrass with its reliance on an unconventional approach to the music. Hensley's unique arrangement of familiar tunes was outside of the box of normal thinking and added to the fresh and inspiring sound of the album. The style joined a growing number of younger artists who were playing traditional-based music, which, while still centered on classic bluegrass instrumentation, was moving in a new, pro-gressive direction that drew heavily from any number of influences, most notably rock 'n' roll.

"The 1970s was a decade of experimentation in bluegrass music," says Baltimore Blue Grass Inc. owner Steve Cunningham. He cites the Jerry Garcia-led bluegrass super group, Old and in the Way, as "an experimental blend of instruments and styles" and acknowledges their impact on a growing legion of younger, more adventurous bluegrass bands. But he says that more than that it was "the introduction of chromatic scales that was the greatest influ-ence on bluegrass instrumentation," as this allowed the music to move away from its traditional roots and find a more exploratory, wider-appealing sound. Cunningham mentions "Bill Keith, Tony Trischka, Peter Wernick, and Sam Bush as gaining an earnest following" for their innovative approach to blue-grass. Many of these younger bands started spreading across the stage, each member with his own microphone instead of jockeying for position around one mic. Some of the bands even began adding electric pick-ups to their instruments, which allowed them to patrol the stage like the rock bands of the time. It also allowed their music to be played at louder volumes, much to the consternation of many older traditional fans who believed that blue-grass music equaled acoustic music. Cunningham says this "produced a gen-eration of players who knew the songs but lacked the original excitement of the music and the subtle 'ommp-chuck-a' bluegrass timing."[41]

Often the most glaring differences between these two different approaches to bluegrass were in the style of the musicians themselves, most recognizably the bushy beards, long hair, and scruffy jeans the younger, pro-gressive pickers wore. This was in contrast to the usual clean-cut, button-up collared shirt aesthetic of most traditional bluegrass bands. While the appear-ance of Hensley with his perfectly coifed hair on the cover of *Pickin' on New Grass* would never be confused with the wild unkempt look many of these younger musicians sported, the music he made on that album was seen by many as being just as progressive.

A young Sam Bush was bowled over by Hensley's picking and the new, dynamic sound he was creating on his revolutionary album. Bush loved bands he felt were pushing the progressive edge of bluegrass—bands like the Coun-try Gentlemen, Jim and Jesse, and the Dillards, bands he said were playing the first newgrass style. His discovery of *Pickin' on New Grass* fed into this desire to find new, adventurous sounds in bluegrass. "When Walt put his record out, it was exciting because it wasn't the same bluegrass I was listening to, what I had grown up around. It was nice to hear people take a departure away from what was going on," says Bush. "Walt was what I define as newgrass."

The term newgrass was still relatively new at the time but was starting to be applied to the bluegrass those younger, often bearded musicians were playing. The thirty-six-year-old Hensley may have not fit in with those younger musicians, with his conservative fashion sense and rural upbringing, but Bush believed the music he made was just as forward-thinking, "For Walt to call the album *Pickin' on New Grass* was a signal of the changing of the guard. That a new style of bluegrass was being played." Bush recognized the genius in Hensley was that, despite his playing being deeply rooted in the Scruggs style, what he played was a "departure" from the "same bluegrass" being played by every other picker of the day. "Let's face it, when you play Scruggs style banjo does it get any better than Earl [Scruggs]?," asks Bush. "No. But obviously there are people who have taken Earl's style and made it more of an art form. That was Walt."[42] Hensley was ahead of his time, and was willing to try new ideas and add unique techniques to his banjo repertoire to help keep the instrument alive through the years.

Bush gives credit to bandmate bassist Ebo Walker for coming up with the name for their new band, though Hensley was clearly on his mind as well when Bush and Walker, along with guitarist Curtis Burch and banjo picker Courtney Johnson debuted their new band, New Grass Revival. New Grass Revival was at the forefront of the newgrass revolution in bluegrass. They incorporated lengthy instrumental jams into their songs, similar to what San Francisco area bands like the Grateful Dead, Jefferson Airplane, and Quicksilver Messenger were doing at the time. With these lengthy jams and the way they seemed to revel in bucking convention, "New Grass Revival was breaking ground by resynthesizing the folk and popular elements of bluegrass."[43] Hensley would again be on Bush's mind years later when he immortalized the legendary Baltimore banjo picker on his 2006 album, *Laps in Seven*. In the song "Riding That Bluegrass Train," Bush sings of trading an old guitar for a ticket all the way to Baltimore. He says, "I wrote 'Riding that Bluegrass Train' with my friend John Pennell. The song talks about loving horse racing, losing money at the track, and getting mugged on Church Street. Walt Hensley was a banjo player out of Baltimore and he did an album called *Pickin' on New Grass* back in the '60s. At the end of 'Riding that Bluegrass Train' we wrote the lines 'riding that new grass train to Baltimore' as a tribute to him."[44]

Despite the appeal Hensley's album had among younger, newgrass musicians and the inspiration they found on it and the way they viewed it as so forward-thinking, Hensley did not see his album that way. He declared, in an interview in 1978 with the *Baltimore Sun* when asked about the newgrass sound in bluegrass, "I like to listen to some of that progressive stuff, but I don't like it enough to want to play it."[45]

Despite the high praise and adulation heaped by Bush onto Hensley and *Pickin' on New Grass* not much changed for Hensley after the release of the album. He continued to play with his band, the Dukes of Bluegrass, in and around Baltimore. The lineup for his band, like many other bands in the area, would fluctuate but generally featured Hensley, his brother Jim on guitar, Hooper on Dobro, and Frankie Short on mandolin. Bass players would come and go, no one player holding the spot permanently. They would use a rotating cast of fiddlers until they added emerging local hotshot Jon Glik to the lineup. Glik was a few years younger but was "an intensely rhythmic, bluesy fiddler, with such soul and passion in his playing," and had no trouble fitting in with his older and more experienced bandmates.[46] Since his start with Hensley, Glik has played and record with a number of bluegrass legends including David Grisman, Frank Wakefield, Peter Rowan, and Bob and Danny Paisley. He also appeared on Del McCoury's 1988 album, *Don't Stop the Music*.

The Dukes of Bluegrass at Pete's Lounge in Baltimore in 1978 (from left): Jon Glik, Walt Hensley, and Frankie Short, Sr. (courtesy Russ Hooper).

Hensley seemed happiest when he was playing in small bars in Baltimore or Cincinnati. Part of the reason is because that's where he had grown up playing. It was his comfort zone. He loved the people at those bars and they loved him back. Jim McCall's son Dwight would say years later about his dad and Hensley, "They had so many chances to cross that line to a bigger audience, but in my mind they just didn't want it. They were happy where they were, playing to forty people who were there to have a good time."[47] The other reason for Hensley's reluctance to put himself in unfamiliar situations and his desire to play close to home in the same bars over and over was his extreme lack of confidence in his own talent. He was notorious for agreeing to play a show or festival, then finding out there would be some other banjo player of renown on the bill, and freezing up and not being able to play the show.

In 1974 Hooper was playing with Hensley in the Dukes of Bluegrass. The band was booked to play a festival in Reedsville, North Carolina. They were not able to travel down from Baltimore together and had planned to meet up at the festival grounds the Saturday of the show. Hooper left Baltimore Friday after work and drove down by himself. Saturday morning he went to the festival grounds to find the rest of the band. After an hour of searching he bumped into Mike Auldridge of Seldom Scene. Auldridge and Hooper were old friends and chatted a bit. Hooper asked if he had seen Hensley or any of the other guys from the band. Auldridge said he had not. Hooper began to get worried and went back to his hotel and started making some phone calls. He eventually got hold of Frankie Short's wife at home. Short was in the band at the time and was supposed to be in North Carolina for the festival. Short's wife told Hooper that Frankie was definitely not in North Carolina, as he was out working right then. She told Hooper that Frankie had said the rest of the band had decided not to go at the last minute.

Hooper, who could feel his anger rising at the long drive he had just made for nothing, figured out what had happened. "It had to do with the fact that J.D. Crowe was going to be playing at the festival, and it was Walt's attitude that he didn't think he was good enough to play there with him," says Hooper. "The sad thing is I have conversations with J.D. and he tells me that Walt is one of his idols."[48] (As a sign of his respect for Hensley, Crowe would later include the Hensley tune "Walt's Breakdown," renamed "Stony Mountain Twist," on his 1986 album, *Straight Ahead*.) After Hooper discovered the band had not made the trip he continued making phone calls until he was finally able to get Hensley's brother Jim on the line. Hooper, who was still full of rage, told Jim, "Tell your brother to shove it sideways until his eyes bleed and not to call me anymore." Hensley and Hooper would not play together for the next decade.[49]

This did not mark the end of Hensley's discomfort in the spotlight. In 1986 Hensley was among a select few invited to play at the rededication ceremony of the Statue of Liberty over the July 4 weekend. This was a huge honor for Hensley and recognition of what he had achieved as a pioneer in bluegrass. But instead of playing the show and being exposed to a national audience that, for most in attendance, would be experiencing Hensley's playing for the first time, Hensley decided not to go. He told friends that he felt the trip to New York would end up costing more money than it was worth. Few of those close to Hensley bought this explanation and rightly suspected his nerves and limited confidence got the best of him. Years later Hensley would admit to bandmate James Reams before a show at the Delaware Valley Bluegrass Festival that he suffered from debilitating stage fright and this is what had held him back over the years.[50]

Regardless of whether it was stage fright, a lack of confidence in his abilities, or a belief that he was not as good as others told him he was, the same drawbacks had dogged him since he was a young man standing backstage at Carnegie Hall in 1959, "shaking like he was in a windstorm."[51] Whatever it was caused him to struggle in the presence of Boots Randolph and the Jordanaires when he went to work on his first solo album and to not show up for shows and festivals that featured other great players like him. It led him to happily relinquish his spot in the Country Gentlemen so he could return to the same old bars in Baltimore, or (as rumored) to turn down Lester Flatt when asked to join Flatt's band after Flatt and Scruggs broke up. It was what kept the man known as the Banjo Baron of Baltimore from displaying just as much talent as any of those early second-generation players and instead relegated him to the role of forgotten innovator. Hensley seemed to be the only person who never truly recognized how good he was. Hooper, with clear disappointment in his voice, says, "I don't think Walter ever realized how important he was and how much people liked his stuff."[52]

9

"The one thing they all had was talent"

Recommended listening: Frank Solivan and Dirty Kitchen's 2013 album, *On the Edge*, with its mix of hard-driving traditional-style songs and forward-thinking jazz and rock-flavored numbers, helps highlight the differences Baltimore bluegrass was experiencing in the seventies as a new crop of younger bands started pushing that familiar traditional sound into new directions. The presence of Mike Munford's banjo on *On the Edge* only serves to strengthen this connection.

"Bluegrass in this town has gone through what I call peaks and valleys," explains Russ Hooper. "If all of sudden you see an ad on TV where there is a fiddle or banjo playing in the background there is an upsurge of interest in this music…. When the interest waned and the music was down in the valleys again the only people who supported the music would be the people here who were brought up with this stuff."[1] These peaks Hooper spoke of were much like the growth and interest the genre experienced during the folk revival in the fifties and sixties when a brand new audience of younger, often college-educated fans started discovering bluegrass. It's similar to the modern-day revival with bands like Mumford and Sons, the Avett Brothers, the Infamous Stringdusters, and Yonder Mountain String Band, who have all dipped their toes into the bluegrass pool and are riding a wave of popularity at the end of the first decade of the 21st century. It seems as if bands have rediscovered the beauty of the string-band sound and are incorporating banjos, fiddles, and acoustic instruments into their music like never before. For a time in the fifties and sixties Baltimore was at the top of one of those peaks, as bands from the tight-knit community of musicians in the city all seemed to be gaining the attention of the rest of the bluegrass world.

Mike Seeger got things started with the release of his *Mountain Music Bluegrass Style* album, which heavily featured Baltimore bands Earl Taylor and the Stoney Mountain Boys and Bob Baker and the Pike County Boys.

The Stoney Mountain Boys' pioneering appearance at Carnegie Hall as part of the Folksong '59 Concert and the subsequent release of *Folk Songs from the Blue Grass: Earl Taylor and His Stoney Mountain Boys* and *Bluegrass Taylor-Made* helped increase the Baltimore buzz. The release of Walt Hensley's groundbreaking pair of albums, *5-String Banjo Today* and *Pickin' on New Grass*, continued this high peak. *Who's That Knocking?*, the debut album by Hazel Dickens and Alice Gerrard released in 1965, helped push this peak into new, uncharted directions. But as the seventies dawned, bluegrass in Baltimore drifted into one of those valleys Hooper spoke of.

Hazel Dickens attributes some of the decline bluegrass experienced in Baltimore to the aging of the first crop of musicians who hailed from the city and the fans who packed the bars to see them. She says, "When those hillbillies in Baltimore got old, they hung it up and the old audience wasn't there anymore."[2] While it's true many of the original players and fans had gotten older and started families and many of them had moved out of the city, thus making their trips to see these bands play less frequent as the demands of home and family became greater with age, there were still some of those original musicians around who were playing like they had back in the old days. These bands had been some of the most popular in the region at one time and still had strong followings in the area.

The rise and fall of bluegrass in Baltimore in the sixties also seemed to parallel the economic fortunes of the city. The decade began on a high, as the city was still in the midst of the post–World War II economic boom that saw the election of a young, handsome president who seemed to usher in a new age for the country. But that excitement would not last as the Vietnam War, civil rights struggles, and a spate of political assassinations dominated the second half of the decade, which coincided with an economic downtown in the manufacturing sector in Baltimore. Bethlehem Steel at Sparrows Point was still the largest steel mill in the country in 1971, but it was already starting to experience massive layoffs, which affected the job fortunes of many of the original migrants and their families.

The notoriously reserved homebody Hensley, who had his moment in the glare of the bright big-time spotlight and a brief brush with fame, was content to stay close to home and just play on the weekends. He had a good job working as an exterminator during the week, and the harsh realities and low pay that went along with being in a regular touring band were no longer appealing to the thirty-seven-year-old Hensley. The grind of playing every night of the week like he used to do back in the day with Earl Taylor was not an option. For these aging musicians and their similarly aging fans, late nights out at shows during the week when combined with early-morning alarms for work and the daily grind of raising a family led to fewer numbers at shows during the week. Instead, weekend shows became packed events. Hensley, along with his band, the Dukes of Bluegrass, would hold down regular weekend residencies at the Cub Hill Inn and Pete's Lounge throughout the seventies.

The differences between the scenes in Washington and Baltimore grew greatly at this time. Whereas in the previous two decades there was an abundance of cross-pollination between the two cities, as the seventies dawned the interaction between the two started to dwindle to almost nothing. This dwindling interaction can be attributed to the aging core of the Baltimore bluegrass players and their desire to stay where they were comfortable, as well as a lack of motivation to get out and pursue gigs as they once had when they were younger. While there was a younger crop of musicians who would eventually follow in those aging legends' footsteps, it would be years before the newcomers would establish themselves as renowned players. It would not be until the eighties that interaction between the two neighboring cities would pick back up as those new, younger Baltimore musicians found the confidence and respect to start playing with the more established musicians from the D.C. area and the scene centered around the historic Birchmere in Alexandria, Virginia, just outside the D.C. city limits.

As the Washington bands Seldom Scene and Country Gentlemen became national superstars in the seventies, Baltimore musicians seemed to withdraw, retreating to the safety of the familiar confines of the well-worn bars and venues and going about business as usual. This retreat seemed only to heighten the growing differences between the two cities. Both had well-established bluegrass scenes, with Baltimore's predating D.C.'s by a few years. Unlike its neighbor to the south, Baltimore drew on the large presence of Appalachian migrants who heavily populated that city, while D.C. relied more on suburban hillbillies. While often lumped together as one indistinguishable scene, this does not accurately give credit to each city, which each had its own separate personalities. While D.C. and Baltimore shared a geographical region, as they are separated by less than fifty miles, they were two entirely unique scenes that should be viewed as individual entities, not as one combined scene. Many of the musicians would cross-pollinate and play with each other over the years, yet the differences between the two were always there and always came down to the background of the people making and listening to this music.

"What was happening in D.C., and this is a vast generalization, is it was much more of those college-educated or partly educated college, middle-class kids in D.C. and more of the hillbillies in Baltimore," says Alice Gerrard, who was familiar with both cities, as she lived in D.C. but regularly traveled to Baltimore to play.[3] Hooper agrees with Gerrard's assessment and believes these differences were noticeable not only in the musicians but also in the fans and venues of the two cities. He says the makeup of each scene was "totally different" and the only "respectable" places he knew that supported bluegrass were in the D.C. area, that people went to those places to "listen and nothing else." Whereas in Baltimore, he says, "You had these little dumps that would fit thirty or forty people, and they would fill up. And for those people it was just an excuse to drink."[4] Patrick McAvinue emerged out of Baltimore in 2003 as one of the most inspiring, young fiddle talents in the country. Despite the passage of time since Dickens and Hooper first began playing in Baltimore, the differences they noted between Baltimore and D.C. still held true for McAvinue: "When I think of Baltimore musicians I think of blue-collar music, whereas D.C. musicians to me are cerebral. I think Baltimore musicians can swing a hammer just as well as they can play music."[5]

Dickens credits D.C.'s fan base for helping their scene become more popular and stay more relevant than the one in Baltimore. She explains that "in Washington, a lot of the audience was college-educated people who stayed interested in the music."[6] This helped create an audience that was long-lasting and, unlike in Baltimore, one that did not thin out as they grew older.

Slowly over time D.C. garnered more and more attention for the groundbreaking work of bands like the Country Gentlemen and Seldom Scene, while their peers to the north seemed to be forgotten. This was troubling to Chris Warner, who had gotten his start in the bars of Baltimore playing with local luminaries like Kimball Blair, Frankie Short, Del McCoury, and Delmar Delaney before joining Jimmy Martin's band in 1968. He says, "Baltimore was every bit as important if not more [than D.C.] but has not gotten its due notice for its bluegrass scene."[7] Carroll Swam played with the Franklin County Boys in the sixties and observed the gap grow between the two. He believes that more than anything it was the way those D.C. bands were able to take advantage of the opportunities they were presented that separated the two cities. "I think to some extent D.C. is credited with being the hotbed of bluegrass activity, but really I think there was just as much if not more in the Baltimore area. They [musicians in Baltimore] just didn't capitalize on it the same way."[8]

As the fortunes of Baltimore changed so did the makeup of the musicians there. Some of the early leaders of the bluegrass movement in Baltimore had moved away, in some cases on to bigger things. Hazel Dickens, Alice Gerrard, and Mike Seeger were all experiencing varying degrees of success on a national level with the release of a variety of albums throughout the seventies.

The Dukes of Bluegrass at Pete's Lounge in Baltimore in 1978 (from left): Walt Hensley, Jon Glik, Frankie Short, Sr., and Barry Glickman (courtesy Russ Hooper).

They had since moved away from Baltimore, and their ties to the city existed mostly as memories, though Dickens still had family in the area, most notably her nephew Buddy Dickens, who remained an active part of Baltimore's modern bluegrass community. Earl Taylor, Jim McCall, and Boatwhistle had relocated to Cincinnati, where they continued to play together in a steady stream of bands. Although the three would find regular work there they would never replicate the success or fame they experienced in the late fifties and early sixties when they played at Carnegie Hall and recorded a couple of well-received albums.

Those who remained of the old guard in Baltimore were still an active presence. Russ Hooper played with a variety of bands and continued his steady session work. Walt Hensley regularly played at the Cub Hill Inn with his Dukes of Bluegrass, which featured original Baltimore players Frankie Short, Curtis Cody, Dee Gunter, and Hensley's brother Jim. Another local band at the time, Grass on the Rocks, was led by Hooper's old pals Bob Arney, Danny Curtis and Lamar Grier (whose son David would go on to become one of the premier flat-picking guitarists in the world), who were all part of the original jam sessions in Baltimore. This old guard was keeping alive the flame of their youth, but there was also a younger generation beginning to emerge in the area that was more tied to the hippy new-grass style of bluegrass than to the traditional style of old.

The background of this younger generation was worlds away from the music they were discovering. The majority of the original bluegrass players in Baltimore had ties that stretched back to Appalachia. Many were born in that region and moved to Baltimore as children or young adults looking for work. This new, younger generation had little or no connection to Appalachia beyond an appreciation for the music that came from that region. The new crop of players was not tied to the mountains in anyway and was reflective of the times, as they were associated with the hippy newgrass side of the music with their long hair, bushy beards, casual attire, and wholly different approach to the music. This new scene was centered on a store in northeast Baltimore called Baltimore Blue Grass Inc.

Baltimore Blue Grass Inc. storefront in 1976. The store served as the center for the next generation of bluegrass pickers in Baltimore upon its opening in 1975 (courtesy Steve Cunningham).

Opened by Steve Cunningham in November of 1975, at 5502 Belair Road, two and half miles inside the Baltimore Beltway, Baltimore Blue Grass Inc. was a string-music institution for twenty-five years. It was recognized both locally and nationally for its unparalleled instrument repair. Baltimore Blue Grass Inc. served as the center and social hub of the next generation of bluegrass pickers in the city. They bought their instruments there, brought them back to have them repaired, and most likely joined in an impromptu picking session around the fabled potbelly stove that sat in the corner of the picking room. The store's slogan as advertised on local radio station WPOC during its Sunday night bluegrass show said it all: "Baltimore Blue Grass Inc., bluegrass has a home in the city."

Cunningham had developed a love of bluegrass as a twelve-year-old when he discovered the banjo. He soon was playing in a number of local bands. As a young man in his twenties he decided "on whim"[9] to open the

One of the many famous visitors who stopped by Baltimore Blue Grass Inc. over the years, Steve Cunningham (right), with legendary Josh Graves at the store in 1980 (courtesy Steve Cunningham).

Tony Trischka leads a banjo lesson for a lucky few at Baltimore Blue Grass Inc. in 1984 (courtesy Steve Cunningham).

store. He and a friend, Jack Snodgrass, had driven to Pennsylvania to see banjo master Chris Warner about fixing some frets on Cunningham's banjo. On the drive back home they were bemoaning the lack of a quality acoustic music store in the area and thought it would be cool if they opened up their own bluegrass shop. Back at Cunningham's apartment the pair began brainstorming and making lists of everything they would need to open their own store. "We started writing things like location, advertising, inventory, and other things like insurance," Cunningham remembers. "We would write each category on a piece of paper and put it on the floor. Pretty soon the darn floor was filled with these sheets of paper. He [Snodgrass] gathered up half and I gathered up the other half and we went looking into it."[10]

Snodgrass lacked the passion of Cunningham for the project and turned his half of the research over to him. Cunningham realized he would have plenty of time to devote to this undertaking if he quit his job, so he did just that and spent the summer working on everything he would need to open the store. Before choosing a location for it, Cunningham conducted a survey of several of the bluegrass musicians in the area. He asked about all of the venues where they had played music in the previous ten years and marked those on a map to try to figure out the best location of his proposed store. He found the northeast corner of the city seemed to be bustling with activity through the presence of a number of bluegrass friendly bars in the area. Most notably the area had the Cub Hill Inn, where Cunningham had spent many an evening "eating hot dogs and sauerkraut and listening to Walt Hensley and the Dukes of Bluegrass," who played a regular residency there.[11] Cunningham went to the northeast area of the city and drove up and down the streets until he spotted a "For Rent" sign on an empty storefront. "That was the luckiest move I've made," he later said.[12] A few short months after conceiving the idea, Baltimore Blue Grass Inc. opened its doors, in November of 1975.

At the time, Cunningham was playing in a local band, Windy Ridge. Windy Ridge was made up of younger musicians who played bluegrass that did not strictly adhere to the traditional style prevalent among the older, established bands in the city. The Cub Hill Inn was not the typical brownstone bar of years past, but a larger, more modern establishment, and it was looking to expand its demographic beyond the aging blue-collar fan that made up the bulk of the crowd for Walt Hensley and the Dukes of Bluegrass. The Inn wanted to include this younger crop of musicians and hired Windy Ridge for a regular Thursday night residency to help attract a different clientele. Cunningham used Windy Ridge's Thursday night shows at the Cub Hill Inn as well as his other gigs around town to help promote the grand opening of his new store. His strategy worked. "Sure enough, the first day we were open we were busy, more busy than I would have liked as a guy who did not know what he was doing," jokes Cunningham. "I literally did not know anything about anything."[13]

Cunningham had always envisioned his store as being more than just a place to buy instruments. He believed bluegrass was a "communal type of music, a sharing type of music,"[14] and he wanted his store to reflect that. He wanted Baltimore Blue Grass Inc. to be somewhere you could just pop in and have people to play with whenever you wanted. This openness was partly fostered by Cunningham through the décor of the store with the inclusion of the potbelly stove that sat in the picking room and the old-timey wood paneling that adorned the walls. "We wanted it to suggest an open, welcoming, warm atmosphere," he says.[15]

Baltimore Blue Grass Inc. also hosted open weekly jam sessions. Cunningham says his store was probably the first place on the East Coast to hold open jam sessions like this. "We would have as many as seventy people in the store and out on the sidewalk," he proudly declares. "Cops would stop and listen. It was probably the safest place in town on a Friday night." These jam sessions would stretch well past the posted 10:00 p.m. closing time and reach into the wee hours of the night. Baltimore Blue Grass Inc. was the place where everybody would go to find someone to pick with or a musician to fill out a band. The store also became the go-to spot in Baltimore for visiting bluegrass royalty. Everyone from Charlie Monroe to Josh Graves to Vassar Clements to Pete Wernick to Kenny Kosek stopped by to have a pick by the famous potbelly stove, get a damaged instrument repaired, and maybe give a group lesson to a lucky few. Famous visitors were not limited to musicians. Cunningham remembers actor Keith Carradine hanging around the store for a week when he was in town performing in a play.

The opening of Baltimore Blue Grass Inc. helped revitalize the bluegrass scene in Baltimore. As the next generation of Baltimore's bluegrass musicians began to develop, a new, more diverse, and at times upscale clientele started to be seen at bluegrass shows in Baltimore. Whereas bluegrass bars and music were once solely the domain of hillbilly migrants or musically like-minded folkies who had a taste for string-band music, the audience at shows in the mid-seventies began to reflect a much larger demographic. At places like the Cub Hill Inn or Pete's Lounge, middle-class suburbanites mixed easily with everyone—"college students, motorcyclists, working-class people and old timers—persons who have little in common, except for their love of the music."[16] From its opening in 1975 until it shuttered its doors twenty-five years later, the store would serve as the focal point for all of those people who came from various walks of life but were united by their love of bluegrass music.

Initially Cunningham had brought his good friend Jeep Watson into the business as the only other employee, as Watson knew about retail and the business-related aspects of running a store that Cunningham was still trying to figure out. The pair soon realized they need another person to help out because they both played in bands and could not always cover all the hours the store was open. Through Snodgrass, Cunningham had met a local seventeen-year-old banjo-picking fanatic who "was just learning how to play, but was already tearing it up."[17] The youngster, named Mike Munford, was totally into bluegrass and a J.D. Crowe fanatic, and Cunningham thought he would be perfect to help out with the store.

Munford was born in 1958 in St. Louis. His family moved to the Roland Park neighborhood of Baltimore shortly after he was born. He discovered bluegrass as a fifteen-year-old, as so many others had before, through the sweet sounds of Earl Scruggs. A friend had invited him over to check out his new banjo and played Munford a cut from Scruggs' scintillating *Live at Kansas State* album. "It was the banjo and 'Foggy Mountain Breakdown' that really nailed me right to the floor," Munford says.[18] Like so many others in Baltimore Munford got his daily bluegrass fix via Ray Davis' regular weekday radio shows. He dove into bluegrass headfirst, absorbing all he could, and became one of the best young pickers in the city. The opening of Baltimore Blue Grass Inc. was an eye-opening event for the teenaged Munford. He had met Cunningham previously and recalls going to the store the first or second day it was open. With its commitment to bluegrass, acoustic, and string music, the store was a life-affirming event for the young Munford: "I remember that sense of feeling like I had a found this place, this oasis, a music store dedicated to this music I had just discovered."[19]

Munford was a regular at the Friday night jam sessions before he was approached by Cunningham to work at the store. Munford thought it was the perfect opportunity as he realized he was not interested in college or a real job. So the day after he graduated from high school in 1976, Munford started working at Baltimore Blue Grass Inc. Cunningham and Watson had other commitments the day Munford started and they left their brand-new, seventeen-year-old employee in charge. When they checked in with him later that day, Cunningham was impressed to find out that Munford had not only

Mike Munford works on a banjo at Baltimore Blue Grass Inc. in 1994. Munford worked at the store from 1976 until it closed in 2000 (courtesy Steve Cunningham).

be able to handle the store but actually was able to sell an instrument—the always tough to sell dulcimer—while they were away. Cunningham and Watson were soon involving Munford in all facets of the store business.

After a couple of years Watson left the business and Munford was promoted to Watson's old position of vice president. Due to Cunningham's meticulous nature and strong organizational skills there were generally only three employees working at Baltimore Blue Grass Inc. at any given time. During its busiest years the store had as many as six employees but, Cunningham says, "Mike and I were just so efficient that we really didn't need all those employees. They would just end up standing around and drinking coffee and smoking cigarettes."[20] From the time he first started to work at Baltimore Blue Grass Inc. the day after he graduated from high school Munford would stay with Cunningham for the next twenty-five years, until the store finally closed for good in 2000.

In addition to his normal work at the store, Munford also started teaching music lessons and doing instrument repairs to help support himself financially. "What I started to learn early on was you don't really need that much to survive," states Munford, "if that one thing you're doing for a living is something you really enjoy."[21] This levelheaded approached allowed Munford to carve out a full-time living through some of the less glamorous opportunities afforded to musicians, like giving lessons and repairing instruments. In addition to his growing musical prowess, he began to develop a reputation as one of the premier instrument repairmen and setup guys in the country. Munford would literally help write the book on the banjo when he contributed a chapter on banjo maintenance to Ross Nickerson's book *The Banjo Encyclopedia: Bluegrass Banjo from A to Z*, which is one of the most extensive, thorough examinations of the instrument.

Over the years, many bluegrass elites would call on the humble Baltimore musician to help them when their instruments became damaged or fell into disrepair. Banjo icon Tony Trischka had obtained an old prewar flat-head banjo that had been previously owned by Sonny Osborne. While it had been always a great-sounding instrument, something was not quite right with it. Trischka had tried a number of different repairmen and friends to see what else he could coax out of the old Gibson. It was not until Munford went to work on it that the "true power and glory" of it became apparent.[22] Through Trischka, Munford would find himself in the living room of comedian legend and longtime banjo aficionado Steve Martin in 2008, fixing the former *Saturday Night Live* standout's banjo on the coffee table. The ever humble Munford called it an incredible thrill to be able to help him out.[23]

While focusing on working at the store, giving lessons and becoming

known as an elite instrument repairman allowed him to support himself
financially through music (which is the unquestionable desire of every working musician), doing so definitely limited the amount he played outside of
Baltimore. Munford never viewed his pragmatic approach to making a living,
which stunted the amount of national attention he received, as a negative.
Instead he felt fortunate that he lived "in an area where there was always
some kind of steady work." He says that "pretty much since he started with
Windy Ridge in the mid-seventies, all but one or two years, I've had a steady
gig; whether it's the Cub Hill Inn or playing the Sandpiper with Danny Paisley
and Jon Glik."[24] Despite his lack of exposure Munford was not completely
unknown on the national radar at this time. He was well known throughout
the country by other musicians, and many big-time acts would ask him to
sit in when they were in the area or to join them for special shows at festival
across the country. He even played on Peter Rowan's 1997 Grammy-
nominated album *Bluegrass Boy*. Generally though, despite the odd foray into
the big-time, Munford seemed content to stay close to home and make a
steady, practical living working at Baltimore Blue Grass Inc. and playing his
regular gigs around the area.

This lack of exposure and Munford's quiet nature led to his becoming
one of the more enigmatic figures in bluegrass, with Hot Rize banjoist Pete
Wernick calling him the "gentle giant of the banjo." But Munford's quiet
nature left even some as knowledgeable as Wernick guessing how great he
truly was. "[He] is so unassuming that it took me a while to catch on to how
much he's capable of," says Wernick. It was not until years after first hearing
of this "gentle giant" that Wernick finally was able to meet and play with him
at a festival. Wernick was instantly "amazed by how deep and wide his knowledge was." He explained: "He [Munford] seemed to have a bead on every
style, so many tunes and techniques, and was eager to add to his stockpile
with a gung-ho enthusiasm that went on into the wee hours that night." While
getting to know Munford up close allowed Wernick to finally be able to appreciate the talents of the Baltimore banjo picker it also left him more baffled as
to why Munford was not better known and playing on more records. Wernick
tried to persuade Munford to go into the recording studio more. It was a
futile effort, as Munford told Wernick he was "content to be giving lessons
and being, a 'go-to guy' when somebody good came to town or someone
needed a sub."[25] Munford's longtime friend, banjo legend Trischka, was also
frustrated by the lack of attention Munford received and coined an acronym
for him, TDWR, which he says stands for Talent Deserving of Wider Recognition.[26]

A strange thing then happed one day. A few years after Baltimore Blue

Mike Munford (center) plays at the 2013 Charm City Folk and Bluegrass Festival with Chris Eldridge (right) and bandmate Frank Solivan (left), who leans in for a closer look at Munford's picking (photograph by the author).

Grass Inc. closed, Munford, who estimates that he has played over 1500 shows in the Baltimore-Washington, D.C., area, upped and joined a national touring band, Frank Solivan and Dirty Kitchen, in 2009. The move took everyone by surprise, as they had become accustomed to the homebody version of Munford, who never seemed to stray too far from the Baltimore area. Solivan, an Alaska native who had moved just outside of Washington had been creating quite a buzz with his impressive, powerhouse mandolin work since the release of his debut album, *I Am a Rambler*, in 2002. Solivan and Munford first crossed paths in 2004 when Solivan was still playing in the Country Current, the United States Navy Band. The two played together a few times, and Munford guested on Solivan's 2006 album, *Selfish Tears*. The chemistry between them was evident and Solivan asked Munford if he would like to join his band full time. Munford was a bit hesitant, but Solivan eventually persuaded him to join. Munford was drawn to Solivan's singing and songwriting, which he says is "a great vehicle for being able to play Scruggs-Crowe style and melodic style as well, which sums up my overall approach to the banjo."[27]

The move allowed Munford to reveal his seldom-seen talents to a much wider audience.

With Munford onboard, Frank Solivan and Dirty Kitchen was born, and the attention being paid to the band increased. Pete Wernick was excited and relieved to see Munford step out from the shadows. "Thank goodness he finally hooked up with an ambitious band and became increasingly noticed," he says.[28] When Solivan is asked what it is about Munford that makes him so special, he answers bluntly, "If you were to name a handful of upper-echelon players like Bela Fleck or Jens Kruger or Noam Pikelny or any of those players, they would all say, 'Oh, Mike Munford, he's pretty much a badass."[29] Unsurprisingly, as soon as Munford started touring nationally with Frank Solivan and Dirty Kitchen the accolades began pouring in and culminated in 2013 in Munford's first IBMA nomination for banjo player of the year and winning the award. It was a long-overdue but well deserved recognition of one of Baltimore's most talented sons.

Throughout the 1970s Baltimore Blue Grass Inc. and the few bluegrass-friendly bars in the surrounding area were not the only places to support this type of music in town. Blue Seas Studio in Hunt Valley, just outside the Baltimore city limits, had quietly become one of the hidden gems of the recording studio world, and over that decade would host a number of notable bluegrass recording sessions. The studio was owned by ex–Lovin' Spoonful bassist Steve Boone, who had taken it over in 1973 with the help of Little Feat's Lowell George. George had first become interested in the studio through his association and work with producer and engineer George Massenburg. Massenburg is from Baltimore and one of the most innovative and well-respected music engineers in the recording industry. Since first getting into the music business in the late sixties he has worked on over 400 albums for such luminaries as James Taylor, Billy Joel, Herbie Hancock, Lyle Lovett, Journey, and Linda Ronstandt. He also served as the engineer for Walt Hensley's groundbreaking 1969 *Pickin' on New Grass*, which owes much of its unique sonic power to Massenburg's highly innovative approach to recording.

As an electrical engineering student at Johns Hopkins University in Baltimore Massenburg became interested in parametric equalization, an advanced recording technique that allows engineers more precise control over the sounds they record. He dropped out of school as a sophomore to devote his time fully to music-engineering, recording, and the development of recording equipment. He eventually became involved in a new studio being built in Hunt Valley, Maryland. Through Massenburg's involvement this new facility became one of the premier studios in the area. Unfortunately, after only a short time it fell into financial ruin through poor management. Despite the setback, the equipment and studio that Massenburg helped build were still considered top-notch and were a valuable commodity. Recognizing its value, Boone stepped in and bought the studio, renaming it Blue Seas for his love of sailing. By the time Boone took ownership of the studio, Massenburg, who had grown frustrated with the ownership situation there, had moved away from Baltimore and on to other projects.

Through a mutual friend Boone met George and found out he was looking for a place to record Little Feat's next album. George was already familiar with Massenburg's elite skills as an engineer from work they had done a few years earlier in Los Angeles and he knew of his past association with Blue Seas Studio. Familiar with the high quality of Massenburg's work in setting up a studio, George agreed to bring Little Feat to Baltimore to work on their next album at Blue Seas. He then convinced Massenburg to return from Paris, where he had been living, to help with the recording of the album. Thus the classic Little Feat album *Feats Don't Fail Me Now* was created.

Shortly after the release of *Feats Don't Fail Me Now*, because of pressure exerted by some of the more buttoned-up, business-minded neighbors who shared a building with the studio and were not fond of a bunch of scruffy long-hair musician types lurking around, Boone moved the studio to a floating barge at Pier 4 in Baltimore's Inner Harbor. The studio continued to produce stellar work, cranking out albums by Robert Palmer, Bonnie Rait, Emmylou Harris, and Linda Ronstadt over the years. Blue Seas would prove to be a bluegrass friendly studio as well. The 1976 album *Breakfast Special*, which featured notable bluegrass stars Tony Trischka, Ken Kosek, and Andy Statman, was recorded at the famed studio. Ricky Skaggs and the Seldom Scene's Mike Auldridge both recorded at Blues Seas throughout the decade. It was through Auldridge that a young, emerging band would get their first taste of time in the studio at Blue Seas.

As the recently christened New Grass Revival, Sam Bush, Ebo Walker, Courtney Johnson, and Curtis Burch were beginning to build a name for themselves when they started in 1971. They were soon regularly traveling to the Washington area, where they became friends with the Country Gentlemen. When the Country Gentlemen hit the road for a tour, they would often ask their friends in New Grass Revival to cover their weekly spot at the Shamrock Club on M Street in downtown D.C. Through their time in D.C. Bush and New Grass Revival would also become friendly with John Duffey. Duffey had been an original member of the Country Gentlemen but had since left it and started the Seldom Scene with Mike Auldridge, Ben Eldridge, Tom Gray, and John Starling. Through Duffey, New Grass Revival met Auldridge, who was in the process of recording his first solo album, *Dobro*, at Blue Seas Studio.

Auldridge and New Grass Revival discovered they had a mutual friend in photographer Jim McGuire, who was helping to produce Auldridge's album. McGuire arranged it so that when Auldridge took a lunch break from recording one afternoon New Grass Revival could come into the studio while he was gone and work on a couple of tracks. The band's session was a blur as the band tried to get through a couple of songs in the short time they had. As was the norm at Blue Seas, Massenburg was the engineer working the board throughout the New Grass Revival session. Bush says their short session at Blue Seas was the first time the band was ever in the studio under the New Grass Revival moniker. The tapes from those sessions were never released and Bush says it is not known for sure what happened to them.[30] They were most likely lost forever Christmas Day 1977 when Blue Seas Studio sank into the Inner Harbor amidst rumors of foul play over legal and money issues. "We salvaged most of our electronic gear, but the tapes all tipped over and fell into the salt water," said studio owner Boone. "We lost all our master tapes, safeties, and backups, including stuff by Lowell George and Earth, Wind, & Fire"[31]—and most likely the first ever recordings of New Grass Revival.

Despite this setback, Bush says that New Grass Revival enjoyed the scene in Baltimore. His connection to the city had begun inadvertently a few years before when a young musician-journalist penned the first national story on Bush for a leading publication, *Bluegrass Unlimited*, in a 1969 issue. The writer's name was Alice Foster, though Foster was her married name. Her maiden name was Gerrard and she got her musical start in Baltimore along with Hazel Dickens.

Over the course of the seventies Bush and New Grass Revival began regularly playing at a place in the city called No Fish Today on Eutaw Street. "We loved playing there. It was a small shotgun kind of building and we just dug the place," says Bush. Whenever they performed there the band would usually play two or three sets, but Bush remembers one particular show in 1975 or '76 when they had an opening band which was unusual. Bush recalls the evening:

> There were five guys who came in with armed guards. They were prison inmates and they were given leave to sing. They were a gospel acapela band. They were terrific. It was very emotional. Some of their mothers were there and they probably hadn't heard them sing in a very long time. It was a really amazing thing. We were a little taken a back when we saw armed guards led these guys in, in handcuffs. They took the cuffs off while they sang. When they were done they went back to where they had come from.[32]

As the 1980s dawned, Baltimore continued to see its fortunes rise again, though not to the level the early pioneers in the city had reached. The bluegrass scene in the city seemed to awaken from its seventies slumber and started to become part of the national conversation again as its players became more involved with the dominant Washington scene. As the next generation of pickers in the city emerged, the old guard seemed to get revitalized and many of them began to start playing much more frequently.

On January 28, 1984, Baltimore and bluegrass lost one of its most unheralded pioneers when Earl Taylor suffered a heart attack and died. He had been in poor health for several years due to a stroke. He had been a lifelong smoker and had been known as a hard-drinking man back in the day. Although that was a thing of the past, years of hard living had taken their toll on him. Taylor had relocated to Cincinnati from Baltimore in the mid-sixties and would live out the rest of his life there. Throughout the latter half of that decade Taylor worked with Jimmy Martin and Flatt and Scruggs for a couple of years. He returned to his roots when he and Jim McCall teamed up again for a trio of traditional-style albums (1967's *Bluegrass Favorites* and 1971's *Bluegrass Favorites*, vol. 2, and vol. 3) that would later be rereleased on a pair of compilation albums (1997's *20 Bluegrass Favorites* and 2007's *24 Bluegrass Favorites*). The music on these albums was what writer Jon Weisberger called "stout":

> The music here isn't for the faint of heart; it's raw, and not in a mountain sense, but in an industrial one, made to appeal to the homesick tastes of migratory factory workers over the hubbub of a hard night's drinking. The album itself was thrown into the market with little regard for the niceties of music-as-art, and that's almost as true of the reissue as of the original release, which is probably why a misidentification of the supporting musicians remains uncorrected (for the record, the banjo was supplied by Vernon McIntyre Jr., not Tim Spradlin, and the bass by his father, "Boatwhistle" McIntyre, not Charlie Hoskins; the occasional fiddle most likely comes from Scotty Stoneman).[33]

Each album tested the relationship of Taylor and McCall, as long-simmering tenses would always arise each time they began working together. These tensions would finally come to a head in 1975 when Taylor took an ill-fated trip to Florida in hopes of working with McCall there. McCall had taken a job working as a staff musician at Frontierland in Disney World with Nelson Young and the Sandy Valley Boys. Taylor took his family, as well Gary Bushorn, Chris Montgomery, and Jeff Roberts, who were playing in Taylor's band at the time, to Orlando in hopes of working with McCall. Work was extremely scarce and soon the rest of Taylor's band headed back to Cincinnati where work was more plentiful. Shortly after they left, tragedy struck for Taylor and his family. Taylor's son Billy drowned in a local pond in a swimming accident. His death shattered Taylor and his wife, Ellen. McCall's son Dwight believes that Taylor blamed McCall in a way for his son's death, as Taylor had moved there to work with McCall. Dwight says that after the tragic death of Taylor's son the two families were never together in the same place again. The death of his son seemed to sap the will to make music from Taylor. As the years wore on he became gradually less active musically. He would play sporadically over the years in Cincinnati, but it was never with the same passion or ambition.

Taylor never reached the same level of fame that many of his contemporaries achieved, but he is an important and vital link between the earliest second-generation bluegrass performers whose Appalachian roots branded them as authentic and the next generation of bluegrass players whose origins were less authentic and more widely varied. Many of them had perhaps spent long nights listening to Taylor and the Stoney Mountain Boys on the Alan Lomax-released album, *Folk Songs from the Blue Grass*; or maybe they discovered him, as Jerry Garcia did, on Mike Seeger's *Mountain Music Bluegrass Style*; or perhaps they first heard of his pioneering appearance at Carnegie

A latter-day version of the Dukes of Bluegrass play at famed Lucketts Schoolhouse in Leesburg, Virginia, in 1984 (from left): Jon Glik, Russ Hooper, Walt Hensley, and Jim McCall (courtesy Russ Hooper).

Hall. Taylor was an influential second-generation bluegrass figure who never received the attention he was due. Tom Ewing, who played with Taylor in the seventies and later would join Bill Monroe's band, thinks that this lack of attention was fine by Taylor. "I'm not sure Earl wanted 'the big time,'" says Ewing. "He seemed content to play the bars and then go home every night." Ewing adds that Taylor was most proud of "having worked with 'the bigs': Flatt & Scruggs and Jimmy Martin, recording with the Stanleys, and of securing his major label success [with Capitol Records]."[34]

A few months after Taylor's death, Russ Hooper received a phone call. As soon as he answered he recognized the voice of Walt Hensley on the line. Hensley wasted no time and asked Hooper if he would like to rejoin the Dukes of Bluegrass. The two men had not spoken since Hensley had left Hooper stranded without a band at a North Carolina bluegrass festival ten years before. Hooper, who still felt the sting of Hensley's no-show a decade earlier, reminded him that he must have a short memory, as Hooper told Hensley he would never work with him again. Despite Hooper's reluctance to speak with him, Hensley's affable nature and the deep friendship the two had shared for so long eventually won Hooper over and he agreed to join the Dukes of Bluegrass. It also helped that Hensley swore "up and down it would never happen again" to Hooper.[35]

Hensley's Dukes of Bluegrass were an all-star roster of Baltimore talent at the time. In addition to Hooper the band featured Frankie Short on mandolin, Jim McCall on guitar, and a rotating trio of fiddlers in Warren Blair, Curt Cody, and Jon Glik. The bass spot was in constant flux, but for a while it was held down by Jerry McCoury. Soon after Hooper joined the Dukes, Short, whose health had been in decline, died.

Short had been an integral part of the Baltimore scene since he first moved there in 1958 from his home in West Virginia. He was one of the most admired lead singers around and could play just about anything with strings. Over the years, he played with seemingly every band of renown from Baltimore, though he himself never saw much recognition from outside the area. Short's musical legacy has been carried on by his son Frankie Short, Jr., who still plays in a Baltimore-based band with the son of another longtime Baltimore bluegrass picker, Warren Blair. Blair's father was famed local fiddler Kimball Blair, who, like Frankie Short, Sr., had been a mainstay of the Baltimore bluegrass community since the fifties.

With the loss of Short, Hensley needed to find a replacement mandolin player for the Dukes. McCall's sixteen-year-old son, Dwight, had recently begun playing the mandolin. Despite his young age and lack of experience, Dwight impressed his seasoned Dad with not only his playing, but also his singing. McCall had Dwight try out for Hensley, who agreed he was perfect for the band. Despite his impressive musical skills, in the company of such veteran musicians like his dad, Hensley, Hooper, and Glik, young Dwight still had a lot to learn. On his first few shows with the band Hooper remembers that Dwight did not "do much more than just chop rhythm."[36] For the teenaged Dwight it was an eye-opening experience, as he had long admired the musicians he was now playing with. He learned from his veteran bandmates quickly and was soon more than able to hold his own. As his ability and ambition grew he left the Dukes of Bluegrass and formed his own band, Union Springs. He joined Charlie Waller and the Country Gentlemen in 1992. He played with Waller for four years, during which time he began to develop a reputation as one of the finest young mandolin pickers in bluegrass. This led to an invitation to join legendary J.D. Crowe's band, New South, in 1996, and allowed him to carry the torch of Baltimore bluegrass to the rest of the country. He stayed with Crowe and New South until Crowe retired in 2012. After Crowe's retirement, Dwight, along with other members of New South, formed their own band, American Drive.

No matter how far Dwight's musical career has taken him away from Baltimore he always remembers those musicians he first encountered and idolized there as a youngster. "To this day I talk of the musicians that were and still are in the Baltimore area and hold them up on a pedestal no matter how much they drank or what chances they missed," he says, "because the one thing they all had was talent."[37]

10

"Bluegrass with funky Americana undertones"

Recommended Listening: At the start of the 21st century there was a resurgence of roots-based, bluegrass-tinged music in Baltimore. This resurgence was best exemplified by a trio of albums, Smooth Kentucky's 2004 self-titled release, Caleb Stine's 2008 album, *I'll Head West Again*, and the Bridge's 2011 album, *National Bohemian*. All three albums are the sound of Baltimore pushing its bluegrass roots forward in new sonic directions while still singing with the mountain soul from which the music was birthed.

On a cold February night in 2012, five musicians are huddled onto the small stage in the back corner of a bar on Charles Street in downtown Baltimore. There is a joyous quality to the band's playing, reflected by the crowd wedged in between the tables and bar stools. The dangerous, violent tension so pervasive from the patrons at the Chapel Café forty years earlier when Del McCoury and Jack Cooke were playing there is nonexistent this night. It has been replaced by an almost party-like atmosphere at the Charles Street bar, Mick O'Sheas. The band onstage has been together for years, and unlike their predecessors some of the musicians on stage have already established themselves on a national level. The band this evening, Smooth Kentucky, is a collection of longtime friends who have played together for years in a number of musical guises. Smooth Kentucky's music straddles a divide that has Bill Monroe and Townes Van Zandt on one side and Jerry Garcia and Bob Dylan on the other. Their sound is a trip through the spirit of American music. They have a bluegrass soul but play with a rock 'n' roll heart. The crowd packed into Mick O'Sheas has clearly been with the band and musicians for years, as they sing along, shout out friendly requests, and banter with the band throughout the night. When the quiet singer on the right of the stage in the baseball cap and glasses sings the line "Baltimore city, one horse town," from their song "Get Yourself in Line," there is a definite roar of approval of hometown pride from the crowd.

Much like the times at the Chapel Café when Del and Jerry McCoury, Jack Cooke, Kimball Blair, and a cast of many others were onstage, the band playing tonight represent some of the best talent in Baltimore. The reed-thin, youthful-looking fiddler has been mesmerizing audiences for over half his life since being attracted to bluegrass as a musically precious six-year-old when a friend's father introduced him to the fiddle. When he lays into yet another tasty solo while on stage at Mick O'Sheas his baby-face appearance belies the wealth of experience and the overflowing fountain of skill evident with each pull of the bow across his fiddle's strings. Much like the youthful-looking fiddler, the bearded guitarist standing to his left plays with an air of wizened maturity that hides his age. He sings with an old-man soul voice that has been compared to the impassioned wail of Warren Haynes and the southern-fried, gravely, timbre of Little Feat's Lowell George. Playing local bars since he was in high school, the bearded guitarist has long been a part of the city's musical fabric. The fiddler and guitarist are quite simply some of Baltimore's most talented musicians in the first decade of the 21st century. They first met when the fiddler joined Smooth Kentucky, but their musical partnership runs much deeper than that now.

Smooth Kentucky was formed when the quiet singer in the hat and

Smooth Kentucky plays at Mick O'Sheas, January 7, 2011 (from left): Dave Frieman, Tim Pruitt, Cris Jacobs, Patrick McAvinue, and Ed Hough (photograph by Jordan August).

glasses, Ed Hough, and the bearded guitarist, his longtime friend Cris Jacobs, found the band's name on the back of a whiskey bottle when they put the band together in 2003 to play as part of the Baltimore Brewing Company's regular Friday night bluegrass happy hour. The two have been playing together since Jacobs was in high school and they have developed a musical language that highlights their brotherly harmonies. They first came together when Hough answered a musician wanted ad hanging in the Gordon Miller Music Store on Joppa Road in Towson in the summer of 1994. The ad featured a badly drawn Grateful Dead logo that read, "Drummer wanted, Deadhead preferred" and had been placed by sixteen-year-old Jacobs, who was putting together his first band with some high school friends. Twenty-four-year-old Hough answered the ad and showed up for rehearsal, "in his VW bus with hair down to his ass."[1] Hough was initially hesitant at the youth and inexperience of his potential bandmates but was awed by the unlimited potential he saw in Jacobs' exuberant guitar playing. Hough stuck around and a deep musical partnership, which is nearing twenty years, was forged between Jacobs and him.

When Hough and Jacobs were putting together a lineup for their first shows as Smooth Kentucky they brought in another friend, mandolinist BJ Lazarus. At one of their first gigs, bassist Dave Frieman dropped off his card and was added to the band. They played as a four-piece for a couple of years but wanted to augment their sound and decided to add a fiddler. While playing on a local radio show on WTMD they announced they were looking for a fiddler and received a phone call from the youthful-looking fiddler's mom. The fiddler's mom said she had heard them on the radio and told them her son, Patrick McAvinue, was a fiddler looking for a band. Hough and Jacobs were initially skeptical of the fifteen-year-old McAvinue's age, but like Hough a decade earlier, they put their skepticism aside. McAvinue, who was still in the 10th grade, had to be driven to the audition by his mom as he was not old enough to drive yet. The older musicians were worried as McAvinue walked into their rehearsal room that his youth might be a hindrance, both musically and where he would be allowed to play professionally. Any fears of his age quickly evaporated. "He walked in and was baby faced and we were hesitant, but all I did was hear him tune up and I was done," says Hough. "That was it. He was that good."[2] Jacobs was running late to rehearsal and heard McAvinue start playing through the window as he walked up and remembers thinking, *Holy shit, this kid can play!*[3] McAvinue blasted through a couple of tunes with his soon-to-be bandmates and fit in immediately. McAvinue recognized the tight musical chemistry that existed between Hough and Jacobs and says he is "thankful that I can weave myself into their creativity. It's such a beautiful thing."[4] Jacobs and Hough approached McAvinue's parents and asked if they would have a problem with their young son playing in the bars where they played many of their shows. McAvinue's parents quashed any concerns about his age, as they said he had already been traveling from Maine to Florida to play music professionally for the past few years.

As a child, McAvinue was introduced to the fiddle by a family friend and remembers "thinking as a six-year-old, this is what I want to do."[5] He proved to be a prodigy on the instrument, mastering many different styles of the fiddle at a young age, which led him to be named the Delaware state fiddle champion three straight years, from 2003 to 2005. It was during this time, in 2004, that he joined Smooth Kentucky. His profile exploded from there and he was soon recording and sharing the stage with many of the biggest names in bluegrass, including Marty Stuart, J.D. Crowe, Bobby Osborne, and Del McCoury. For a short time he also played in a Baltimore band featuring Mike Munford. McAvinue credits his brief time working with Munford as being a huge learning experience in his growth as a musician. In 2005 McAvinue began to work with banjo player Chris Warner, who would prove instrumental in helping the young fiddler land his next big opportunity when he arranged an audition for McAvinue to try out for ex–Sunny Mountain Boy Audie Blaylock's band Redline. At his audition, the still teenaged McAvinue was told by Blaylock to play "Fire on the Mountain" as fast as he could. Like he had with Hough and Jacobs the previous year, McAvinue wowed the older musicians with his prodigious skills. Blaylock asked him to join on the spot. The exposure McAvinue gained from joining Audie Blaylock and Redline saw more validation for his immense talents, as he was named a candidate for IBMA fiddler of the year in 2009, 2010, 2012, and 2014. At an age when many of his musical peers are just trying to figure things out, McAvinue is already one of the most inspiring young talents in bluegrass, with a long, impressive resume. His bandmate Blaylock calls him "the most inventive fiddler in bluegrass today."[6]

In Baltimore, a town nicknamed Small-timore by locals, it is not surprising that guitarist Jacobs' roots run deep and intertwine with the city's long musical history. As a child, Jacobs remembers hearing stories from his bluegrass-loving grandfather about Baltimore and Washington's rich bluegrass traditions. Jacobs' grandfather owned a clothing store and had firsthand access to one of the top players in the area; one of his employees was bluegrass heavyweight Bill Harrell. As a seventeen-year-old, Jacobs would cross paths with one of Baltimore's legendary sons, Mike Munford, when he and a friend first visited Baltimore Blue Grass Inc. Jacobs was into the banjo at the time

Patrick McAvinue (left) and Cris Jacobs (center) play at the 2014 Charm City Folk and Bluegrass Festival. They are joined by McAvinue's bandmate Audie Blaylock (right) (photograph by the author).

and took one lesson at the store. Years later he realized it was Munford who had given him his one and only banjo lesson. While his interest in the banjo waned, Jacobs began to focus all his energy on guitar, soon purchasing his first Martin guitar at the fabled Baltimore store, where he started "going all the time to listen to records."[7]

After graduating from the University of Massachusetts, Jacobs returned to Baltimore, where he ran into an old friend at a house party where guitarist David Grier (son of famed Baltimore banjo player Lamar Grier) was playing. The friend, Kenny Liner, like Jacobs, had just returned to Baltimore from Hawaii, where he had been living. Liner had recently started playing the mandolin and the two budding musicians, inspired by the intimate set they had just seen from world-class guitarist Grier, went back to Liner's house to "pick some tunes for a few hours."[8] The pair was soon getting together frequently to play and pick and from those sessions between two old friends a brand new band, the Bridge, was born. While the music the Bridge made, with its hints of New Orleans funk and Grateful Dead–inspired improvisation was more akin to the Americana soul of the Band or the roots-rock of Little Feat, Jacobs readily admits, "If it wasn't for bluegrass there would have been no Bridge."[9] After forming in 2001 the Bridge became a touring machine, criss-crossing the country many times over the years, playing at some of the biggest festivals each year, including Bonnaroo, All Good, Jam Cruise, and Wakarusa during their ten-year run.

Over the course of their decade together their brand of American roots music would find them sharing the stage with a diverse roster of musicians including Mike Gordon from Phish, Russell Batiste from the Funky Meters, and Steve Berlin of Los Lobos (who would produce their final album, *National Bohemian*, in 2011). One of the true shames and mysteries is how a band that seemingly had everything going in its favor—creativity, original songwriting, unmatched musicianship, a wholly unique sound, a passionate fan base, and the support of many famous musician friends—could not find a larger audience across the country, which forced the band to call it quits in 2011. After the end of the Bridge, Jacobs began to establish himself as a solo artist and one of the most versatile guitarists around, easily sharing the stage with a diverse list of musicians such as Steve Winwood, Anders Osborne, Greensky Bluegrass, Sturgill Simpson, and Eric Lindell. He also became an in-demand

Bluestone plays the Carroll Arts Theater in 2012 (from left): Jon Glik, Russ Hooper, Heath Laird, Dick Laird, Carroll Swam, and Tom Neal (courtesy Russ Hooper).

studio guitarist, recording with Deanna Bogart, Ivan Neville, John Ginty, and Arty Hill, among others.

As McAvinue and Jacobs felt the tug of their other musical commitments, Smooth Kentucky became more of a local phenomenon. They settled into playing locally, at regional festivals and opening for national acts on the way through Baltimore. Despite the local phenomenon tag, Smooth Kentucky continued to see some of the region's most talented players file through its ranks, including the late Dave Giegerich on Dobro and guitarists Jordan Tice and Tim Pruitt. The band would release two well-received albums, 2004's *Smooth Kentucky* and 2009's *A Few More Miles*, which featured Mike Munford and was an album *Bluegrass Unlimited* called "a good, solid production from a young band making their mark in the Mid-Atlantic."[10] *Honest Tune* magazine says both albums "explore the backwoods and the front porch ... all the while soothing your soul with the sounds of a tall glass of whiskey in your hand and the sun shining in your face."[11] Smooth Kentucky's music is what Hough refers to as "bluegrass with funky Americana undertones."[12]

As younger bands and artists like Smooth Kentucky, the Bridge, and Caleb Stine push that rootsy, bluegrass-tinged Baltimore sound forward, Russ Hooper and Bluestone have kept the flame of the past burning with a lineup whose origins stretch back to the earliest days of bluegrass in Baltimore. In addition to Hooper, Bluestone features some of the pioneering practitioners of bluegrass in that city. Guitarist Carroll Swam has been an integral part on the Baltimore scene since the sixties and would serve as a mentor to a young fiddle prodigy named Patrick McAvinue. Banjo picker Tom Neal played bass on Del McCoury's first album and later filled in on banjo for Don Reno in the Tennessee Cut-Ups. Mandolinist Dick Laird was a high school friend of Chris Warner who inspired him to start playing bluegrass.

Fiddler Jon Glik, better known as "Baltimore Johnny," has been a part of the bluegrass fabric in Baltimore since the early seventies. Laird's sons Heath, on bass, and Jeff, on guitar, complete the Bluestone lineup. For a short time while Glik battled health problems Bluestone recruited McAvinue to fill in on fiddle. With a lineup whose lineage includes some of the pioneering musicians of hillbilly music in Baltimore it is not surprising the music they make seems unchanged from the time a handful of like-minded musicians first gathered at Bob Baker's house on Calvert Street to spend many a long night filling the air with the sounds of their sweet picking. As the sound of bluegrass evolves and changes, to the consternation of some, Bluestone forges on like a band of modern-day missionaries of mountain music. Hooper proudly says the music Bluestone plays is still true to its roots: "We are doing what we consider traditional—Flatt and Scruggs and stuff like that. Other people, if you went up and asked them what it is we play, would probably say it is hard-driving bluegrass."[13] In 2014 Bluestone entered the studio to record their fourth album, *What Goes On*. It is an album Hooper says continues to stay true to the hillbilly and bluegrass music he first heard as a young man when he came to Baltimore.

While Bluestone, like many other musicians and bands from their generation, continues to play a more traditional style, the next generation of musicians in the city have created their own scene, one not as beholden to the sounds and styles that came before. This new generation are just as enamored of the first generation of bluegrass musicians as their musical forefathers in the city were, but they are more than willing to push that sound in new directions. The new crop of pickers was exposed to and interested in many different styles and genres of music and would combine and incorporate all of them together. Much like the musicians in the seventies who identified more with a progressive or newgrass style, the latest incarnation of pickers in Baltimore (while serious about their bluegrass) are more closely associated with a roots-based sound that for many was born from the improvisational approach and vast repertoire of the Grateful Dead, a repertoire that dipped freely into the deep well of the songs that Jerry Garcia and Sandy Rothman taped on their cross-country road trip in 1964 to find bluegrass music at its roots.

The importance and impact of the Grateful Dead (and to a lesser degree Phish) on the introduction of new fans to bluegrass cannot be overstated. Many fans from this new younger generation in the eighties and nineties first discovered bluegrass when they heard the Grateful Dead play an old traditional number like "Dark Hollow," "Deep Elm Blues," or "Sitting on Top of the World." Or perhaps they were first exposed to it via Garcia and David Grisman's string-band super group, Old and In the Way, which featured bluegrass heavyweights Vassar Clements on fiddle and Peter Rowan on guitar. Athens, Georgia, banjo picker "the Reverend" Jeffrey Mosier had been deeply into bluegrass but was ignorant of the rock world as a young man growing up in the eighties until he encountered the Grateful Dead. "I saw half a Grateful Dead show in 1989 or 90, and I just got it," he says. "Peter Rowan and Vassar Clements I had known about, but Jerry Garcia I had no idea, then I heard Old and In the Way and I got the connection."[14]

Discovering the connection between the bluegrass he had listened to and the more popular rock sound he was starting to be exposed to proved to be a life-changing event for Mosier. He would bring his traditional bluegrass background and banjo to the rock and jam-band world when he rose to fame after joining the experimental outfit Aquarium Rescue Unit in the late eighties. He would later help teach a young jam band from Vermont how to play bluegrass. Mosier first encountered this young band at a show, in his hometown of Athens, which, he remembers, "was loud and they were jumping up and down on trampolines."[15] The band on the trampolines was named Phish and they would invite Mosier on the road with them. He taught them how to play bluegrass music, which they began regularly incorporating into their sets. It was during this time that Phish also discovered the music of Del McCoury through a tape passed on to them by Mosier's Aquarium Rescue Unit bandmate Matt Mundy. "One day, sometime around '92 he [Mundy] gave me a record and it was *Blue Side of Town*, Del McCoury," remembers Phish guitarist Trey Anastasio. "That became the road music in our van with Phish. I must have listened to that record fifty million times. You know, 'Queen Anne's Lace' and 'Beauty of My Dreams' and all those great songs."[16] Phish would help introduce a brand-new audience to the golden voice of Del McCoury when they invited him to play at their 1999 summer festival in Oswego, New York, in front of 80,000 fans.

Kagey Parrish, one-half of the folk-duo Honey Dewdrops, discovered

(From left): Anders Beck, Patrick McAvinue, and Cris Jacobs play together at the 2nd Annual Charm City Folk and Bluegrass Festival in 2014 (photograph by the author).

bluegrass like many others his age through the wide-ranging influence of the Grateful Dead. "We came into that music through the Grateful Dead. Finding out about the various offshoots they did—jug bands and bluegrass bands, Jerry Garcia's work with David Grisman—and then branching out from there to Bill Monroe and older stuff from him. We had an interest in the Grateful Dead and realized they had an interest in doing more than just electric stuff. Thank God for them! Otherwise I don't know when we would have discovered it."[17] The Honey Dewdrops, originally from southern Virginia, have developed a close friendship with Baltimore's Caleb Stine and have become a ubiquitous presence at Stine's annual Around the Mountain acoustic roots shows and other events in the city. Parrish and bandmate Laura Wortman also played on Stine's 2014 album, *Maybe God Is Lonely Too*.

Cris Jacobs gives voice to this next generation of pickers who have discovered bluegrass through nontraditional avenues such as the Grateful Dead and Phish, and who have decided to incorporate that bluegrass sound into the other strains of music they were playing: "I have never considered myself a bluegrass purist. I don't feel qualified to say that. I feel like it is one of those things you have to do full-on. I feel like there was a period I could have really gone strictly for playing bluegrass and been a traditionalist about it and not playing electric guitar and I thought about doing that, but I thought I would make bluegrass more one of the various vocabularies I work with and genres that I explore."[18] Anders Beck, Dobro player from Greensky Bluegrass, has shared the stage with Jacobs over the years and they toured together and played in the Everyman Orchestra in 2014. He recognizes Jacobs' ability to infuse a diverse palate of sounds into whatever he does, resulting in an uncommonly unique style. "Cris is one of my favorite musicians and also one of my favorite kind of musicians. He bends genres and has soaked up all of his eclectic influences to create his own sound," explains Beck. "The next crop of great bluegrass musicians studied bluegrass and can play fiddle tunes for days, but they also studied Trey Anastasio and Jerry Garcia and Slash. Cris is from this school and to my ear he is one of the best, most creative players out there."[19]

In 2013 a pair of men in Baltimore sought to reignite the connection between the old and the new, to remind the next generation of the importance of bluegrass in Baltimore and to show the larger bluegrass community the music was still alive and well in the city. That idea was born from summer afternoons when two friends would "pick on the porch, goof off, and sip bourbon" in their neighborhood of Hampden in downtown Baltimore. Jordan August and Phil Chorney, with the support of their local community, who enjoyed what they were doing on their porch, decided to start the Charm City Folk and Bluegrass Festival.

Their neighborhood of Hampden has long been friendly to local artists and musicians and is close to the location of some of the original hillbilly ghettos in Baltimore. Many of the musicians who inspired August and Chorney live in Hampden and the surrounding area. The two have deep connections to the close-knit musical community in Baltimore. August is one of the leading live-music photographers in the area and a singer/songwriter. He is also partners with Chorney in the Baltimore Management Agency, which helps oversee the careers of a number of local musicians. With their deep love of the city they call home, August and Chorney wished to "bring the bluegrass back to Baltimore city,"[20] focusing on the music being made there. With a lineup focused on local talent and topped by headliners Tim O'Brien and Tony Trischka, the inaugural Charm City Folk and Bluegrass Festival did just that.

The impressive local talent that filled the day, including Caleb Stine, Cris Jacobs, Letitia VanSant, Chester River Runoff, and Feinwood, represented some of the best bands in Baltimore and was a showcase for many of

No act at the inaugural Charm City Folk and Bluegrass Festival better represented both the past and present of Baltimore's bluegrass community than the all-star band Cris Jacobs assembled for the day (from left): Patrick McAvinue, Ed Hough, Cris Jacobs, Mike Munford, and Jake Leckie (photograph by the author).

The second Charm City Folk and Bluegrass Festival nearly tripled in size from its first year when it moved to the picturesque setting of Druid Hill Park in 2014 (photograph by the author).

those who are on the verge of much bigger days and more recognition. The collection of local talent also helped signal the resurgence of Baltimore's roots, folk, and bluegrass scene as an important, vital community. Stine in particular has been singled out for his important contributions to not only keeping alive the musical tradition started years before, but for his highly intense songwriting, which is at times very Baltimore-centric in its themes. It is a style of writing that Charm City Festival founder Chorney refers to as "reverberant."[21] Jacobs calls Stine an "important link in the chain" in the history of Baltimore, someone who "gets what roots music is all about."[22] As with any musical scene on the cusp of bigger days there is a special feeling that permeates the air. McAvinue, who despite the lengthy amount of time spent away from the city while on the road with Audie Blaylock and Redline, can still sense what is happening in his hometown. "The scene is growing. It is really on the brink of something," he says. "It makes me proud to be part of this scene. It is a cool time. I feel for a long time not much was happening and people had migrated away from it."[23]

Charm City Folk and Bluegrass Festival founders, Phil Chorney (left) and Jordan August (right), along with Kenny Liner, thank the crowd at the second annual event in 2014 (photograph by the author).

No act at the inaugural festival better represented both the past and present of Baltimore's bluegrass community than the all-star band Jacobs assembled for the day. Comprising Jacobs, his Smooth Kentucky bandmates McAvinue and Ed Hough, jazz bass wizard Jake Leckie, and Mike Munford on banjo, their set was an emotional highlight of the day for both fan and performer. The pairing of Jacobs and McAvinue along with Munford was a truly special moment in the long history of bluegrass in the city, as it brought the brightest talents from two different generations together onstage for the first time. For Jacobs the chance to play with Munford along with McAvinue, Hough, and Leckie was a dream lineup. "In my mind I thought, I want to put together a band of the best players I can." He had special praise for Munford: "He played with Tony Rice and Peter Rowan. Hearing him play the banjo like that and thinking he is just a local guy, it is pretty unbelievable. To me he is just like Bela Fleck."[24]

The overwhelming success of the sold-out-in-advance festival surprised August and Chorney. "The festival did much better than we anticipated," said

August, "and the response from the attendees and local business and community members made it really easy to continue and start planning the next one in 2014."[25] The sold-out festival was a far cry from the polarizing days when people either hated bluegrass or loved it, with those who loved it most likely being too embarrassed to admit it. In those long-gone days Baltimore bluegrass icon and radio DJ Ray Davis remembered how folks would turn down the radios in their cars at stoplights so people would not know they were listening to bluegrass. Jacobs happily proclaimed, "What the Charm City Fest did was fantastic. It brought everybody together and showed you how many people around town are into bluegrass and how many people are still good at playing it."[26] The Charm City Folk and Bluegrass Festival showed that while much has changed in Baltimore over the last fifty years, on some levels things are still very much the same. Although not every picker in the city has roots that run back to Appalachia, the Charm City Folk and Bluegrass Festival proved that bluegrass in Baltimore in the 21st century is alive and well.

The second edition of the Charm City Folk and Bluegrass Festival continued to exhibit this as it almost tripled in size from its first year and moved from the cozy confines on the grounds of the Union Craft Brewery to the gorgeous setting of Druid Hill Park. The move also unintentionally served to tighten the ties to the past, as Druid Hill Park was the same location where, forty-five years earlier, Walt Hensley posed for his iconic cover shot in his immaculate suit and perfectly coifed hair for his 1969 album, *Pickin' on New Grass*. For its third year in 2015, the Charm City Folk and Bluegrass Festival again returned to Druid Hill Park and again featured a lineup that reflected the city's strong ties to not only bluegrass' glory days but also its place in modern bluegrass. The addition of headliners the Travelin' McCourys speaks to both of these ideals, as the band features the two sons of Del McCoury, Rob on banjo and Ronnie on mandolin, who both spent time in the Baltimore region with their dad. With a lineup that also included such heavyweight acts as the Seldom Scene and Frank Solivan & Dirty Kitchen the Charm City Folk and Bluegrass Festival has continued to develop its reputation as one of the premiere bluegrass festivals on the East Coast.

The runaway success has emboldened festival founders August and Chorney. Recognizing the special history of the city, the pair hope to not only enlighten the festival patrons as to Baltimore's history, but also to create a destination event. "I want to turn this event into a weekend long, all day, and late-night experience that the whole region and country want to be part of," says August. "I want to make our community of bluegrass and folk music unique and desirable to travel to."[27] He cites New Orleans' Jazz and Heritage Festival and Philadelphia's Folk Festival as examples of what Chorney and he hope to achieve.

The success of the Charm City Festival perfectly encapsulates the dichotomy that is Baltimore in 2014. At the same time as the Charm City Festival has begun to draw national attention to Baltimore for its thriving folk and bluegrass scene, the city still is experiencing an exploding crime and murder rate that ranks among the worst in the United States. This juxtaposition that defines Baltimore is described by songwriter Stine: "I don't think there are too many major cities in America that are this interesting and alive right now. We're dealing with huge problems, but also experiencing a multitude of rebirths." This juxtaposition in a city Stine calls "vibrant, passionate, and troubled" inspires him, as he sings of these problems and rebirths in many of his songs.[28]

Baltimore's legacy was brought to the forefront a few months after Charm City Folk and Bluegrass Festival. While Del McCoury has moved well beyond the dingy downtown bars of Baltimore he once played so regularly,

Entering its third decade, the Del McCoury Band is at the top of its game. The band plays at the 2013 Delfest in Cumberland, Maryland (from left): Ronnie McCoury, Jason Carter, Rob McCoury, Alan Bartram, and Del McCoury (photograph by the author).

it is clear that his time in Charm City left a lasting impression on him as demonstrated by the release of his 2013 album, *The Streets of Baltimore*. Starting with the title track, the often-covered Tompall Glaser and Harlan Howard song "Streets of Baltimore," the album is a reflective look back for Del; the track listing of the album is populated with a number of country songs that would have been a standard part of many bluegrass band's set-lists in Baltimore in the late fifties and early sixties. It is an album that found Del looking

Russ Hooper (left) visits with his longtime friend and bandmate Walt Hensley at Hensley's home in 2012 (courtesy Russ Hooper).

back on his past and reflecting on where he got his start. In January of 2014, *Streets of Baltimore* won the Grammy for best bluegrass album. It was Del's second such honor following his win in 2006 for *The Company We Keep*. His second win helped further cement his status as one of the truly iconic figures in bluegrass. "When you look at what Del and his band have done for bluegrass, it's hard to top their contribution. By now it's monumental," says Hot Rize's banjoist, Pete Wernick. "Of course he played with great musicians all along, but once the band had [sons] Ronnie and Rob in it, and Jason [Carter], and Alan [Bartram], there was a powerful entity that had the talent and authority to represent bluegrass far and wide. And now that band is in its third decade. That's a long time, longer than the whole Flatt & Scruggs band's career. It's especially impressive to hear how they stay at the top of their game even with Del past seventy, still leading the way."[29] A song cowritten by bassist Bartram and Jon Weisberger that debuted in 2014 called "The Old Boy Is Still in the Game" perfectly summed up Wernick's feelings about Del as it sang of the grey-haired crooner's immeasurable importance to bluegrass.

A few short months after the release of *Streets of Baltimore*, and almost exactly two months before the album won its Grammy, Baltimore lost one of its most legendary bluegrass sons. On November 25, 2013, Walt Hensley, the Banjo Baron of Baltimore, lost his long battle with cancer and passed away. The highest compliment a musician can receive is the respect of fellow musicians, and upon his death Hensley received the upmost respect from those musicians as accolades poured in. Longtime Hensley fan Sandy Rothman says, "He was my hero ever since I was a kid as a banjo player. He was the most important unheralded banjo player."[30]

James Reams played with Hensley near the end of the legendary banjo player's long career. Reams' excitement and enthusiasm to work with his lifelong idol had stirred some of the best playing ever from Hensley and the resulting 2002 album, *The Barons of Bluegrass,* was an unqualified success, being nominated by the IBMA for the 2002 recorded event of the year. His short time playing with Hensley had a lifelong impact on Reams. "Working with and knowing Walter Hensley was one of the sweetest times of my life. He opened my eyes to so much. One minute, a story of a wayward trip with Charlie Moore, the next a tale of Pee Wee Lambert's generosity. Having Walter as a mentor, friend and bandmate was history and musical ecstasy all in the same package," says Reams. He memorably summed up the enigma that was Hensley's long, at times anonymous, career of excellence: "Mention his name to someone and you may get a blank stare, but anyone who ever heard him play, never forgot it."[31]

Hensley was a humble man who cared more about playing music than promoting it, so the gushing accolades he received from friends and music peers were the ultimate sign of respect for the shy banjo picker. The music he made over the course of his lifetime did what music was supposed to do. It inspired. It made the day's troubles seem a little less overwhelming. It was some of the most creative, explosive, traditional-style bluegrass ever picked on a banjo. It was quite simply hard drivin'.

Baltimore was a proving ground, a place for many young bluegrass musicians to apprentice. It was similar to many other midwestern cities that supported their own bluegrass scenes. But Baltimore separated itself from those other cities with its unmatched talent—talent that, unfortunately, was not always well known. "Man, all of the great music that has been played in the Baltimore area is amazing when you think about it," says Dwight McCall. "I grew up around Walter Hensley, Warren Blair, Jon Glik, Danny Paisley, Frankie Short, and Russ Hooper and actually got the chance to play with them. I got to see Buzz Busby, Del, Ronnie, and Rob McCoury, Porter Church, Don Stover, Bill Sage, Paul Silvius, James King, Chubby Wise, and more that I can't remember. And I got to sit in with my Dad and Walt. They were very respected by their peers and I witnessed all of it. I am really lucky to have seen all of the talented people that I got to see in such a short time."[32]

That was what it was all about—the talented musicians who played their hearts out for a couple of bucks at some of the worst dive bars Baltimore has ever known and the folks who regularly packed those places to see them play. From the earliest days of Russ Hooper and Dickie Rittler picking away at Fred Walker's Music Store; the first bluegrass band of Bob Baker, Mike Seeger, and Hazel Dickens playing for tips at the Blue Jay; the rough-and-tumble times that Earl Taylor, Walt Hensley, and the Stoney Mountain Boys witnessed from the stage at the 79 Club; the discovery of Del McCoury at the dingy joint that was the Chapel Café; the picking sessions led by Steve Cunningham and Mike Munford that spilled onto the sidewalk out in front of Baltimore Blue Grass Inc.; the celebration of the music that continues at the Charm City Folk and Bluegrass Festival, to the next generation of musicians who are just starting and who spend many a long night playing at the 8x10 Club or 1919 on Fleet Street or some other small corner bar like musicians have for years, it has always been about just the music. Whether played for a handful of drunks at the Stonewall Inn, a gathering of like-minded folkies in Alyse Taubman's living room, or in front of a packed house at Carnegie Hall, it was the hard-driving spirit fostered in Baltimore that set the music apart from that of other cities. Jerry McCoury, who has been part of the music made in the city for over fifty years and seen all the city has to offer, sums it up simply: "At the time, I just couldn't figure out why the people loved us so much. Looking back I guess it was 'cause the music was pretty good."[33]

Chapter Notes

Introduction

1. Carroll Swam, interview with author, February 2, 2012.

2. Jerry McCoury, interview with author, June 6, 2012.

3. Ben Windham, "'Legend' Pays Tribute to Bill Monroe," *Tuscaloosa News*, February 21, 2003.

4. Neil V. Rosenberg, *Bluegrass: A History* (Urbana: University of Illinois Press, 1985), 28.

5. Alan Lomax, "Bluegrass Background: Folk Music with Overdrive," *Esquire*, October 1959.

6. Levon Helm with Stephen Davis, *This Wheel's on Fire* (Chicago: Chicago Review Press, 1993), 19–20.

7. Michael Streissguth, *Outlaw: Walyon, Willie, Kris, and the Renegades of Nashville* (New York: HarperCollins, 2013), 30–31.

8. Jerry McCoury, June 6, 2012.

9. Neil Rosenberg and Charles K. Wolfe, *The Music of Bill Monroe* (Urbana: University of Illinois Press, 2007), 149.

10. Del McCoury, interview with author, January 29, 2011.

11. Vince Gill [Liner Notes], *Celebrating 50 Years of Del McCoury*, McCoury Music, 2009.

12. Chris Pandolfi, "Bluegrass Manifesto," http://chrispandolfi.com/ (accessed October 17, 2013).

13. Grant Alden and Peter Blackstock, eds., "Hazel Dickens," *The Best of No Depression: Writing About American Music* (Austin: University of Texas Press, 2005), 204.

14. Geoffrey Himes, "From the Hills: How Mid-Century Migrants from the Mountains Brought Bluegrass—and More—to Baltimore," *Baltimore City Paper*, January 12, 2000, http://www.citypaper.com/news/story.asp?id=3636 (accessed June 7, 2012).

15. Bill Friskics-Warren, "Hazel Dickens, Folk Singer, Dies at 75," *New York Times*, April 22, 2011.

16. Himes, "From the Hills."

17. Del McCoury, January 29, 2011.

18. Himes, "From the Hills."

19. Tina Aridas [Liner Notes], *James Reams & Walter Hensley: The Barons of Bluegrass*, Copper Creek Records, 2002.

20. Sam Bush, interview with author, August 24, 2012.

21. James Reams, email with author, September 5, 2012.

22. Dwight McCall, email with author, October 31, 2012.

23. Del McCoury, January 29, 2011.

24. Russ Hooper, interview with author, June 24, 2013.

25. Chris Warner, interview with author, April 10, 2013.

26. Tom Ewing, email with author, September 24, 2012.

27. Alice Gerrard, interview with author, April 2, 2012.

28. Artie Werner, email with author, March 27, 2012.

Chapter 1

1. Bill Malone and Hazel Dickens, *Working Girl Blues: The Life and Music of Hazel Dickens* (Urbana: University of Illinois Press, 2008), 36.

2. *Ibid.*

3. William Connery, "Point of Entry:

213

Baltimore, the Other Ellis Island," Baltimore md.com http://www.baltimoremd.com/charm/pointofentry.html (accessed July 12, 2012).

4. John Alexander Williams, *Appalachia: A History* (Chapel Hill: University of North Carolina Press, 2001), 312.

5. Mary Battiata, "A High & Lonesome Sound: Hazel Dickens…," *Washington Post*, June 24, 2011.

6. "Vast Traffic Jam Daily Engulfs Workers Outside Baltimore Bomber Plant," *Life Magazine*, December 8, 1941.

7. Neil Rosenberg. *Bluegrass: A History* (Urbana: University of Illinois Press, 1985), 82.

8. Anthony Harkins, *Hillbilly: A Cultural History of an American Icon* (New York: Oxford University Press, 2003), 99.

9. "Hillbilly Music and Epilepsy," *Baltimore Sun*, October 28, 1953.

10. Jo Ann Harris, "Baltimore: Hillbilly Haven," *Baltimore Sun*, August 4, 1974.

11. Geoffrey Himes, "Drinking Songs," *Baltimore City Paper*, http://www2.citypaper.com/special/story.asp?id=20427 (accessed June 7, 2013).

12. Kurt Wolfe and Orla Duane, "On My Journey Home: The Story of Bluegrass," *Country Music: A Rough Guide* (New York: Penguin, 2000), 209.

13. *Ibid.*

14. Jon Weisberger, "Earl Taylor & Jim McCall 20 Bluegrass Favorites," *No Depression Magazine*, July–August 1998.

15. Bud Dickens and Tony Bonta, "Russ Hooper interview with Baltimore Bluegrass Meet-up Group," Meetup.com, http://www.meetup.com/Baltimore-Bluegrass/pages/Russ_Hooper_-_Part_1/ (accessed December 2, 2013).

16. Russ Hooper, interview with author, May 10, 2012.

17. Dean Sapp, email to author, June 6, 2012.

18. Dwight McCall, email with author, November 24, 2012.

19. Dave Reimer, "Russ Hooper: Baltimore's Resonator Pioneer," *Bluegrass Unlimited*, November 2002, 39.

20. Bill Vernon [Liner Notes], *Rebel Records: 35 Years of the Best in Bluegrass*, Rebel Records, 1997.

21. Russ Hooper, June 18, 2013.

22. Reimer, "Russ Hooper," 36.

23. Russ Hooper, May 10, 2012.

24. *Ibid.*

25. *Ibid.*

26. Mike Seeger [liner notes], *Mountain Music Bluegrass Style*, Smithsonian/Folkway Records, 1959.

27. Russ Hooper, May 10, 2012.

28. Jerry McCoury, interview with author, June 6, 2012.

29. Russ Hooper, May 10, 2012.

30. Bob Dylan, *Chronicles, Volume 1* (New York: Simon & Schuster, 2004), 69–70.

31. Battiata, "A High & Lonesome Sound."

32. Malone, *Working Girl Blues*, 9.

33. Bill Malone, *Music from the True Vine: Mike Seeger's Life & Musical Journey* (Chapel Hill: University of North Carolina Press, 2011), 56.

34. Stringbean would go on to a grisly death. He had a lifelong distrust of banks and was known to stash thousands of dollars in his cabin in Ridgetop, Tennessee. In November of 1973, upon returning from a show at the Opry, Stringbean and his wife found two men in their house ransacking it, looking for money. The intruders shot and killed both Stringbean and his wife. The two men never found any money and were eventually caught and sentenced to 99 years in prison. Twenty years later, the new owner of Stringbean's cabin found $20,000 in rotting bills behind a loose brick in the fireplace.

35. Russ Hooper, May 10, 2012.

36. Christopher Lehmann-Haupt, "Earl Scruggs, Bluegrass Pioneer, Dies at 88," *New York Times*, March 29, 2012.

37. Chris Pandolfi, interview with author, July 9, 2013.

38. Russ Hooper, May 10, 2012.

39. Marc Smirnoff, ed., "Sam Perkins," *The Oxford American Book of Great Music Writing* (University of Arkansas Press, 2008), 344.

40. Sandy Rothman, interview with author, September 17, 2012.

41. Dennis McNally, *A Long Strange Trip: The Inside History of the Grateful Dead* (New York: Broadway Books, 2002), 69–72.

42. Sandy Rothman, September 17, 2012.

43. Jimbo Juanis, "Old and Even More in the Way: An Exclusive Interview with Sandy Rothman," *Relix*, 2 (August 1998): 15–18.

44. *Bill Monroe: Father of Bluegrass Music*, dir. Steve Gebhardt, MVD Visual, 1999 [DVD].

45. Rosenberg, *Bluegrass: A History*, 101–102.

46. Stephanie P. Ledgin, *Homegrown*

Music: Discovering Bluegrass (Westport, CT: Praeger, 2004), 24.

47. Robert Shelton, "Bluegrass Style: Mountain Music Gets Serious Consideration," *New York Times*, August 30, 1959.

48. Hunter S. Thompson, *The Proud Highway: Saga of a Desperate Gentleman 1955–1967* (New York: Ballantine, 1997), 303–306.

49. Ledgin, *Homegrown Music*, 24–25.

50. Russ Hooper, email with author, April 3, 2014.

51. Ledgin, *Homegrown Music*, 25.

52. The research author Stephanie Ledgin conducted for her book *Homegrown Music: Discovering Bluegrass* is interesting. Looking through a random selection of dictionaries from 1958 to 1996 she could find not find the word bluegrass with its music definition in any dictionary until 1988.

53. Ralph Rinzler [liner notes], *American Banjo: Three Finger & Scruggs Style*, Smithsonian/Folkways, 1957.

Chapter 2

1. Alice Gerrard, interview with author, April 2, 2012.

2. Ibid.

3. Hank Schwartz, email with author, June 10, 2013.

4. Bill Malone, *Music from the True Vine: Mike Seeger's Life & Musical Journey* (Chapel Hill: University of North Carolina Press, 2011), 65.

5. Lisa Chiera [liner notes], *Galax, Va: Old Fiddlers' Convention*, Smithsonian Folkways, 1964.

6. Ray Allen, *Gone to the Country: The New Lost City Ramblers & the Folk Music Revival* (Urbana: University of Illinois Press, 2010), 19–20.

7. Malone, *Music from the True Vine*, 65.

8. Bill Malone and Hazel Dickens, *Working Girl Blues: The Life and Music of Hazel Dickens* (Urbana: University of Illinois, 2008), 7.

9. *Ibid.*

10. Folk Alliance, "Hazel Dickens 2002 Folk Alliance International Lifetime Achievement Award Recipient," Youtube.com, http://www.youtube.com/watch?v=tRplbVzw_64 (accessed November 16, 2013).

11. Malone, *Working Girl Blues*, 11.

12. Russ Hooper, interview with author, May 10, 2012.

13. Folk Alliance, "Hazel Dickens."

14. Ray Allen, *Gone to the Country: The New Lost City Ramblers & the Folk Music Revival* (Urbana: University of Illinois Press, 2010), 19.

15. Alice Gerrard [liner notes], *Hazel Dickens & Alice Gerrard: Pioneering Women of Bluegrass*, Smithsonian Folkways, 1996.

16. Ibid.

17. Malone, *Music from the True Vine*, 71.

18. Gerrard, April 2, 2012.

19. *Ibid.*

20. Gerrard [liner notes], *Hazel Dickens & Alice Gerrard*.

21. Gerrard, April 2, 2012.

22. Gerrard [liner notes], *Hazel Dickens & Alice Gerrard*.

23. Folk Alliance, "Hazel Dickens."

24. Bill Friskics-Warren, "Hazel Dickens & Alice Gerrard," *No Depression*, Nov.–Dec. 1998.

25. Sandy Rothman [liner notes], *Ragged but Right*, Jerry Garcia Family LLC, 2010.

26. Bob Dylan [liner notes], *World Gone Wrong*, Columbia, 1993.

27. Malone, *Working Girl Blues*, 13.

28. Malone, *Music from the True Vine*, 59.

29. Sandy Rothman, interview with author, September 17, 2012.

30. Jay Orr [liner notes], *True Vine*, Smithsonian/Folkways, 2003.

31. Neil Rosenberg, *Bluegrass: A History* (Urbana: University of Illinois Press, 1985), 147.

32. Ellen Wright, *Pressing On: The Roni Stoneman Story* (Urbana: University of Illinois Press, 2007), 38–42.

33. Mike Seeger [liner notes], *American Banjo: Three Finger & Scruggs Style*, Smithsonian Folkways, 1957.

34. Rosenberg, *Bluegrass: A History*, 110.

35. Ralph Rinzler [liner notes], *American Banjo: Three Finger & Scruggs Style*, Smithsonian Folkways, 1957.

36. Allen, *Gone to the Country*, 21.

37. Malone, *Music from the True Vine*, 72.

38. Rosenberg, *Bluegrass: A History*, 153.

39. Sandy Rothman, email with author, October 12, 2012.

40. "Review of Mountain Music Bluegrass Style," *Billboard Magazine*, August 17, 1959, 32.

41. Mike Seeger [liner notes], *Mountain Music Bluegrass Style*, Smithsonian Folkways, 1959.

42. Russ Hooper, May 10, 2012.

43. Russ Hooper, June 24, 2013.

44. Sandy Rothman, September 17, 2012.

45. Jimbo Juanis, "Old and Even More in the Way: An Exclusive Interview with Sandy Rothman," *Relix*, 2 (August 1998): 17.

Chapter 3

1. Greg Cahill, "Mando Mania: David Grisman Just Keeps Pickin'," *Sonoma County Independent*, March 9–15, 2000.

2. Bill Malone, *Country Music USA*, 2d ed. (Austin: University of Texas Press, 2002), 52.

3. Jay Orr [liner notes], *True Vine*, Smithsonian/Folkways Records, 2003.

4. Sandy Rothman, October 12, 2012.

5. Sandy Rothman, interview with author, September 17, 2012.

6. Walt Hensley, interview with Sandy Rothman for KALW Radio, San Francisco, January 10, 1998 [CD].

7. Sandy Rothman, September 17, 2012.

8. Tom Ewing, "Earl Taylor: One of the Bluegrass Greats," *Bluegrass Unlimited*, September 1976, 10–14.

9. Jeff Roberts, email with author, March 27, 2012.

10. Colin Escott [liner notes], *Earl Taylor & Jim McCall with the Stoney Mountain Boys: 24 Bluegrass Favorites*, Rural Rhythm, 2007.

11. [liner notes], *Scotty Stoneman: Live in L.A. with the Kentucky Colonels*, Rural Rhythm, 2003.

12. Oliver Trager, *The American Book of the Dead* (New York: Simon & Schuster, 1997), 132.

13. Mike Seeger [liner notes], *Mountain Music Bluegrass Style*, Smithsonian Folkways Records, 1959.

14. Ewing, "Earl Taylor," 11.

15. *Ibid.*

16. Seeger [liner notes], *Mountain Music Bluegrass Style.*

17. Artie Werner, email with author, March 27, 2012.

18. Sandy Rothman, September 17, 2012.

19. Artie Werner, March 27, 2012.

20. Rosenberg, *Bluegrass: A History*, 42–43.

21. Ewing, "Earl Taylor," 11.

22. Tom Ewing, email to author, September 27, 2012.

23. Marty Godbey, *Crowe on Banjo* (Urbana: University of Illinois Press, 2011), 44.

24. "5 Licenses Suspended," *Baltimore Sun*, October 11, 1957.

25. Russ Hooper, interview with author, May 10, 2012.

26. Geoffrey Himes, "From the Hills: How Mid-Century Migrants from the Mountains Brought Bluegrass—and More—to Baltimore," *Baltimore City Paper*, January 12, 2000, http://www.citypaper.com/news/story.asp?id=3636 (accessed June 7, 2012).

27. Ewing, "Earl Taylor," 12.

28. Himes, "From the Hills."

29. Hensley, interview with Sandy Rothman, November 15, 1997.

30. James Reams, "A Tribute to the Banjo Baron of Bluegrass, Walter Hensley 1936–2012," Cybergrass.com, http://www.cybergrass.com/node/2006 (accessed July 1, 2013).

31. Hensley, interview with Sandy Rothman, January 10, 1998.

32. Tina Aridas [liner notes], *James Reams & Walter Hensley: The Barons of Bluegrass*, Copper Creek Records, 2002.

33. This album was a big comeback for Hensley. By 2002 he had not recorded in years and begun to pull away from the music business. This album would go on to be nominated for IBMA's 2002 Recording Event of the Year, and help introduce Hensley to a new generation of bluegrass fans.

34. James Reams, email with author, September 5, 2012.

35. Hensley, interview with Sandy Rothman, January 10, 1998.

36. Sandy Rothman, September 17, 2012.

37. Russ Hooper, May 10, 2012.

38. Jerry McCoury, interview with author, June 6, 2012.

39. James Reams, September 5, 2012.

40. Alan Lomax [liner notes], *Folk Songs from the Blue Grass: Earl Taylor and His Stoney Mountain Boys*, United Artists, 1959.

41. Dean Sapp, email with author, April 18, 2012.

42. Sandy Rothman, September 17, 2012.

43. Russ Hooper, May 10, 2012.

44. Sandy Rothman, September 17, 2012.

45. Russ Hooper, June 18, 2013.

46. Roy Cole, interview with author, December 4, 2013.

47. Russ Hooper, June 18, 2013.

48. Lomax [liner notes], *Folk Songs from the Blue Grass.*

49. Hooper, February 28, 2014.

50. "Classified ads," *Baltimore Sun*, November 22, 1954.

51. Bill Vernon [liner notes], *Rebel Records: 35 Years of the Best in Bluegrass*, Rebel Records, 1997.

52. Himes, "From the Hills."

53. Russ Hooper, May 10, 2012.

54. Del McCoury, interview with author, January 29, 2011.

55. Vernon [liner notes], *Rebel Records: 35 Years of the Best in Bluegrass*.

56. Dave Freeman, email with author, August 28, 2012.

57. Del McCoury, January 29, 2011.

58. Jerry McCoury, June 6, 2012.

59. Escott [liner notes], *Earl Taylor & Jim McCall with the Stoney Mountain Boys: 24 Bluegrass Favorites*.

Chapter 4

1. Walt Hensley, interview with Sandy Rothman on KALW Radio, San Francisco, January 10, 1998 [CD].

2. Geoffrey Himes, "From the Hills: How Mid-Century Migrants from the Mountains Brought Bluegrass—and More—to Baltimore," *Baltimore City Paper*, January 12, 2000, http://www.citypaper.com/news/story.asp?id=3636 (accessed June 7, 2012).

3. Walt Hensley, interview with Sandy Rothman, January 10, 1998.

4. John Wilson, "Program Given by Alan Lomax: Folklorist Offers Impressive Array of American Artists in Carnegie Hall Concert," *New York Times*, April 4, 1959.

5. Wilson, "Program Given by Alan Lomax."

6. Ronald Cohen, *Alan Lomax: Selected Writings 1934–1997* (New York: Routledge, 2003), 189.

7. Neil Rosenberg, *Bluegrass: A History* (Urbana: University of Illinois Press, 1985), 151.

8. Richard D. Smith, *Can't You Hear Me Callin': The Life of Bill Monroe, Father of Bluegrass* (Cambridge, MA: Da Capo Press, 2001), 148.

9. Del McCoury, interview with author, July 30, 2013.

10. Russ Hooper, interview with author, June 18, 2013.

11. Alan Lomax [liner notes], *Folk Songs from the Blue Grass: Earl Taylor and His Stoney Mountain Boys*, United Artists 1959.

12. John Morgan, "Walter Hensley," *Bluegrass Unlimited*, March 1972, 17–18.

13. Walt Hensley, interview with Sandy Rothman, January 10, 1998.

14. Cohen, *Alan Lomax*, 188.

15. John Szwed, *Alan Lomax: The Man Who Recorded the World* (New York: Viking Penguin, 2010), 310–311.

16. Wilson, "Program Given by Alan Lomax."

17. Cohen, *Alan Lomax: Selected Writings 1934–1997*, 188.

18. Ronald Cohen, *Rainbow Quest: The Folk Music Revival and American Society 1940–1970* (Amherst: University of Massachusetts Press, 2002), 140.

19. Bill Malone, *Music from the True Vine: Mike Seeger's Life & Musical Journey* (Chapel Hill: University of North Carolina Press, 2011), 114.

20. Robert Shelton, "Bluegrass Style: Mountain Music Gets Serious Consideration," *New York Times*, August 30, 1959.

21. Tom Ewing, "Earl Taylor: One of the Bluegrass Greats," *Bluegrass Unlimited*, September 1976, 12.

22. Hensley, interview with Sandy Rothman, January 10, 1998.

23. James Reams, email with author, July 16, 2013.

24. Russ Hooper, June 18, 2013.

25. James Reams, September 11, 2012.

26. Ewing, "Earl Taylor," 12.

27. Hensley, interview with Sandy Rothman, January 10, 1998.

28. Sandy Rothman, email with author, September 19, 2012.

29. Russ Hooper, June 18, 2013.

30. Del McCoury, July 30, 2013.

31. Artie Werner, email with author, April 9, 2012.

32. Walt Hensley, interview with Sandy Rothman, January 10, 1998.

33. Sandy Rothman, September 17, 2012.

34. *Ibid.*

35. *Ibid.*

36. Dwight McCall, email with author, October 30, 2012.

37. *Ibid.*

38. *Ibid.*

39. Del McCoury, July 30, 2013.

40. Tom Ewing, email with author, September 24, 2012.

41. Sandy Rothman, September 17, 2012.

42. Chris Warner, interview with author, April 10, 2013.

43. Del McCoury, July 30, 2013.

44. Russ Hooper, May 10, 2012.

45. Dwight McCall, October 31, 2012.

Chapter 5

1. Russ Hooper, interview with author, May 10, 2012.
2. Russ Hooper, June 18, 2013.
3. Ibid.
4. Roy Cole, interview with author, December 4, 2013.
5. Dean Sapp, email with author, April 17, 2012.
6. Carroll Swam, email with author, May 14, 2012.
7. Roy Cole, December 4, 2013.
8. Russ Hooper, June 18, 2013.
9. Stinson Barth interview with Steve Keleman, "Stinson Barth: I'll Forget You Woman," http://www.rockabillyhall.com/StinsonBarth.html (accessed August 7, 2013).
10. John Morgan, "Walter Hensley," *Bluegrass Unlimited*, March 1972, 18.
11. Del McCoury, interview with author, July 30, 2013.
12. Neil Rosenberg [liner notes], *Hazel Dickens & Alice Gerrard: Pioneering Women in Bluegrass*, Smithsonian Folkways, 1996.
13. Russ Hooper, November 7, 2013.
14. Henry Scarpua, "Country Comes to Baltimore," *Baltimore Sun*, August 5, 1973.
15. James Reams, email with author, September 5, 2012.
16. Carroll Swam, February 2, 2012.
17. Chris Warner, interview with author, April 10, 2013.
18. Ibid.
19. Patrick McAvinue, interview with author, August 1, 2013.
20. *Ibid.*
21. Carroll Swam, February 2, 2012.
22. Del McCoury, interview with author, January 29, 2011.
23. Karen Warmkessel, "Bluegrass Isn't Just 'Hillbilly' Music to Its Many Area Fans," *Baltimore Sun*, December 11, 1977.
24. Richard Thompson, "Ray Davis Celebrates 60 Years on the Radio," Bluegrasstoday.com http://bluegrasstoday.com/ray-davis-celebrates-60-years-on-radio/ (accessed July 26, 2013).
25. Bluegrass Country, "WAMU's Bluegrass Country Host Ray Davis Profiled by PBS." Youtube.com. http://www.youtube.com/watch?v=wr5hb0DbTew (accessed July 26, 2013).
26. Russ Hooper, November 7, 2013.
27. Mark Yacovone [liner notes], *Red Allen Featuring Frank Wakefield: The Folkways Years 1964–1983*, Smithsonian Folkways, 2001.
28. Russ Hooper, May 10, 2012.
29. Roy Cole, December 4, 2013.
30. Geoffrey Himes, "Drinking Songs," *Baltimore City Paper*, http://www2.citypaper.com/special/story.asp?id=20427 (accessed June 7, 2013).
31. Dean Sapp, April 18, 2012.
32. Chris Warner, April 10, 2013.
33. *Ibid.*
34. Del McCoury, July 30, 2013.
35. Russ Hooper, June 18, 2013.
36. Russ Hooper, May 10, 2012.
37. Alice Gerrard, interview with author, April 2, 2012.
38. Russ Hooper, May 10, 2012.
39. *Ibid.*
40. Chris Warner, April 10, 2013.
41. *Ibid.*
42. Carroll Swam, May 14, 2012.
43. Jerry McCoury, interview with author, June 6, 2012.

Chapter 6

1. Yonder Mountain String Band, Concert recorded at Delfest, Cumberland, Maryland, May 25, 2012.
2. Trey Anastasio Band, Concert recorded at Delfest, Cumberland, Maryland, May 24, 2013.
3. Del McCoury Band, Concert recorded at Jazz and Heritage Festival, New Orleans, Louisiana, April 27, 2008.
4. Chris Pandolfi, interview with author, July 9, 2013.
5. *Ibid.*
6. Del McCoury, interview with author, January 29, 2011.
7. Del McCoury, July 30, 2013.
8. Russ Hooper, interview with author, June 18, 2013.
9. Hooper, August 7, 2013.
10. http://dcrecords.org/Empire.htm (accessed August 8, 2013).
11. Russ Hooper, June 18, 2013.
12. Randi Henderson, "You Won't Get Rich Pickin 'n' Grinnin', but Bluegrass Is Catchy," *Baltimore Sun*, December 1, 1978.
13. Jerry McCoury, interview with author, June 6, 2012.
14. Del McCoury, July 30, 2013.
15. *Ibid.*
16. *Ibid.*
17. Howard Sounes, *Down the Highway:*

The Life of Bob Dylan (New York: Grove Press, 2001), 100.

18. Bill Monroe and His Bluegrass Boys, Concert recorded at New York University, New York City, New York, February 8, 1963.

19. Sara Refiman, "David Grisman interview with Sara Refiman," Gratefulweb.com, http://www.gratefulweb.com/node/6032# (accessed August 9, 2013).

20. Pete Wernick, email with author, September 3, 2013.

21. Sam Bush, interview with author, August 24, 2012.

22. Del McCoury, July 30, 2013.

23. *Ibid.*

24. Chris Stewart, "Del McCoury: Leading Man," in Randy Rudder, ed., *Country Music Reader 2007* (Mt. Juliet, TN: Music City Publishing, 2006), 122.

25. Del McCoury, July 30, 2013.

26. Jerry McCoury, June 6, 2012.

27. Del McCoury, July 30, 2013.

28. Del McCoury, January 29, 2011.

29. Jerry McCoury, June 6, 2012.

30. Chris Hillman, email with author, August 27, 2013.

31. "Reflections: Jerry Garcia's Life and Legacy," *Relix Magazine*, Relix.com, http://www.relix.com/articles/detail/reflections-jerry-garcia-s-life-and-legacy-john-bell-del-mccoury-ethan-mill (accessed March 10, 2014).

32. Frank Overstreet, "SPBGMA Preservation Hall of Greats Inductee 1989: Del McCoury," http://www.spbgma.com/level2/delmccoury.html (accessed August 12, 2013).

33. Rudder, *Country Music Reader 2007*, 123.

34. Tony Trischka, email with author, August 13, 2013.

35. Russ Hooper, November 7, 2013.

36. Russ Hooper, May 10, 2012.

37. Del McCoury, July 31, 2013.

38. Stewart, "Del McCoury," in Rudder, ed., *Country Music Reader 2007*, 121.

39. Tony Trischka, August 13, 2013.

40. Dean Sapp, email with author, April 10, 2012.

41. Pete Wernick, September 2, 2013.

42. Chris Pandolfi, July 9, 2013.

43. Stewart, "Del McCoury," in Rudder, ed., *Country Music Reader 2007*, 120.

44. Chris Pandolfi, July 9, 2013.

Chapter 7

1. Tim Newby, "Caleb Stine: Music Is Life," Honesttune.com, http://www.honesttune.com/caleb-stine-music-is-life/ (accessed August 26, 2013).

2. Cris Jacobs, interview with author, August 15, 2013.

3. William Hughes, "Fancy Hillbilly Folk Art," *Cecil County Guardian*, August 1, 2013.

4. Murphy Hicks Henry, *Pretty Good for a Girl: Women in Bluegrass* (Urbana: University of Illinois Press, 2013), 37.

5. Paula Hathaway Anderson-Green, *A Hot-Bed of Musicians: Traditional Music in the Upper New River Valley-Whitetop Region* (Knoxville: University of Tennessee Press, 2002), 238.

6. Hugh Campbell, interview with author, August 18, 2013.

7. Eric Siegel, "Music Close to the Land, Faith During Hard Times," *Baltimore Sun*, August 24, 1975.

8. Hugh Campbell, August 18, 2013.

9. Jeff Place [liner notes], *Ola Belle Reed: Rising Sun Melodies*, Smithsonian Folkways, 2010.

10. Anderson-Green, *A Hot-Bed of Musicians*, 36.

11. Dean Sapp, email with author, July 2, 2012.

12. Russ Hooper, interview with author, October 16, 2013.

13. Ed Okonwicz, "A Cecil Family's Musical Legacy," *Cecil Soil Magazine* 4, no. 1 (November/December 2007): 40.

14. Frances Mann Riale, Comments about Ola Belle Reed from Journey Stories: A Musical Journey: The Life of Ola Belle Reed August 4, 2012, at the Cecil County Library, courtesy of Travis Kitchens.

15. Place [liner notes], *Ola Belle Reed: Rising Sun Melodies*.

16. Mike Seeger, "Late News Report from Sunset Park, West Grove, Penn., Five-String Banjo Picking Contest," in Thomas Goldsmith, ed., *The Bluegrass Reader* (Urbana: University of Illinois Press, 2004), 124–126.

17. Russ Hooper, October 16, 2013.

18. *Ibid.*

19. Neil Rosenberg, *Bluegrass: A History* (Urbana: University of Illinois Press, 1985), 109.

20. Alice Gerrard, interview with author, April 2, 2012.

21. Alice Gerrard [liner notes], *Hazel Dickens & Alice Gerrard: Pioneering Women of Bluegrass*, Smithsonian Folkways, 1996.

22. Bill Malone, *Music from the True Vine: Mike Seeger's Life & Musical Journey*

(Chapel Hill: University of North Carolina Press, 2011), 57.

23. Carroll Swam, interview with author, February 2, 2012.

24. David Dodd, *The Complete Annotated Grateful Dead Lyrics* (New York: Free Press, 2005), 106.

25. Eddie Dean, "O Brother Where Art the Sunsets of Yesteryear," *Philadelphia Weekly*, October 31, 2001.

26. Okonwicz, "A Cecil Family's Musical Legacy," 41.

27. Dan DeLuca, "Sunset Park, Where Country's Still Country," Philly.com, http://articles.philly.com/1995–08–06/entertainment/25707712_1_marty-stuart-country-music-lester-flatt (accessed October 28, 2013).

28. Russ Hooper, October 16, 2013.

29. Jerry McCoury, interview with author, June 6, 2012.

30. Jerimy Campbell, interview with author, August 18, 2013.

31. Hugh Campbell, August 18, 2013.

32. Isaac Rehert, "A 'Hillbilly' Doctorate," *The Baltimore Sun*, June 13, 1978.

33. Hugh Campbell, August 18, 2013.

34. Ava Voshell, "Cecil County's Pioneers of Country & Bluegrass," *Cecil Soil Magazine* 5, no. 2 (January/February 2009): 33.

35. Hugh Campbell, August 18, 2013.

36. Ola Belle Reed [liner notes], *My Epitaph*, Smithsonian Folkways, 1976.

37. Place [liner notes], *Ola Belle Reed: Rising Sun Melodies.*

38. *Ibid.*

39. Jerimy Campbell, August 18, 2013.

40. Hugh Campbell, August 18, 2013.

41. Heather Coffey, email with author, October 24, 2013.

42. Voshell, "Cecil County's Pioneers of Country & Bluegrass," 61.

43. Hugh Campbell, August 18, 2013.

Chapter 8

1. Del McCoury, interview with author, July 30, 2013.

2. Russ Hooper, interview with author, June 18, 2013.

3. Russ Hooper, November 7, 2013.

4. Russ Hooper, May 10, 2012.

5. Bud Dickens and Tony Bonta, "Russ Hooper interview with Baltimore Bluegrass Meet-up Group," Meetup.com, http://www.meetup.com/Baltimore-Bluegrass/pages/Russ_Hooper_-_Part_1/ (accessed December 2, 2013).

6. Tom Adams, "Tom Neal, interview with Tom Adams," Banjonews.com, https://banjonews.com/2014–01/tom_neal.html (accessed March 5, 2014).

7. Chris Warner, interview with author, April 10, 2013.

8. Russ Hooper, May 10, 2012.

9. Carroll Swam, interview with the author, February 20, 2012.

10. Chris Warner, April 10, 2013.

11. Tom Ewing, "Earl Taylor: One of the Bluegrass Greats," *Bluegrass Unlimited*, September 1976, 13.

12. Tom Ewing, email with author, February 24, 2014.

13. Dwight McCall, email with author, October 30, 2012.

14. *Ibid.*

15. Sandy Rothman, email with author, November 8, 2013.

16. Sandy Rothman, interview with author, September 17, 2012.

17. Sandy Rothman, November 8, 2013.

18. Russ Hooper, November 1, 2013.

19. Walt Hensley, interview with Sandy Rothman on KALW Radio, San Francisco, November 15, 1997 [CD].

20. Russ Hooper, November 7, 2013.

21. Walter Hensley [liner notes], *The 5-String Banjo Today*, Capitol Records, 1964.

22. Hensley, interview with Sandy Rothman, November 15, 1997.

23. Sandy Rothman, November 8, 2013.

24. Russ Hooper, June 18, 2013.

25. Russ Hooper, November 1, 2013.

26. Geoffrey Himes, "From the Hills: How Mid-Century Migrants from the Mountains Brought Bluegrass—and More—to Baltimore," *Baltimore City Paper*, January 12, 2000, http://www.citypaper.com/news/story.asp?id=3636 (accessed June 7, 2012).

27. Russ Hooper, November 1, 2013.

28. Russ Hooper, November 7, 2013.

29. Roy Cole, interview with author, December 4, 2013.

30. Russ Hooper, June 18, 2013.

31. *Ibid.*

32. *Ibid.*

33. *Ibid.*

34. Eddie Stubbs [liner notes], *Rebel Records: 35 Years of the Best in Bluegrass*, Rebel Records, 1997.

35. Russ Hooper, June 18, 2013.

36. Sandy Rothman, November 8, 2013.

37. John Morgan, "Walter Hensley," *Bluegrass Unlimited*, March 1972, 20.

38. Sandy Rothman, November 8, 2013.

39. Tom Adams, "Tom Neal, interview with Tom Adams," Banjonews.com, https://banjonews.com/2014-01/tom_neal.html (accessed March 5, 2014).

40. Russ Hooper, November 1, 2013.

41. Steve Cunningham, email with author, January 2, 2014.

42. Sam Bush, interview with author, August 24, 2012.

43. Neil Rosenberg, *Bluegrass: A History* (Urbana: University of Illinois Press, 1985), 298.

44. Joe O'Gara, "Sam Bush Tests Bluegrass Limits," Nuvo.net, http://www.nuvo.net/indianapolis/sam-bush-tests-bluegrass-limits/Content?oid=1205754 (accessed April 23, 2012).

45. Randi Henderson, "You Won't Get Rich Pickin' 'n' Grinnin', but Bluegrass Is Catchy," *Baltimore Sun*, December 1, 1978.

46. Ira Gitlin, "Mike Munford," Banjonews.com, https://banjonews.com/2011-09/mike_munford.html (accessed May 19, 2014).

47. Dwight McCall, email to author, October 31, 2012.

48. Russ Hooper, May 10, 2012.

49. Russ Hooper, June 18, 2013.

50. James Reams, email with author, September 5, 2012.

51. Hensley, interview with Sandy Rothman, November 15, 1997.

52. Russ Hooper, June 18, 2013.

Chapter 9

1. Russ Hooper, interview with author, May 10, 2012.

2. Geoffrey Himes, "From the Hills: How Mid-Century Migrants from the Mountains Brought Bluegrass—and More—to Baltimore," *Baltimore City Paper*, January 12, 2000, http://www.citypaper.com/news/story.asp?id=3636 (accessed June 7, 2012).

3. Alice Gerrard, interview with author, April 2, 2012.

4. Russ Hooper, May 10, 2012.

5. Patrick McAvinue, interview with author, July 31, 2013.

6. Himes, "From the Hills."

7. Chris Warner, interview with author, April 10, 2013.

8. Carroll Swam, interview with author, February 2, 2012.

9. Eric Siegel, "A Sad Note on Belair Road," *Baltimore Sun*, June 2, 2000.

10. Steve Cunningham, interview with author, November 26, 2013.

11. *Ibid.*

12. "An Evening of Pickin' by a Pot-Belly Stove," *Baltimore Sun*, October 29, 1978.

13. Steve Cunningham, November 26, 2013.

14. Karen E. Warmkessel, "Bluegrass Isn't Just 'Hillbilly Music' to Its Many Area Fans," *Baltimore Sun*, December 11, 1977.

15. Steve Cunningham, November 26, 2013.

16. Warmkessel, "Bluegrass Isn't Just 'Hillbilly Music' to Its Many Area Fans."

17. Steve Cunningham, November 26, 2013.

18. Bud Dickens and Tony Bonta, "Mike Munford interview with Bud Dickens and Tony Bonta," Meetup.com, http://www.meetup.com/Baltimore-Bluegrass/pages/Mike_Munford_-_Part_1/ (accessed November 26, 2013).

19. *Ibid.*

20. Steve Cunningham, November 26, 2013.

21. Wesley Case, "Mike Minford, Master of Banjo, Honed Skills in Baltimore," *Baltimore Sun*, December 14, 2013.

22. Tony Trischka, email with author, August 13, 2013.

23. Case, "Mike Munford, master of banjo."

24. Dickens, "Mike Munford interview with Bud Dickens and Tony Bonta."

25. Pete Wernick, email with author, September 3, 2013.

26. Tony Trischka, August 13, 2013.

27. Ira Gitlin, "Mike Munford," Banjonews.com, https://banjonews.com/2011-09/mike_munford.html (accessed May 19, 2014).

28. Pete Wernick, September 3, 2013.

29. Case, "Mike Munford, Master of Banjo."

30. Sam Bush, interview with author, August 24, 2012.

31. Marti Smiley Childs, *Echoes of the Sixties,* Kindle ed. (EditPros LLC, 2011).

32. Sam Bush, August 24, 2012.

33. Jon Weisberger, "Earl Taylor & Jim McCall 20 Bluegrass Favorites," *No Depression,* July–August 1998.

34. Tom Ewing, email with author, September 24, 2012.

35. Russ Hooper, June 18, 2013.

36. *Ibid.*

37. Dwight McCall, email with author, October 31, 2012.

Chapter 10

1. Cris Jacobs, email with author, August 12, 2009.

2. Ed Hough, interview with author, January 27, 2009.

3. Cris Jacobs, August 15, 2013.

4. Patrick McAvinue, interview with author, July 31, 2013.

5. *Ibid.*

6. "Bio," Patrickmcavinue.com, http://www.patrickmcavinue.com/bio/ (accessed March 20, 2014).

7. Cris Jacobs, August 15, 2013.

8. Cris Jacobs, August 22, 2007.

9. Cris Jacobs, August 15, 2013.

10. "Reviews: Smooth Kentucky, *A Few More Miles,*" Bluegrassmusic.com, http://bluegrassmusic.com/content/reviews/reviews-november–2009/ (accessed May 29, 2014).

11. Tim Newby, "Smooth Kentucky: Funky Undertones," Honesttune.com, http://www.honesttune.com/smooth-kentucky-funky-undertones/ (accessed April 9, 2014).

12. Ed Hough, January 27, 2009.

13. Russ Hooper, interview with author, February 28, 2014.

14. Tim Newby, "Jeff Moiser: Lessons Learned," Honesttune.com, http://www.honesttune.com/jeff-mosier-lessons-learned/ (accessed March 4, 2014).

15. Ibid.

16. Trey Anastasio Band, concert recorded at Delfest, Cumberland, Maryland, May 24, 2013. Author's collection.

17. Tim Newby, "Honey Dewdrops: Heartfelt Honest Songs," Honesttune.com, http://www.honesttune.com/honey-dewdros-heartfelt-honest-songs/ (accessed March 3, 2014).

18. Cris Jacobs, August 15, 2013.

19. Anders Beck, email with author, June 4, 2014.

20. Jordan August, email with author, March 13, 2014.

21. *Ibid.*

22. Cris Jacobs, August 15, 2013.

23. Patrick McAvinue, July 31, 2013.

24. Cris Jacobs, August 15, 2013.

25. Jordan August, March 13, 2014.

26. Cris Jacobs, August 15, 2013.

27. Jordan August, March 13, 2014.

28. Tim Newby, "Caleb Stine: Music is Life," Honesttune.com, http://www.honesttune.com/caleb-stine-music-is-life/ (accessed August 26, 2013).

29. Pete Wernick, email with author, September 13, 2013.

30. Sandy Rothman, interview with author, September 17, 2012.

31. James Reams, email with author, March 6, 2014.

32. Dwight McCall, email with author, October 31, 2012.

33. Jerry McCoury, interview with author, June 6, 2012.

Bibliography

Books

Alden, Grant, and Peter Blackstock, eds. *The Best of No Depression: Writing About American Music.* Austin: University of Texas Press, 2005.

Allen, Ray. *Gone to the Country: The New Lost City Ramblers & the Folk Music Revival.* Urbana: University of Illinois Press, 2010.

Anderson-Green, Paula Hathaway. *A Hot-Bed of Musicians: Traditional Music in the Upper New River Valley-Whitetop Region.* Knoxville: University of Tennessee Press, 2002.

Childs, Marti Smiley. *Echoes of the Sixties,* Kindle ed. EditPros LLC, 2011.

Cohen, Ronald. *Alan Lomax: Selected Writings 1934–1997.* New York: Routledge, 2003.

_____. *Rainbow Quest: The Folk Music Revival and American Society 1940–1970.* Amherst: University of Massachusetts Press, 2002.

Dodd, David. *The Complete Annotated Grateful Dead Lyrics.* New York: Free Press, 2005.

Dylan, Bob. *Chronicles, Volume 1.* New York: Simon & Schuster, 2004.

Fleischhauer, Carl, and Neil V. Rosenberg. *Bluegrass Odyssey: A Documentary in Pictures and Words, 1966–86.* Urbana: University of Illinois Press, 2006.

Godbey, Marty. *Crowe on Banjo.* Urbana: University of Illinois Press, 2011.

Goldsmith, Thomas, ed. *The Bluegrass Reader.* Urbana: University of Illinois Press, 2004.

Harkin, Anthony. *Hillbilly: A Cultural History of an American Icon.* New York: Oxford University Press, 2003.

Helm, Levon, and Stephen Davis. *This Wheel's on Fire.* Chicago: Chicago Review Press, 1993.

Henry, Murphy Hicks. *Pretty Good for a Girl: Women in Bluegrass.* Urbana: University of Illinois Press, 2013.

Ledgin, Stephanie P. *Homegrown Music: Discovering Bluegrass.* Westport, CT: Praeger, 2004.

Malone, Bill. *Country Music U.S.A.,* 2d ed. Austin: University of Texas Press, 2002.

_____. *Music from the True Vine: Mike's Seeger's Life & Musical Journey.* Chapel Hill: University of North Carolina Press, 2008.

_____, and Hazel Dickens. *Working Girl Blues: The Life and Music of Hazel Dickens.* Urbana: University of Illinois Press, 2008.

McNally, Dennis. *A Long Strange Trip: The Inside History of the Grateful Dead.* New York: Broadway, 2002.

Nickerson, Ross. *The Banjo Encyclopedia: Bluegrass Banjo A to Z.* Pacific, MO: Mel Bay, 2003.

Rosenberg, Neil V. *Bluegrass: A History.* Urbana: University of Illinois Press, 1985.

_____, and Charles K. Wolfe. *The Music of Bill Monroe.* Urbana: University of Illinois Press, 2007.

Rudder, Randy, ed. *Country Music Reader 2007.* Mt. Juliet, TN: Music City Publishing, 2006.

Smirnoff, Marc, ed. *The Oxford American Book of Great Music Writing.* Fayetteville: University of Arkansas Press, 2008.

Smith, Richard D. *Can't You Hear Me Callin': The Life of Bill Monroe, Father of Bluegrass.* Cambridge, MA: Da Capo Press, 2001.

Sounes, Howard. *Down the Highway: The Life of Bob Dylan.* New York: Grove Press, 2001.

Streissguth, Michael. *Outlaw: Waylon,*

Willie, Kris, and the Renegades of Nashville. New York: HarperCollins, 2013.

Szwed, John. *Alan Lomax: The Man Who Recorded the World*. New York: Viking Penguin, 2010.

Thompson, Hunter S. *The Proud Highway: Saga of a Desperate Gentleman 1955–1967*. New York: Ballantine, 1997.

Trager, Oliver. *The American Book of the Dead*. New York: Simon & Schuster, 1997.

Williams, John Alexander. *Appalachia: A History*. Chapel Hill: University of North Carolina Press, 2001.

Wolfe, Kurt, and Orla Dune. *Country Music: A Rough Guide*. New York: Penguin Press, 2000.

Wright, Ellen. *Pressing On: The Roni Stoneman Story*. Urbana: University of Illinois Press, 2007.

Magazines

Ewing, Tom. "Earl Taylor: One of the Bluegrass Greats." *Bluegrass Unlimited*, March 1972.

Friskics-Warren, Bill. "Hazel Dickens & Alice Gerrard." *No Depression*, November–December 1998.

Hughes, William. "Fancy Hillbilly Folk Art." *Cecil County Guardian*, August 1, 2013.

Juanis, Jimbo. "Old and Even More in the Way: An Exclusive Interview with Sandy Rothman." *Relix*, August 1998.

Lomax, Alan. "Bluegrass Background: Folk Music with Overdrive." *Esquire*, October 1959.

Morgan, John. "Walter Hensley." *Bluegrass Unlimited*, March 1972.

Okonowicz, Ed. "A Cecil Family's Musical Legacy." *Cecil Soil Magazine*, November–December 2007.

Reimer, Dave. "Russ Hooper: Baltimore's Resonator Pioneer." *Bluegrass Unlimited*, November 2002.

"Review of Mountain Music Bluegrass Style." *Billboard Magazine*, August 17, 1959.

"Vast Traffic Jam Daily Engulfs Workers Outside Baltimore Bomber Plant." *Life*, December 8, 1941.

Voshell, Ava. "Cecil County's Pioneers of Country & Bluegrass." *Cecil Soil Magazine*, January–February 2009.

Weisberger, Jon. "Earl Taylor & Jim McCall 20 Bluegrass Favorites." *No Depression*, July–August 1998.

Newspapers

Battiata, Mary. "A High and Lonesome Sound; Hazel Dickens became a mountain music legend while working a day job in Georgetown. And in the age of dot-coms, welfare reform and NAFTA, this daughter of Appalachia still has plenty to say." *Washington Post*, June 24, 2011.

Cahill, Greg. "Mando Mania: David Grisman Just Keeps Pickin'." *Sonoma County Independent*, March 9–15, 2000.

Case, Wesley. "Mike Munford, Master of Banjo, Honed Skills in Baltimore." *Baltimore Sun*, December 14, 2013.

"Classified Ads." *Baltimore Sun*, November 22, 1954.

Dean, Eddie. "'O' Brother Where Art the Sunsets of Yesteryear." *Philadelphia Weekly*, October 31, 2001.

"An Evening of Pickin' by a Pot-Belly Stove." *Baltimore Sun*, October 29, 1978.

"5 Licenses Suspended." *Baltimore Sun*, October 11, 1957.

Friskics-Warren, Bill. "Hazel Dickens, Folk Singer Dies at 75." *New York Times*, April 22, 2011.

Harris, Jo Ann. "Baltimore: Hillbilly Haven." *Baltimore Sun*, August 4, 1974.

Henderson, Randi. "You Won't Get Rich Pickin' 'n' Grinnin', but Bluegrass Is Catchy." *Baltimore Sun*, December 1, 1978.

"Hillbilly Music and Epilepsy." *Baltimore Sun*, October 28, 1953.

Kelly, Jacques. "Olga Amy, 94, Accompanist for 1950s Baltimore TV shows." *Baltimore Sun*, April 30, 1999.

Lehmann-Haupt, Christopher. "Earl Scruggs, Bluegrass Pioneer Dies at 88." *New York Times*, March 29, 2012.

Rehert, Isaac. "A Hillbilly Doctorate." *Baltimore Sun*, June 13, 1978.

Scarpua, Henry. "Country Comes to Baltimore." *Baltimore Sun*, August 5, 1973.

Shelton, Robert. "Bluegrass Style: Mountain Music Gets Serious Consideration." *New York Times*, August 30, 1959.

Siegel, Eric. "Music Close to the Land, Faith During Hard Times." *Baltimore Sun*, August 24, 1975.

_____. "A Sad Note on Belair Road." *Baltimore Sun*, June 2, 2000.

Warmkessel, Karen. "Bluegrass isn't just 'hillbilly' music to its many area fans." *Baltimore Sun*, December 11, 1977.

Wilson, John. "Program Given By Alan

Lomax: Folklorist Offers Impressive Array of American Artists in Carnegie Hall Concert." *New York Times*, April 4, 1959.

Windham, Ben. "'Legend' Pays Tribute to Bill Monroe." *Tuscaloosa News*, February 21, 2003.

Liner Notes

Aridas, Tina. *James Reams & Walter Hensley: The Barons of Bluegrass*. James Reams, Walter Hensley and the Barons of Bluegrass. Copper Creek Records, CCCD 0214, 2002.

Celebrating 50 Years of Del McCoury. Del McCoury. McCoury Music, 2009.

Chiera, Lisa. *Galax, VA: Old Fiddlers' Convention*. Various Artists. Smithsonian Folkways, FW02435, 2000.

Dylan, Bob. *World Gone Wrong*. Bob Dylan. Columbia, CK57590, 1993.

Escott, Colin. *24 Bluegrass Favorites*. Earl Taylor & Jim McCall with the Stoney Mountain Boys. Rural Rhythm, RHY-CD 320, 2007.

The 5-String Banjo Today. Walter Hensley. Capitol Records, T2149, 1964.

Gerrard, Alice. *Hazel Dickens & Alice Gerrard: Pioneering Women of Bluegrass*. Hazel Dickens and Alice Gerrard. Smithsonian Folkways, SFW40065, 1996.

Lomax, Alan. *Folk Songs from the Blue Grass: Earl Taylor and His Stoney Mountain Boys*. United Artists, UAL 3049, 1959.

Orr, Jay. *True Vine*. Mike Seeger. Smithsonian Folkways, SFW 40136, 2003.

Place, Jeff. *Classic Bluegrass from Smithsonian Folkways*. Various Artists. Smithsonian Folkways, SFW40092, 2002.

_____. *Ola Belle Reed: Rising Sun Melodies*. Ola Belle Reed. Smithsonian Folkways, SFW40202, 2010.

Reed, Ola Belle. *My Epitaph*. Ola Belle Reed. Smithsonian Folkways, FW02493, 1976.

Rinzler, Ralph, and Mike Seeger. *American Banjo: Three Finger & Scruggs Style*. Various Artists. Smithsonian Folkways, SFW40037, 1990.

Rothman, Sandy. *Ragged but Right*. Jerry Garcia Acoustic Band. Jerry Garcia Family LLC, JGCD 1003, 2010.

Schwartz, Hank. *Notes Along the Way: Old-Time and New-Time Renditions of 5-String banjo tunes with vocal accompaniment*. Hank Schwartz. Hank Schwartz Design,

1999.

Scotty Stoneman: Live L.A. with the Kentucky Colonels. Scotty Stoneman. Rural Rhythm, Sierra 6029, 2003.

Seeger, Mike. *Mountain Music Bluegrass Style*. Various Artists. Smithsonian Folkways, SFW40038, 1991.

Vernon, Bill. *Rebel Records: 35 Years of the Best in Bluegrass*. Various Artists. Rebel Records, REB 4000, 1997.

Yacovone, Mark. *Red Allen Featuring Frank Wakefield: The Folkways Years 1964–1983*. Red Allen and Frank Wakefield. Smithsonian Folkways, SFW40127, 2001.

Online

Adams, Tom. "Tom Neal, interview with Tom Adams." Banjonews.com, https://banjonews.com/2014-01/tom_neal.html (accessed March 5, 2014).

Bluegrass Country. "WAMU's Bluegrass Country host Ray Davis profiled by PBS." Youtube.com. http://www.youtube.com/watch?v=wr5hb0DbTew (accessed July 26, 2013).

Bluegrass Music. "Reviews: Smooth Kentucky, *A Few More Miles*." Bluegrassmusic.com. http://bluegrassmusic.com/content/reviews/reviews-november-2009/ (accessed May 29, 2014).

Connery, William. "Point of Entry: Baltimore, the Other Ellis Island." Baltimoremd.com. http://www.baltimoremd.com/charm/pointofentry (accessed June 10, 2013).

DC Records. "Empire Records." *Dcrecords.org*. http://dcrecords.org/Empire.htm (accessed August 8, 2013).

Deluca, Dan. "Sunset Park, Where Country's Still Country." Philly.com. http://articles.philly.com/1995-08-06/entertainment/25707712_1_marty-stuart-country-music-lester-flatt (accessed October 28, 2013).

Dickens, Bud, and Tony Bonta. "Mike Munford interview with Bud Dickens and Tony Bonta." Meetupwww. http://www.meetup.com/Baltimore-Bluegrass/pages/Mike_Munford_-_Part_1/ (accessed November 26, 2013).

_____, and _____. "Russ Hooper interview with Baltimore Bluegrass Meet-up Group." Meetup.com. http://www.meetup.com/Baltimore-Bluegrass/pages/Russ_Hooper_-_Part_1/ (accessed December 2, 2013).

Folk Alliance. "Hazel Dickens 2002 Folk Alliance International Lifetime Achievement Award Recipient." Youtube.com. http://www.youtube.com/watch?v=tRp1bVzw_64 (accessed November 16, 2013).

Gitlin, Ira. "Mike Munford." Banjonews. com. https://banjonews.com/2011–09/mike_munford.html (accessed May 19, 2014).

Himes, Geoffrey. "Drinking Songs." *Baltimore City Paper*, http://www2.citypaper.com/special/story.asp?id=20427 (accessed June 7, 2013).

_____. "From the Hills: How Mid-Century Migrants from the Mountains Brought Bluegrass—and More—to Baltimore." *Baltimore City Paper*, http://www.citypaper.com/news/story.asp?id=3636 (accessed June 7, 2012).

Keleman, Steve. "Stinson Barth: I'll Forget You Woman." Rockabillyhall.com. http://www.rockabillyhall.com/StinsonBarth.html (accessed August 7, 2013).

Newby, Tim. "Caleb Stine: Music Is Life." Honesttune.com. http://www.honesttune.com/caleb-stine-music-is-life/ (accessed August 26, 2013).

_____. "Honey Dewdrops: Heartfelt Honest Songs." Honesttune.com. http://www.honesttune.com/honey-dewdrops-heartfelt-honest-songs/ accessed (March 3, 2014).

_____. "Jeff Moiser: Lessons Learned." Honesttune.com. http://www.honesttune.com/jeff-mosier-lessons-learned/ (accessed March 4, 2014).

_____. "Smooth Kentucky: Funky Undertones." Honesttune.com. http://www.honesttune.com/smooth-kentucky-funky-undertones/ (accessed April 9, 2014).

O'Gara, Joe. "Sam Bush Tests Bluegrass Limits." *Nuvo.net.* http://www.nuvo.net/indianapolis/sam-bush-tests-bluegrass-limits/Content?oid=1205754 (accessed April 23, 2012).

Pandolfi, Chris. "Bluegrass Manifesto." Chrispandolfi.com. http://chrispandolfi.com/ (accessed October 17, 2013).

PatrickMcAvinue.com. "Bio." Patrickmcavinue.com. http://www.patrickmcavinue.com/bio/ (accessed March 20, 2014).

Reams, James. "A Tribute to the Banjo Baron of Bluegrass, Walter Hensley 1936–2012." Cybergrass.com. http://www.cybergrass.com/node/2006 (accessed July 1, 2013).

Refiman, Sara. "David Grisman interview with Sara Refiman." Gratefulweb.com. http://www.gratefulweb.com/node/6032# (accessed August 9, 2013).

Relix Magazine. "Reflections: Jerry Garcia's Life and Legacy." Relix.com. http://www.relix.com/articles/detail/reflections-jerry-garcia-s-life-and-legacy-john-bell-del-mccoury-ethan-mill (accessed March 10, 2014).

Thompson, Richard. "Ray Davis Celebrates 60 Years on the Radio," Bluegrasstoday.com. http://bluegrasstoday.com/ray-davis-celebrates-60-years-on-radio/ (accessed July 26, 2013).

Weisberger, Jon. "Del McCoury et al. Are Winners Again." Countrystandardtime.com. http://www.countrystandardtime.com/d/article.asp?fn=delmccoury.asp (accessed August 2, 2013).

Live Recordings

Bill Monroe and His Bluegrass Boys. Concert recorded at New York University, New York City, New York, February 8, 1963. Author's Collection.

Del McCoury Band. Concert recorded at Jazz and Heritage Festival, New Orleans, Louisiana, April 27, 2008. Author's Collection.

Trey Anastasio Band. Concert recorded at Delfest, Cumberland, Maryland, May 24, 2013. Author's Collection.

Walt Hensley. Interview with Sandy Rothman, San Francisco, California, November 15, 1997, broadcast on KALW Radio. Author's Collection.

Walt Hensley. Interview with Sandy Rothman, San Francisco, California, January 10, 1998, broadcast on KALW Radio. Author's Collection.

Yonder Mountain String Band. Concert recorded at Delfest, Cumberland, Maryland, May 25, 2012. Author's Collection.

DVD

Bill Monroe: Father of Bluegrass. Directed by Steve Gebhardt. 1999. MVD Visual. DVD.

Index